FALLING SHORT

# FALLING SHORT

The Bildungsroman and
the Crisis of Self-Fashioning

Aleksandar Stević

*University of Virginia Press*
CHARLOTTESVILLE AND LONDON

University of Virginia Press
© 2020 by the Rector and Visitors of the University of Virginia
All rights reserved
Printed in the United States of America on acid-free paper

*First published 2020*

9 8 7 6 5 4 3 2 1

Library of Congress Cataloging-in-Publication Data

Names: Stević, Aleksandar, 1980– author.
Title: Falling short : the bildungsroman and the crisis of self-fashioning / Aleksandar Stević.
Description: Charlottesville : University of Virginia Press, 2020. | Includes bibliographical references and index.
Identifiers: LCCN 2019045936 (print) | LCCN 2019045937 (ebook) | ISBN 9780813944029 (hardcover) | ISBN 9780813944036 (paperback) | ISBN 9780813944043 (epub)
Subjects: LCSH: Bildungsromans—History and criticism. | European literature—History and criticism. | Failure (Psychology) in literature. | Maturation (Psychology) in literature. | Self-realization in literature.
Classification: LCC PN3448.B54 S74 2020 (print) | LCC PN3448.B54 (ebook) | DDC 809.3/034—dc23
LC record available at https://lccn.loc.gov/2019045936
LC ebook record available at https://lccn.loc.gov/2019045937

*Cover art/frontispiece: Self-Portrait,* Edvard Munch, 1886 (© Munch Museum/Munch-Ellingsen Group/ARS 2019; photo: Borre Hostland/The National Museum of Art, Oslo, © 2019 Artists Rights Society [ARS], New York); page proofs with handwritten revisions from the *Galaxy,* Henry James, July 1869 (Henry James Collection, Harry Ransom Center, The University of Texas at Austin)

*To Milica*

# CONTENTS

Acknowledgments  ix

Introduction: On Taking Failure Seriously  1

1  Lucien de Rubempré and the Politics of Usurpation in Post-Napoleonic France  23

2  The Great Evasion: Dickensian Bildungsroman and the Logic of Dependency  52

3  Charlotte Brontë and the Governess as a Liberal Subject  77

4  Portrait of the Hero as an Ideologue, ca. 1885–1914  112

5  Madame de Guermantes and Other Animals: Proust and the Forms of Pleasure  149

Epilogue: Historicizing the Bildungsroman  179

Notes  187

Bibliography  219

Index  245

## ACKNOWLEDGMENTS

This book began as a doctoral dissertation at Yale University, where I was particularly fortunate to work under the supervision of Maurice Samuels and Katie Trumpener. I am immensely grateful for their unwavering support, which extends to this day. I am also grateful to Katerina Clark, Emily Greenwood, and Ruth Yeazell, all of whom read the completed dissertation during my time at Yale and offered detailed feedback. The late Alexander Welsh generously offered to read a version of chapter 2, and his kind comments went a long way in persuading me that there just might be a Dickens scholar in me.

On the institutional side of things, I wish to thank Yale University for its generous financial support over the years, as well as the Mrs. Giles Whiting Foundation for a grant that supported me during the final year of my graduate studies. Without the vast resources of Yale libraries this project would have been impossible to pursue. I am equally grateful to King's College, Cambridge, a truly unique intellectual community, for the time it afforded me to further pursue my work on this book.

At both Yale and Cambridge, I am indebted to a long line of scholars and friends for their guidance, encouragement, and engagement with my work. Thanks in particular to Peter Brooks, Peter de Bolla, Moira Fradinger, Pericles Lewis, Barry McCrea, David Quint, Christopher Prendergast, Haun Saussy, and Nicholas White. Thanks also to Jeanne-Marie Jackson for sharing her wisdom on the book publication process, and to Chris Hurshman, who once delved into the stacks at the Sterling Memorial Library at Yale when I needed a book checked from half a world away. At University of Virginia Press, I am grateful to my readers for their detailed and generous engagement with the

## ACKNOWLEDGMENTS

manuscript, and to my editor, Eric Brandt, for his unwavering faith in this project.

Finally, there are debts less immediately connected to my work on this book, but equally significant. My interest in the bildungsroman harks backs to Belgrade, in the early years of the century, where I was fortunate to be taught by Dragan Stojanović, whose reading of Mann's *The Magic Mountain* and translation of *Doctor Faustus* were my true gateway drugs to this genre. It was about the same time that Nataša Marković asked me for an essay on the bildungsroman and *Künstlerroman* that forced me to think about the difficult issues of genre theory that are central to this book. Tanja Popović has been—and continues to be—a constant source of support. Thanks is also due to Marjan Čakarević for many years of conversations about literature (and everything else), and to many friends who sustained me over the years, including Grant Wiedenfeld, Lucian Ghita, Gabi Stoicea, Goran and Bojana Vidović, Michael Rand, and Hagar Ben-Zion.

The making of this book is in some ways a record of my own *Lehrjahre* and *Wanderjahre*. I started to think seriously about the bildungsroman in Belgrade, wrote most of what follows in New Haven, revised it substantially in Cambridge, and added bits and pieces in the most unlikely places: during a wonderful year spent in Amherst and New Salem, Massachusetts (population 990), during the summer sojourns in Belgrade, Paris, and Montreuil, and in our current desert abode in Doha. My deepest gratitude goes to my wife, Milica, for her love and support during these endless travels (this is our third, and, hopefully, *not* final continent), and to Nađa and Đole, the two wonderful rootles cosmopolitans we had along the way, for being such a unique source of joy.

Two parts of this book have been published before. A version of chapter 2 appeared in *Dickens Studies Annual* 45 (2014): 63–94, and the final section of chapter 4 appeared in the *Journal of Modern Literature* 41, no. 1 (2017): 40–57.

FALLING SHORT

# INTRODUCTION

## On Taking Failure Seriously

If you intend to win, you cannot afford to lose.
—*Max Bunker and Magnus*, Alan Ford

This is a book about the Bildungsroman and crisis. It explores the nineteenth-century Bildungsroman's curious commitment to strife and defeat, and its seemingly obsessive tendency to produce narratives in which the process of individual development is inverted and frustrated or, at the very least, put under extreme pressure. To invoke the obvious examples: at the cusp of success, Stendhal's Julien Sorel (*Le Rouge et le Noir*, 1830) is executed. Honoré de Balzac's Lucien de Rubempré (*Illusions Perdues*, 1837–43, and *Splendeurs et misères des courtisanes*, 1838–47) and Henry James's Hyacinth Robinson (*The Princess Casamassima*, 1885–86) commit suicide. George Eliot's Maggie and Tom Tulliver (*The Mill on the Floss*, 1860), James's Roderick Hudson (*Roderick Hudson*, 1875), and Thomas Hardy's Jude Fawley (*Jude the Obscure*, 1894–95) all die barely reaching adulthood. In different ways, Charlotte Brontë's Lucy Snowe (*Villette*, 1853), George Meredith's Richard Feverel (*The Ordeal of Richard Feverel*, 1859), and Charles Dickens's Pip (*Great Expectations*, 1860–61) are condemned to a diminished existence, their aspirations thoroughly frustrated. And while both shameless social climbers (like Eugène de Rastignac in Balzac's 1835 *Le Père Goriot*) and reasonably scrupulous young men (like the eponymous hero of Dickens's *David Copperfield*, first published in 1849–50) are granted an occasional triumph, the chances of meaningful self-fulfillment remain decidedly bleak: the nineteenth century's developmental narratives have a pronounced tendency to turn into narratives of unbecoming, oddly committed to strife and failure, denial and frustration.[1] So much so, in fact, that the crisis of individual development emerges as a significant and, in some ways, defining preoccupation of the nineteenth-century bildungsroman.

Such is the heuristic gambit of *Falling Short:* first, to open up the category of the bildungsroman to this condition of crisis, to the notion that the process of becoming someone that it describes is always contested, invariably caught up in fundamental and often irresolvable disputes about the available ways of living; second, to explore the diverse social pressures that transform the bildungsroman plot into a site of difficult and generally unsuccessful attempts to resolve deep normative conflicts. *Falling Short* will therefore pursue the interpretative possibilities opened up by the hypothesis that the defeat of the aspiring hero tends to reveal a broader crisis in the very assumptions that govern the processes of individual development and social integration.[2]

These claims also address a specific methodological tension that continues to shape our critical engagement with the bildungsroman. On the surface, most contemporary theorists will duly acknowledge that the history of the bildungsroman is rife with humiliating defeats. Franco Moretti, Gregory Castle, and Jed Esty all recognize—on some level, at least—the role of failure in the genre's history.[3] As Castle puts it, "The history of the Bildungsroman is a history of a genre in crisis."[4] On closer scrutiny, however, it quickly becomes apparent that most of the otherwise methodologically diverse work on the bildungsroman continues to embrace an essentially affirmative vision of the genre, a vision difficult to reconcile with a radical questioning of the process of individual development. As a consequence, the reality of failure is generally acknowledged in principle, but is rarely granted full citizenship as a truly consequential structural element of the bildungsroman. At worst, failure is seen as an aberration, a foreign body, extrinsic to the true logic of the genre and recognized only along its historical and geographic periphery—in modernist texts written in the shadow of the Great War or in the postcolonial rewritings of the European bildungsroman, but not in the genre's realist heartlands. At best, it is seen as a part of the ideological mechanism that crushes the hero precisely in order to reinforce the integrative impulses at the heart of the bildungsroman. Consequently, the impossibility of self-realization is simultaneously one of the genre's most persistent features and something like an open secret: we know that it is there, but we don't quite know what to do with it, as it seems to elude our analytical models.

That such a paradox would develop was, perhaps, inevitable, given the history of the bildungsroman as a critical concept whose origins are difficult to disentangle from a broadly affirmative understanding of individual formation. When in 1819 Karl Morgenstern offered the first sustained theoretical reflection on the bildungsroman, he immediately tied the genre both to the defining example of Goethe's *Wilhelm Meister's Apprenticeship* (1795–96) and to the concept of *Bildung* that played such a pivotal role in the intellectual life of late eighteenth-century Germany. As Morgenstern argued, "The task of *Wilhelm Meister's Apprenticeship* appears to be nothing else than to depict a human being who develops toward his true nature by means of a collaboration of his inner dispositions with outer circumstances. The goal of this development is a perfect equilibrium, combining harmony with freedom."[5] In order to describe *Wilhelm Meister*—and, by extension, the genre that Goethe's novel inaugurated—Morgenstern resorted to the rhetoric of fulfillment and reconciliation firmly rooted in Wilhelm von Humboldt's influential understanding of Bildung as a process of social and psychological growth dependent on a productive encounter between the free individual and the world. As Humboldt wrote in 1792, "The true end of Man . . . is the highest and most harmonious *development* of his powers to a complete and consistent whole. Freedom is the grand and indispensable condition which the possibility of such a *development* presupposes."[6] And while Morgenstern's lecture was soon forgotten, the understanding of the bildungsroman as a genre invested in the protagonist's purposeful development toward maturity has very much endured. When in the early twentieth century Wilhelm Dilthey resuscitated the term, he retained an understanding of the bildungsroman as a narrative structure committed to the ideal of the hero's successful social integration. "Life's dissonances and conflicts," Dilthey wrote in 1906, "appear as necessary transitions to be withstood by the individual on his way towards maturity and harmony."[7]

Because it is so firmly rooted in a particular moment of German cultural and intellectual history, this essentially affirmative and conciliatory model of the bildungsroman has become difficult to unsettle, even once the genre's development started to provide us with good reasons to do so. In other words, because both Goethe's prototypical novel and the Humboldtian ideal it narrativizes share an investment in what Dilthey calls "the optimism of personal development,"[8] the hero's successful transition to adulthood has come to be seen not merely as one possible outcome of the developmental process that the bildungsroman describes, but as inherent to the logic of the genre.[9] As a consequence, this conciliatory paradigm, first articulated by Morgenstern and further elaborated by Dilthey, continues to exert considerable pressure on critical approaches to the bildungsroman. Significantly, as we shall see in a moment, this paradigm is operational not only among those scholars who espouse a relatively conservative view of the genre, emphasizing its specifically German cultural provenance and the defining role of Humboldtian Bildung in its history, but also in the recent critical work otherwise attuned to the fact that the bildungsroman functions as an international form relatively independent from the context in which it originated. In other words, and despite proclamations to the contrary, criticism is still haunted by the notion that the bildungsroman—in its "proper" form, at least—is a generic structure that values, above all else, some sort of equitable settlement between the protagonist's inner desires and outer circumstances.

Understandably, this broadly affirmative paradigm of the bildungsroman has encountered significant difficulties when faced with texts that are either incapable of or unwilling to deliver such a settlement, disallowing, instead, the very possibility of successful transition into adulthood. Because the original conceptual lens through which we approach the genre was not designed to account for the possible triumph of centrifugal tendencies within the bildungsroman plot—that is, for the all-too-frequent catastrophic disintegration of the hero's educational trajectory—the discrepancy between the purportedly affirmative logic of the bildungsroman and the seemingly destructive trajectory of so many of its important texts has been the central problem of bildungsroman theory and the key cause of widespread doubts regarding the coherence and legitimate scope of the bildungsroman as a critical concept.[10]

INTRODUCTION

As a consequence, one of the enduring concerns of bildungsroman criticism has been how to resolve this apparent tension between a conceptual framework built around an affirmative understanding of the developmental process and the actual history of the genre in which affirmation of individual development was becoming an increasingly rare occurrence, especially as the bildungsroman was becoming a more international genre. The conservative response to this difficulty has been to shore up the category by introducing a restrictive view of its generic boundaries and, consequently, by excising from the generic sequence those texts that seem to wander too far away from the dominant conciliatory paradigm rooted in Humboldtian Bildung. As Jeffrey Sammons puts it, "Bildungsroman should have something to do with Bildung, that is, with the early bourgeois, humanistic concept of the shaping of the individual self from its innate potentialities through acculturation and social experience to the threshold of maturity."[11] Such a solution comes with some significant advantages. Like the earlier theories of Morgenstern and Dilthey, it identifies the narrow and well-defined set of cultural circumstances that gave rise to the bildungsroman and provides the genre with a firm anchoring point in the late eighteenth-century understanding of Bildung, therefore shielding the bildungsroman from the charge of conceptual anarchy so often leveled at generic categories.[12] In fact, once such a model is accepted, some of the more difficult conundrums of bildungsroman theory can be elegantly dismissed: we no longer need to theorize the dramatic changes that occurred between Goethe's *Wilhelm Meister* and, for instance, Balzac's *Illusions perdues,* because, in this analysis, the latter novel is quite simply not a bildungsroman.[13] Such an elegant solution, however, comes at a price, as it provincializes the bildungsroman and turns it into a peculiarity of German literary culture with only a marginal presence in Britain or continental Europe and effectively forecloses the possibility of a comparative approach to the genre.[14]

Generally unwilling to pay such a high price, recent scholars have sought to construct an understanding of the bildungsroman that would allow them to reconcile its overwhelming interest in failure with the claim that the genre is, at its heart, committed to the ideal of harmonious socialization. One way to achieve this goal has been to acknowledge the reality of failure within the history of the genre, but to limit its significance. This approach has often surfaced in recent work on the modernist bildungsroman, which tends to see the crisis of socialization as a symptom of the genre's breakdown around the turn of the twentieth century. As Esty writes about the fictions of Olive Schreiner, Rudyard Kipling, and Joseph Conrad, "In open and sustained violation of the developmental paradigm that seemed to govern nineteenth-century historical and fictional forms, such novels tend to present youthful protagonists who die young, remain suspended in time, eschew vocational and sexual closure, refuse social adjustment, or establish themselves as evergreen souls via the tender offices of the *Kunstlerroman*" (3). In this interpretation, death, failure, and maladjustment are all implicitly construed as antithetical to the logic of the "traditional" nineteenth-century bildungsroman, while the story of the genre's development is subsumed into the broader narrative about the modernist subversion of realism's formal and ideological structures. The reality of failure is thus recognized but confined to the fringes of the tradition.[15]

A similar push to minimize the significance of failure in the history of the bildungsroman emerges in the work of Gregory Castle, who seeks to describe failed socialization as reconcilable with the bildungsroman's affirmative paradigm. According to this argument, realizing that you can't have it all is a vital part of the process of maturation, and if some novels stage harrowing defeats of individual desires, they do so with a lesson in mind, a lesson directed perhaps not at the defeated hero, but certainly at the reflexive reader. In other words, the bildungsroman's commitment to failure is explained by the genre's presumed pedagogical ambitions. As Castle explains,

> The hero's conflict with social authority (typically a real or symbolic father) ultimately leads to an affirmation of that authority in the social sphere and in the choice of a vocation. The primary function of the classical Bildungsroman up to the turn of the twentieth century had been to narrativize the dialectical harmony of this affirmation. If the process failed, as it often did in the French Bildungsroman, it did not mean that society had somehow

failed in its duty nor that dialectics has failed to signify the ideal relations of the individual to the social totality. Rather, such failures remind the hero (and the reader) that social maturity involves knowing one's limits and accepting one's place in the order of things.[16]

Failed socialization therefore only appears to contradict the bildungsroman's conciliatory logic: even if certain heroes are crushed, their defeat serves as a cautionary tale that, in the final analysis, only reaffirms the integrative ideals at the heart of the genre. *Wilhelm Meister* and *Illusions perdues* thus deliver the same message through different narrative means. While Goethe affirms the ideal of harmonious socialization by describing a hero who learns to live with his own limitations and accepts his place in the grand scheme of things, Balzac affirms the same ideal by portraying a hero who seems utterly incapable of such acceptance. As it soon becomes apparent, for Castle the primary aim of assimilating the novels of French realism to the "dialectical harmony" (12) of the German Enlightenment is to create a relatively unified image of the "classical" bildungsroman against which modernism's interventions are assessed: "In modernist hands, the Bildungsroman is critiqued from the standpoint of its tendency toward dialectical harmony, toward reconciliation of the self and the external social world that is preserved as utopian vision in Goethe and that is mourned as a lost paradisiacal dispensation in the French and English Bildungsromane throughout most of the nineteenth century" (26). Like Esty, Castle seeks to explain away the failure of the educational process: while the former consigns it to the bildungsroman's decadent late phase, the latter implies that the spirit of harmonious socialization is very much at work even in those nineteenth-century novels in which the developmental process seems to fail rather spectacularly. In both interpretations, the nineteenth-century bildungsroman's commitment to Bildung remains largely intact.

Even Franco Moretti—to whose versatile model of the bildungsroman this book has considerable debts—is inclined to see the bildungsroman's stubborn interest in failed socialization as a conscious strategy rather than as a symptom of the genre's struggle to cope with the complexity of the process it seeks to describe. As he argues, in a formulation that will be echoed by Castle (9), among the central tasks of the nineteenth-century bildungsroman was that "it [contain] the unpredictability of social change, representing it through the fiction of youth: a turbulent segment of life, no doubt, but with a clear beginning and unmistakable end" (230). The bildungsroman, in other words, symbolically represents the newfound social dynamism of modernity through the immodest and disruptive aspirations of its hero. When the hero is disposed of and his ambitions are rejected, as is the case with Stendhal's Julien Sorel and Balzac's Lucien de Rubempré, the bildungsroman can symbolically reestablish the conditions of social equilibrium. This, then, is its role: as a therapeutic tool in the hands of modern European culture, a tool used to simultaneously articulate and symbolically quash the unruly impulses of modernity.[17]

What these various approaches have in common—despite significant methodological differences and the diverging accounts of the bildungsroman's history that they ultimately produce—is the tendency to minimize or rationalize the persistence of failed socialization in nineteenth-century fiction. Sometimes this failure is seen as a problem because it contradicts the purportedly affirmative logic of the "true" bildungsroman, and sometimes because it weakens or complicates the argument about the bildungsroman's radical transformation at the hands of modernist authors.

The polemical ambition of this book is precisely to open up the interpretative possibilities closed off by such theorizations. Instead of seeking to diminish or explain away its significance, I wish to embrace the crisis of socialization as a vital feature of the nineteenth-century bildungsroman.[18] Neither an aberration alien to the requirements of the genre nor yet another brick in the great wall of novelistic pedagogy, the all-too-common failure of the nineteenth-century bildungsroman to see through the process of individual development to an equitable outcome testifies to something more consequential than the inadequacy of an odd protagonist whose well-deserved defeat will only reinforce the imperative of social cohesion. What is truly at stake is that the process of socialization—the bildungsroman's main thematic concern—is itself a site of uncertainty, contestation, and crisis. To paraphrase Castle, the nineteenth-century bildungsroman is less a structure dedicated to putting the hero (and the reader) in his place, but rather one that struggles to place him at all.

INTRODUCTION

What can account for this curious internal dynamics? To answer this question is to rethink the bildungsroman's relationship to modernity, the one relationship that has consistently—and with uneven results—preoccupied the historians of the genre. The assumption that the rise of the bildungsroman should be read as a response to the emergence of new social and discursive structures across modern Europe has surfaced under different guises in Morgenstern's early remarks on *Wilhelm Meister* as a text concerned with "modern European man's development"; in Moretti's vision of the bildungsroman as a genre tied to what he describes as modernity's "restlessness" (5); and in Joseph Slaughter's more recent argument about the bildungsroman and the modern discourse of human rights in *Human Rights, Inc.*[19] As the remarkable rhetorical overlap between the sociology of modernity and bildungsroman theory shows, the latter is heavily dependent on the assumption that a new form of the novel emerges in response to a major shift in the structure of social relations. In Mikhail Bakhtin's typically sweeping formulation, the bildungsroman does not merely narrate the "the emergence of a new man," but places individual development in the context of a historical reality that is itself caught up in the process of radical transformation: "The organizing force held by the future is therefore extremely great here—and this is not, of course, the private biographical future, but the historical future. It is as though the very *foundations* of the world are changing, and man must change along with them."[20] Bakhtin's insistence on the fluidity of the world into which the bildungsroman hero emerges—a world trapped in the process of permanent transition—anticipates Anthony Giddens's influential definition of modernity as "a society . . . which unlike any preceding culture lives in the future rather than in the past."[21] Indeed, when Giddens claims that in modernity "the transformation of time and space, coupled with the disembedding mechanisms, propels social life from the hold of preestablished precepts or practices,"[22] he sounds as if he is repeating Bakhtin's comments on *Wilhelm Meister*: "Everywhere, whatever served as and appeared to be a stable and immutable background for all movements and changes became for Goethe a part of emergence, saturated through and through with time, and emergence took on a more essential and creative mobility than ever."[23] In the final instance, the rise of modernity functions as the necessary precondition of the bildungsroman's emergence on the scene of European literature.

However, while the alignment between the rise of the bildungsroman and the rise of what Giddens famously describes as "the post-traditional order" can hardly be disputed, this particular convergence between literary and social history requires further elaboration.[24] As Tobias Boes argues, one of the problems of bildungsroman criticism has been its tendency to perform "a grand leap to very broad claims about temporally and geographically diverse novels and their supposed relationship to abstract concepts such as 'modernity' or 'humanity.'"[25] In other words, in order to avoid slipping into overly abstract arguments, it is necessary to identify specific social processes that are responsible both for the genre's emergence and for its enduring interest in failed socialization.

Some of the much-needed historical specificity is already on display in Moretti's *The Way of the World*. As we have seen in the preceding pages, most scholars tend to associate the bildungsroman's radical transformation with the later stages of its development and, in particular, with the transition from realism to modernism. However, one of Moretti's remarkable insights is that a particularly far-reaching change in the narrative logic of the bildungsroman occurred very early in its history. By 1830—the year in which Stendhal published *Le Rouge et le Noir*—a reasonable rapprochement between self-fulfillment and socialization, so central to Goethe (and, as Moretti argues, to Jane Austen), has become difficult to imagine. This transition, Moretti further claims, is closely tied to the dramatic transformation of European society and politics in the late eighteenth and the early nineteenth century. As he writes about *Wilhelm Meister*, "The definitive stabilization of individual, and of his relationship with the world—'maturity' as the story's final stage—is fully possible *only in the precapitalist world*" (27, emphasis original). My own understanding of this important early stage in the history of the bildungsroman broadly aligns with Moretti's. Goethe's novel explores the question of individual development within a context which is not only predominantly aristocratic (*Way of the World*, 64), but that possesses an almost caste-like rigidity.[26] The defining preoccupations of the bildungsroman from Stendhal onward, including the obsessive desire to break through social barriers and the fantasy of meteoric rise through the ranks, are nowhere to be found in *Wilhelm Meister*. To put it differently, it can be argued that novels like *Le Rouge et le Noir, Illusions perdues,* and *Great Expectations* revolve around a single question: How can a nobody become somebody? Goethe asks no such question. His protagonist is not a penniless parvenu fighting tooth and nail to move up in the world whose social hierarchies are in constant flux, but rather a young man from a well-established bourgeois house who will be gently co-opted into the world of aristocracy through the benevolent schemes of the Society of the Tower. The drama of social mobility can never really materialize in *Wilhelm Meister* because, as Moretti has persuasively argued, the preeminence of aristocracy faces no meaningful challenge.[27]

A different way of expressing this conclusion is to say that Goethe's novel falls on one side of a certain understanding of modernity, whereas the major texts of nineteenth-century realism fall on the other. Central to this vision of modernity is the assumption, articulated most famously by Eric Hobsbawm, that the end of the eighteenth century and the early decades of the nineteenth saw a radical transformation of Western societies, propelled by the rise of industrial economy on the one hand, and by the French Revolution on the other. As Paul Johnson has shown in *The Birth of the Modern,* by 1830 these transformative economic and political developments have thoroughly reshaped at least the most advanced of Western societies. In the process, they have created what Marshall Berman calls "the highly developed, differentiated and dynamic new landscape in which modern experience takes place."[28] As Berman describes it, this landscape is largely urban and industrialized, but—more important for my purposes—it is also simultaneously shaped by distinctly bourgeois ideals, by the lingering power of aristocracy, and by the rise of the working class, and it is characterized by a general sense of accelerated social change, apparent not only in various forms of political upheaval but also in new forms of social mobility.[29]

Unlike Wilhelm Meister, the heroes of the realist bildungsroman must navigate precisely this landscape: every parvenu in the French novel of the 1830s and 1840s must go from the provinces to the metropolis and negotiate between the demands of developing capitalism and the residual forms of aristocratic power. Dickens's young men yearn for a distinctly bourgeois ideal of respectability; the shift from preindustrial to industrial modes of production features prominently in the bildungsromans of Stendhal, Dickens, and Balzac; and the heroes of Balzac's and Gustave Flaubert's novels repeatedly engage in financial speculation. Later in the nineteenth century, when issues of industrial development and class tensions were compounded by the rise of working-class movements and modern nationalism, the bildungsroman will respond accordingly, forcing its heroes to engage these newly articulated political projects. "Modernity" in this sense is therefore more than a byword for the remarkable dynamism of nineteenth-century societies: it is also a set of specific processes that constitute the bildungsroman's most immediate context.

What follows from this analysis is a vision of the bildungsroman not as a genre that originates with Goethe and then persists, in one way or another, in its commitment to the ideal of reconciliation between the hero and the world until it breaks down around the turn of the twentieth century, but, rather, as a genre that begins to explore a fully modern socialization process only several decades after the publication of *Wilhelm Meister* and continues to do so throughout the nineteenth century and into the twentieth. This, of course, is not to say that no meaningful connection can be established between Goethe's novel (and the harmonizing ideal it has come to embody) and the subsequent development of the bildungsroman, but merely to acknowledge that such a connection appears only intermittently and that it does not govern the genre's subsequent trajectory.[30] *Wilhelm Meister* is not so much a prototype as it is a precursor: a text that anticipates many of the issues that subsequent bildungsromans will have to face in a more dramatic and less manageable form. To invoke an obvious example, the early chapters of Goethe's novel forcefully articulate the opposition between Wilhelm's and Werner's understanding of life, the former committed to an inward calling, the latter to practical pursuits of trade. As an exasperated Wilhelm protests when his parents begin to question his commitment to puppet theater: "For goodness' sake, Mother, why is everything useless that doesn't bring money or enlarge our property?"[31] While we can certainly recognize the conflict between "useful" and "useless" pursuits as a distinctly modern dilemma, subsequent bildungsromans will find it quite difficult to articulate such a conflict, mainly because they will struggle to imagine a kind of self-fulfillment that is not already wedded to the logic of capitalism. Balzac briefly introduces a similar opposition in *Illusions perdues* when he pushes Lucien de Rubempré to choose between joining the penniless aesthetes of the Cénacle and the cutthroat world of journalism, but this is not a very serious dilemma: for Lucien artistic ambitions can never be fully dissociated from fame and financial success. Even Dickens, who shows little interest in the details of David Copperfield's career or in his hero's finances, nonetheless assumes that his triumph as a writer comes with appropriate financial rewards. In Flaubert's *L'Éducation sentimentale* (1869), the idea of fully disinterested commitment to art is reduced to parody, and it will only reappear in modernism. In Goethe's world, one may still wonder whether to accept the premises of modern capitalism; in the world of nineteenth-century realism there is no such luxury.[32]

Even more significantly for my argument, it is precisely when the bildungsroman engages with fully developed modernity—the modernity of industrialization, urbanization, and the rise of the bourgeois order—that it begins to struggle to imagine a worthwhile future for its heroes. In other words, and contrary to what is usually assumed, the bildungsroman's interest in the crisis of individual development does not correspond to what Hobsbawm describes as the "end of the world made by and for the bourgeoisie" around the time of the Great War, but rather to the consolidation of that world nearly a century earlier.[33]

Why would this be the case? In my view, the curious position of the bildungsroman as a form simultaneously dedicated to the processes of individual development and social integration yet all too often unable to imagine those processes as successful stems from the peculiar double bind into which modernity places its subjects, simultaneously imposing and complicating the imperative of self-definition. In the words of Zygmunt Bauman, "Needing to *become* what one *is* is the feature of modern living—and of this living alone (not of 'modern individualization', that expression being evidently pleonastic; to speak of individualization and of modernity is to speak of one and the same social condition). Modernity replaces the heteronomic determination of social standing with compulsive and obligatory self-determination."[34] The imperative of individual self-determination gathers a particular sense of urgency in nineteenth-century Europe amid such events as the struggle to upend the traditional political hierarchies (particularly in France) and the social and economic disruption brought on by emerging capitalism (in France as well as in Britain). In different ways, both the ideals of popular sovereignty and those of economic liberalism have created a space in which individual existence can be imagined in terms of radical social mobility: within the frameworks of both French republicanism and liberal individualism, there is a range of social positions (including many toward the top of the social hierarchy) that are imagined as available to any man. Hence in Dickens the fixation on becoming a gentleman; hence the struggle of Stendhal's and Balzac's poor young provincials to make it in Paris.

However, the very condition that makes the project of self-determination "obligatory" is also the condition that turns this project into something of a trap. As Peter Wagner points out, "Although modernity emphasizes autonomy, the right and obligation to self-rule, it does not offer any guidance as to how one should design one's own rules, nor does it provide any criterion with which one should engage in rule deliberation."[35] Because it rejects the relative stability of earlier social arrangements, modernity imposes on its subjects the demand for self-definition, yet it is for that same reason that it cannot provide a definite normative framework within which this obligation can be carried out. Hence Pip's almost farcical pursuit of chimerical "expectations"; hence the abject failure of so many of Balzac's and Stendhal's heroes to achieve anything other than early death.

What modernity offers instead is a series of difficult dilemmas about available and desirable ways of living, courses of individual and collective action, and types of social organization. In a word, modern socialization is inextricably tied to a condition of normative crisis. It is this condition that the bildungsroman must engage: by exploring whether the acquisition of particular social roles is permissible and desirable, and if so, by what means, under what conditions, and at what cost. In doing so, it articulates not only the clash between inward desires and outward social, ethical, and economic pressures (which have traditionally preoccupied the theorists of the genre), but also the conflicting external demands imposed on the process of socialization at specific historical junctions. As I will show, the narratives of individual development are difficult to disentangle from such normative disagreements. Balzac's *Illusions perdues* and *Splendeurs et misères des courtisanes*—my main concern in chapter 1—stage painstaking and ultimately unsuccessful negotiations between opposing visions of social status and political legitimacy rooted variously in the aristocratic commitment to inherited privilege and in the post-Napoleonic fascination with extreme, self-propelling upward mobility. Conversely, as I show in chapter 2, the structure of Dickens's bildungsromans—from *Oliver Twist* (1837–39) to *Great Expectations* two decades later—reflects a fundamental conflict within the Victorian social imaginary between the pervasive liberal celebration of self-sufficiency and moral autonomy and a version of moral sentimentalism that conceives individual existence as fundamentally dependent on the care of others. Finally, the texts of Henry James and James Joyce that I explore in chapter 4 demonstrate how the rise of mass politics around the turn of the century further complicates the project of self-definition by imposing on the bildungsroman hero the demand to choose between conventional bourgeois socialization and a quasi-messianic role dictated by resurgent nationalist and socialist ideologies.

*Falling Short* seeks both to expose the deep normative conflicts and dramatic ruptures within the social imaginary that precipitate the crisis of individual development and to examine the range of strategies that the bildungsroman adopts in the attempt to negotiate these conflicts. The uncertainty surrounding the question of political legitimacy in early nineteenth-century France, the disputes about the limits of liberal individualism in England, and the forceful emergence of new political ideologies across Europe toward the end of the century all impose extreme pressures on the process of socialization. Work on the self is demanded from the heroes, and frustrated, unreasonable goals are imposed from the outside only to be deemed unattainable, while a tolerable—not outstanding, just tolerable—future proves difficult to imagine. Balzac's Lucien de Rubempré is simultaneously told that he can reinvent himself as a fashionable nobleman and punished because he has believed that he can reinvent himself as a fashionable nobleman. Dickens's Pip is both relentlessly nudged to embrace the fanciful "expectations" and then punished for pursuing them. Indeed, Dickens's deep ambivalence toward the hero of *Great Expectations,* and the novel's moralistic undertones (which suggest that Pip might have been better off had he decided to stay put instead of pursuing unrealistic ambitions), reveal a vision of social mobility as simultaneously irresistible and destructive, an inescapable fantasy but also a threat both to precapitalist forms of life and to the hero's moral and psychological well-being. In both Balzac and Dickens, the difficulty is not that the deluded hero pursues unrealistic expectations, but that the question of what the social expectations are and how they are articulated remains unresolved.

As I will show in the chapters that follow, in responding to such paradoxes the bildungsroman persistently vacillates between the temptation to articulate sociohistorical contradictions as forcefully as possible, fully exposing the absence of a normative consensus, and the equally persistent urge to suppress, contain, or escape those contradictions: its history over the course of the long nineteenth century is simultaneously a site of catastrophic confrontations regarding the possible ways of living and of complex maneuvering designed to circumvent such confrontations. Balzac's bildungsromans generally tend to amplify ideological and economic tensions, forcing the protagonist to participate in frantic movement between contrary assumptions about social mobility until he is destroyed, both morally and physically. Dickens follows in many ways the opposite path. If Balzac, in painstaking detail, forces his heroes to engage the economic and political realities of the early nineteenth century, Dickens's bildungsromans can be described as marvelous mechanisms for averting—or, at the very least, mediating—such an encounter. Balzac's novels illustrate the devastating effects of the centrifugal forces of developing capitalism on the process of individual development. For Dickens, however, such demonstration is hardly necessary: in both *Oliver Twist* and *David Copperfield* he offers his heroes an opportunity to lead reasonably content lives precisely by shifting his focus away from the social and economic pressures of capitalist modernity and toward a fantasy of care. As I will show in this book's concluding chapters, a similar dynamics will emerge around the turn of the century. While in James's *The Princess*

*Casamassima* and Joyce's *A Portrait of the Artist as a Young Man* (1914–15) the question of ideological allegiances acquires an existential significance for the protagonist, that same question will be thoroughly trivialized in Flaubert's *L'Éducation sentimentale,* whose hero learns to ignore it, and then curiously suppressed in Marcel Proust's *À la recherche du temps perdu* (1913–27), in which the society's ability to forget the details of the Dreyfus affair serves as the definitive reminder of the destructive workings of time. The bildungsroman, these examples suggest, is a form equally committed to staring modernity in the face and to developing sophisticated mechanisms for looking the other way.

Of course, because modernity is neither something one can easily grasp nor easily look away from, both paths will prove difficult, leading to complex acts of narrative maneuvering: the crisis of self-realization is also a crisis of plotting. The nineteenth-century bildungsroman therefore serves us a long list of troubled texts, including novels that are seemingly interminable, novels with forced endings, and novels unsure of what they are. Balzac's story of Lucien de Rubempré was more than a decade in the making, spaced out over a series of publications, and only belatedly assembled in the present form. Dickens, for his part, struggled with the ending of *Great Expectations,* unsure whether to foreclose the possibility of a joint future for Pip and Estella, and completely elided the narrative of education in *Oliver Twist,* a novel that abruptly ends as soon as the hero is saved from the hands of Fagin and Sykes. Charlotte Brontë's *Villette*—my main concern in chapter 3—offers one of the most oblique conclusions in all of Victorian fiction, suggesting, but not explicitly acknowledging, the death of Paul Emanuel, and hence of Lucy Snowe's dreams of a fulfilling future. Finally, Eliot's *Daniel Deronda* (1876) stands curiously divided between a Victorian courtship plot and the narrative of Daniel's quasi-messianic ambitions, while James's *The Princess Casamassima* can't decide whether it is a dynamitard novel or a Balzacian tale of infatuation with royalty.

Perhaps the most telling symptom of this crisis is the compulsion felt by so many of the bildungsroman's key authors to rewrite their own plots. Between the mid-1830s and late 1840s Balzac obsessively redeployed the bildungsroman form, first in *Le Père Goriot,* and then in the two novels that make up the gargantuan narrative of Lucien de Rubempré's Parisian conquest: in *Illusions perdues* Balzac sends his hero to Paris, returns him to the provinces after he is defeated in the capital, and then promptly sends him to Paris to try again in *Splendeurs et misères des courtisanes.* The pattern is repeated by Dickens, whose bildungsromans, from *Oliver Twist* to *David Copperfield* and *Great Expectations,* vary the narrative of a mistreated orphan's rescue from the forces of abuse and neglect, examining in the process the relationship between individual responsibility and external forces and the meaning of dependency and guardianship within the context of the developing capitalist economy. Finally, Brontë's variations on the theme of the orphaned governess in *Jane Eyre* (1847) and *Villette* reveal the repeated struggle to construct a space for female self-realization within the strict confines of Victorian domestic ideology. Among the key writers of nineteenth-century bildungsromans, social mobility and individual development repeatedly emerge as problems that will need to be revisited several times.

*Falling Short* therefore proposes an understanding of the nineteenth-century bildungsroman as a generic structure within which those processes that can be variously described as maturation, development, social integration, subject formation, and upward social movement are not just examined but vigorously contested. More often than not, the bildungsroman tends to destroy its heroes not because they are inadequate—although inadequate they may very well be—but because it cannot find a way to reconcile the contradictory historical forces to which the nineteenth century has exposed them. The breakdown of the educational process, in other words, should be taken not as a triumph of novelistic pedagogy but rather as the most prominent symptom of the tremendous difficulties that the bildungsroman's developmental paradigm faces throughout the nineteenth century. As I will show in the following chapters, for the nineteenth-century bildungsroman the process of socialization is always already a site of crisis. This crisis, I will further argue, manifests itself both in the catastrophic demise of some of the iconic bildungsroman protagonists and in the formal difficulties so many novelists face as they struggle to control their narratives.

INTRODUCTION

The understanding of the bildungsroman that this book proposes will serve to qualify and upset both some of the rhetoric of exhaustion and breakdown espoused by most historians of the genre and some of the common binaries we tend to invoke when we speak and write about the bildungsroman. My inquiry begins by locating fundamental normative conflicts and a deeply compromised socialization process in precisely those canonical texts that most contemporary scholarship sees as the paradigmatic examples of the nineteenth-century European bildungsroman. My key examples in chapter 1 will be Balzac's *Illusions perdues* and *Splendeurs et misères des courtisanes,* two novels that forcefully exemplify the struggle to reconcile conflicting assumptions about social status and upward mobility in a society hopelessly divided between competing notions of legitimacy, and hence profoundly unsure about what constitutes a permissible claim to social ascent. In chapter 2, I move across the English Channel in order to examine a similarly paradigmatic set of texts and a similarly deep rupture within the social imaginary. My focus is on Dickens's *Oliver Twist, David Copperfield,* and *Great Expectations,* a series of novels that in different ways enact the conflict between the liberal celebration of self-reliance and moral autonomy and a version of moral sentimentalism that invariably conceived individual existence as communally embedded.

Having described the crisis of social integration and individual development at the heart of mid-century realism, I proceed to examine the unpredictable dynamics of continuity and discontinuity, rejection and appropriation, that links these mid-century novels of Balzac and Dickens with some of the texts that are usually seen as comprehensively violating the bildungsroman's generic demands. This line of inquiry will proceed in two directions: toward the female bildungsroman, routinely conceptualized as fundamentally incommensurable with the narratives of male development (and hence excluded from the more comprehensive histories of the genre), and toward the modernist bildungsroman, whose abandonment of the mid-century commitment to bourgeois socialization is usually seen as a sign of the generic crisis that engulfed the bildungsroman around the turn of the twentieth century.

Chapter 3 focuses on Brontë's *Jane Eyre* and *Villette* and argues that the unique cultural significance of Brontë's bildungsromans lies precisely in her ability to appropriate and adopt the typically masculine form of the bildungsroman in order to explore the process of female development within the context of the radical social limitations imposed on genteel femininity in Victorian England. While such a negotiation will prove extraordinarily difficult, in Brontë's hands the constraints imposed on female development will nonetheless serve to galvanize rather than to suppress the bildungsroman plot: paradoxically, it is precisely because Brontë must tread very carefully to reconcile her heroines' disruptive aspirations to the demands of Victorian domestic ideology that her novels approach, however tentatively, the sense of compromise central to traditional definitions of the bildungsroman.

The final two chapters explore some of the divergent paths that the bildungsroman took around the turn of the century. Chapter 4, which offers detailed readings of James's *The Princess Casamassima*, Samuel Butler's *The Way of All Flesh*, and Joyce's *A Portrait of the Artist as a Young Man*, chronicles the bildungsroman's response to the rise of mass politics beginning in the last third of the nineteenth century. While in novels like *Illusions perdues* and *Great Expectations* the central dilemma for the hero is whether to languish in the provinces or to pursue a more ambitious path in the metropolis, by the 1870s and 1880s the question at hand is whether the commitment to a particular political goal should take precedence over the hero's individual ambitions. While Lucien de Rubempré goes to Paris in pursuit of wealth and fame and Pip goes to London to become a gentleman, Eliot's Daniel Deronda goes to Palestine to become a national redeemer, Émile Zola's Etienne Lousteau heads to Paris driven by revolutionary zeal, and Joyce's Stephen Dedalus threatens to abandon Ireland in what I read as a stark rejection of the dominant forms of ethnolinguistic nationalism. As I demonstrate in the final section of the chapter, Joyce's seminal modernist bildungsroman is best understood as an attempt to find release from the ideological and intellectual legacies of the later nineteenth century: Stephen's rebellion against the demands of the Gaelic Revival constitutes a late iteration of the bildungsroman's struggle with ethnic nationalism, a struggle that began forty years earlier with Eliot's *Daniel Deronda*.

Whereas chapter 4 focuses on those novels that explicitly framed the development of their heroes in ideological terms—that is, in terms of inward struggle to accept or reject a definite set of ideological assumptions dictated by various contemporary mass movements—my final chapter focuses on writers who, although faced with the same ideological upheaval, refuse to turn the bildungsroman into an exploration of the force of collective identity. Along with Flaubert, whom I discuss briefly at the beginning, the central concern of chapter 5 is Proust's *Recherche*. Whereas Joyce seeks to displace the question of collective loyalties that preoccupied the genre in the final decades of the nineteenth century, Proust develops an elaborate mechanism that simultaneously invokes and suppresses such ideological concerns and fundamentally transforms the parvenu plot that had dominated the French bildungsroman tradition since Stendhal. Although steeped in the political context of the 1890s and in nineteenth-century theories of sexuality, the *Recherche* appropriates the form of the Balzacian social chronicle only to invert it, displacing the interest in the mechanics of social mobility with an epistemological enquiry into the possibility of intersubjective communication. After a century in which the narrative of individual development kept going awry, the move toward aesthetic education is, above all, an attempt to look beyond the enduring crisis of social apprenticeship.

It is, of course, not at all obvious that such maneuvering is entirely persuasive: after all, Stephen Dedalus will never leave Dublin (even if his creator will), and Proust's Marcel will continue to inhabit a fictional universe that can never fully shed its Balzacian roots. And yet the failure to wholly suppress the ideological and socioeconomic pressures that complicate the task of socialization is to be expected. From Stendhal to Proust, the unusual power of the bildungsroman as a form stems precisely from the fact that it articulates, enacts, intensifies, brings forth, and then struggles with issues that it can never fully resolve. *Falling Short* aims to chronicle and theorize this struggle.

# 1

# LUCIEN DE RUBEMPRÉ AND THE POLITICS OF USURPATION IN POST-NAPOLEONIC FRANCE

It cannot be an accident that Balzac's most extensive reflection on social mobility is also his most extensive reflection on the failure of social mobility. *Illusions perdues* and *Splendeurs et misères des courtisanes,* two books focusing on Lucien de Rubempré's unsuccessful attempts to claim a place for himself among the elites of Restoration France, are also among Balzac's longest novels, with a combined total of some thirteen hundred pages in most modern editions. And although both novels persistently dismiss their hero as naïve, erratic, and unfocused, Lucien has nonetheless managed to occupy Balzac's imagination more stubbornly than any of his other protagonists, including Eugène de Rastignac, the most able social climber of *La Comédie humaine*.[1]

The writing history behind Lucien's saga speaks for itself. In late June 1836 Balzac wrote to Émile Regnault to announce that he had written the first forty pages of a new book and that with another ninety pages he would be done: "In all likelihood, I will finish *Illusions perdues* by next Saturday."[2] In reality, what Balzac published the following year under that title was not more than the first quarter of the novel as we know it today, with further installments to follow in 1839 and 1843. Moreover, long before the full text of *Illusions perdues* was published, Balzac was already writing its sequel, *Splendeurs et misères des courtisanes*. An early version of the first part of *Splendeurs* appeared as *La Torpille* in 1838. The conclusion to *Illusions perdues* and roughly the first half of *Splendeurs* appeared almost simultaneously in the summer of 1843, and the final part of

*Splendeurs* was published in 1847. What was meant to be done in a week took more than a decade to write.

What this complex publication history suggests is that Balzac felt compelled to rewrite the plot of *Illusions perdues* even before he had finished writing it. In *Illusions perdues,* Lucien attempts to penetrate the world of aristocracy by taking the noble name that once belonged to his mother, then struggles to rise through the ruthless economy of Parisian journalism, and, having failed in both endeavors, returns home to the provinces, prepared to commit suicide. Yet even before his initial Parisian adventure was complete, Lucien was already revived as the hero of *Splendeurs* and given another opportunity to try and conquer Paris under the guidance of the master criminal Vautrin, only to fail once more. The way in which Lucien's fate is plotted offers a radical departure from most of the bildungsroman tradition. Although it is not entirely uncommon for bildungsroman heroes to return from the metropolis, such returns are seldom as far-reaching as the one Balzac offers: his decision to *reset* the bildungsroman plot and to rewrite it while it was still being written suggests that the crisis of social mobility by Lucien de Rubempré had transformed into a crisis of plotting for his creator.

This crisis developed from Balzac's struggle to negotiate the unique pressures imposed on the process of socialization in early and mid-nineteenth-century France. Is upward social movement anything more than an exercise in self-invention? Who can assume positions of privilege and how? What kinds of knowledge, social capital, and work on the self make upward mobility possible? Both Lucien's persistent failures and Balzac's obsessive rewriting of Lucien's story stem from the inability to offer a plausible answer to these questions—an inability that plagued Restoration society as much as it plagued Balzac's novels.

With the restoration of the Bourbon Monarchy in 1815, it seemed that France had left behind both the revolutionary experiment of 1789 and Napoleon's imperial fantasy, which marked the early years of the nineteenth century. In reality, however, both of these projects continued to exert tremendous pressure on both the structure of French society and the collective imagination. On the one hand, the French Revolution, however troubling its history, had managed not only to abolish the aristocracy, but also to articulate a compelling meritocratic and egalitarian challenge to the monarchical principle of inherited privilege. On the other, Napoleon Bonaparte's unlikely rise from obscurity offered a paradoxical but far-reaching precedent. While his triumph seemed to confirm the meritocratic assumptions that drove the revolution, he nonetheless proceeded to engineer an aristocratic order of his own: the emperor was also a self-made man. By 1821—the year when Lucien de Rubempré arrives in Paris—France was once again a monarchy ideologically dominated by a reactionary aristocratic class that did its best to suppress the legacy of the revolution and of the self-proclaimed emperor Napoleon, but could not quite forget that only a decade earlier this Corsican nobody managed to conquer Europe. Lucien is therefore attempting to make it in a society that is simultaneously deeply invested in an essentially aristocratic understanding of social status as an inherited privilege and whose elites in practice included an uneasy mix of the old nobility, yesterday's republicans ennobled by Napoleon, and self-appointed parvenus.[3]

Because the social universe Lucien de Rubempré struggles to navigate is defined by an unresolved relationship between competing models of social power, economic and cultural production, and political legitimacy, there is no master model he can rely on in his quest for success. Instead, what he faces is a series of interrelated contradictions. On the one hand, there is the irresistible attraction of ennoblement, understood not simply in terms of rapid rise through the ranks, but as something akin to an instantaneous invention or an almost alchemical conversion; on the other, there is a powerful reactionary discourse committed to defending the legitimacy of traditional aristocratic privilege, yet unable to quell the legacy of dramatic social change on which Lucien's fantasy of extreme and instantaneous upward movement rests. Perhaps most significantly, the clash between the reactionary notions of aristocratic prestige and the fantasies of Napoleonic rise is itself implicated in a powerful exchange economy that needs to be mastered, but that proves fully unnavigable, even for Vautrin.

Balzac's approach to the question of social mobility in both *Illusions perdues* and *Splendeurs* is entirely governed by these contradictions. The simultaneous writing and rewriting of Lucien's story, along with the inevitable failure the hero suffers at the end of both novels, suggests that the oppositions between monarchical and republican visions of social hierarchy and between feudal and capitalist modes of wealth acquisition have created a rupture within the social imaginary that renders the process of socialization effectively unnavigable. This chapter analyzes the failure of navigation that shapes the logic of Balzac's two Lucien novels. First, however, I will take a brief detour through the work of Stendhal, who had already modeled the bildungsroman hero on the Napoleonic example.

## From Self-Fashioning to Self-Invention

When Balzac began to develop the story of Lucien de Rubempré in the mid-1830s, the French novel was already exploring the mechanisms of social mobility in the post-Napoleonic world. Stendhal's *Le Rouge et le Noir* (1830) anticipates the main themes of Balzac's fiction and brings to the fore the figure of the young provincial parvenu who will attempt to conquer Paris, encouraged by the Napoleonic example. For Stendhal's Julien Sorel, vigorous work on the self is the condition of success: he will consciously shape himself in order to emulate the forms of behavior and appearance exhibited by those who hold power and influence. Like Napoleon, he aspires to go from nothing to something—from an obscure lieutenant, as he puts it, to the ruler of the world. He only needs to adopt the model to the circumstances. Twenty years earlier, at the height of Napoleon's power, prestige was associated with the army, and now equivalent power and status are associated with the Church (71, 26).[4] Hence Julien's initial attempt to rise through the Church hierarchy; hence the laborious task of memorizing the New Testament in Latin.

In many respects, Julien's project closely corresponds to the practice of self-fashioning described by Stephen Greenblatt. For Greenblatt, self-fashioning "is linked to manners or demeanor, particularly that of the elite; it may suggest hypocrisy or deception, and adherence to mere outward ceremony; it suggests a representation of one's nature or intention in speech or actions."[5] As Julien quickly understands, what is required in order to make it in the Church is not familiarity with the dogma, but rather the ability to project the image of pious devotion:

> Que de peine ne se donnait-il pas pour arriver à ce front béat et étroit, à cette physionomie de foi fervente et aveugle, prête à tout croire et à tout souffrir, que l'on trouve si fréquemment dans les couvents d'Italie, et dont à nous autres laïcs, le Guerchin a laissé de si parfaits modèles dans ses tableaux d'église. (264)

> (What endless trouble he took to attain that facial expression of fervent and blind faith, ready to believe and suffer anything, that is so often encountered in monasteries in Italy, and of which Guercino has left us laymen such perfect models in his church paintings.) (191)

Stendhal is even meticulous enough to provide the exact reference: "Voir, au musée du Louvre, François duc d'Aquitaine déposant la couronne et prenant l'habit de moine, no 1130" (See, in the Louvre, Francois, Duke of Aquitaine laying down his breastplate and putting on a monk's habit, n.1130; 264n, 191n). Selves are to be shaped according to models, through a vigorous course of observation, practice, and attention to detail.

It hardly needs emphasizing that this elegant plan is profoundly hypocritical: hypocrisy is the sine qua non of Julien's project, though it is by no means its end point. In *Le Rouge et le Noir* dissimulation is a dreadfully serious affair, requiring a frightening degree of self-discipline, and neither *playing a part* nor *self-invention* do justice to this ambitious project. What is at stake is a process that requires constant perfectioning. "What is haunting about such a project," writes Greenblatt about Sir Thomas More, "is the perpetual self-reflexiveness it demands, and, with this self-reflexiveness, perpetual self-estrangement."[6] In other words, self-fashioning works both as a mechanism of forging individual identity, and a mechanism that reveals the artificial nature of what is being forged.

In spite of such contradictions, the problem of selfhood is at least still taken seriously—perhaps too seriously. What seems premodern about Julien is precisely this fusion of the commitment to subjectivity and the commitment to personal achievement, which together generate the irresistible desire to internalize the fictions of his ambition. Julien attempts to overcome what Moretti calls an "opposition between formation and socialization" (131) by calling for the fusion between the two processes. His

"Koran" consists of both Rousseau's *Confessions* (1782) and Las Cases's *Le Mémorial de Sainte-Hélène* (1823), signifying an attempt to reconcile the exploration of interiority with naked ambition (*Le Rouge et le Noir*, 66; *The Red and the Black*, 22). For instance, even when he is presented with a clearly false noble identity that Monsieur de la Mole provided for him, Julien is quick to identify with it in a way that pushes his project far beyond mere hypocrisy:

> Serait-il bien possible, se disait-il, que je fusse le fils naturel de quelque grand seigneur exilé dans nos montagnes par le terrible Napoléon? A chaque instant, cette idée lui semblait moins improbable. . . . Ma haine pour mon père serait une preuve. . . . Je ne serais plus un monstre! (586–87)

> (Could it really be possible, he wondered, that I might be the natural son of some great lord driven into exile in our mountains by the terrible Napoleon? This idea seemed less improbable to him with every passing moment. . . . My hatred for my father would be proof of it. . . . I shouldn't be a monster any more!) (465)

And once he is given the rank of lieutenant and a spot in a regiment to accompany his title, Julien will immediately start to fantasize about military achievements (588, 466), despite the fact that he has no military experience. What is at stake is not so much a question of ethics, of moral legitimation, as it is of an understanding of social mobility that calls both for one's external appearance and for one's interiority to be shaped in accordance with the demands of ambition.

As we turn from Stendhal to Balzac, however, we will face a steady erosion of this thoroughness, and the slow disappearance of this intersection of self-fashioning, learning, and social mobility. Whereas Stendhal's hero is committed to meticulous work on the self that blurs the line between mere hypocrisy and elaborate self-engineering, Balzac introduces a more radical interpretation of the Napoleonic example: Stendhal's Julien Sorel believes that he can turn himself into a Napoleonic figure through intense work on himself, while Balzac's Lucien de Rubempré believes that he can become a Napoleonic figure by pretending that he is a Napoleonic figure.

The transformation of the bildungsroman hero from a master of self-fashioning into a master of self-invention was not instantaneous. In *Le Père Goriot,* Balzac's other key reflection on mobility, social initiation is still understood as a process, and his hero, Eugène de Rastignac, still knows that he needs to learn, and that he will need a tutor:

> Si d'abord il voulut se jeter à corps perdu dans le travail, séduit bientôt par la nécessité de se créer des relations, il remarqua combien les femmes ont d'influence sur la vie sociale, et avisa soudain à se lancer dans le monde, afin d'y conquérir des protectrices: devaient-elles manquer à un jeune homme ardent et spirituel dont l'esprit et l'ardeur étaient rehaussés par une tournure élégante et par une sorte de beauté nerveuse à laquelle les femmes se laissent prendre volontiers? (57–58)

> (If at first he wanted to throw himself wholeheartedly into his work, he was soon diverted by the need to make social contacts, and noticing how influential women are in social life, he suddenly took it into his head to launch out into the world so that he could win some feminine patronage. Could such patronage fail to reward an ardent and witty young man, whose wit and ardour were enhanced by an elegant bearing and the kind of wiry good looks to which women willingly succumb?) (28)[7]

Acquiring a patron is still a serious task, and one complicated by the fact that there is much that Rastignac doesn't know. When visiting Mme de Restaud he makes the mistake of mentioning Goriot, unaware that the old man is the father of the lady of the house; at Mme de Beauséant he addresses her as "ma cousine" showing that he doesn't quite understand their relationship, and prompting a shocked "Hein?" from her (104, 63). But Rastignac, at least, knows that he doesn't know. He seems aware that there is a system of communication, of manners, of phrases and glances that he needs to penetrate, and, above all, that the world of high society poses an epistemological problem. He understands that there are laws, principles, and signs to be learned, and he knows that he will need an instructor. What brings him to Mme de Beauséant after making the gaffe of mentioning old Goriot to Mme de Restaud is "pour vous demander le mot d'une énigme, et vous prier de me dire de quelle nature est la sottise que j'y ai faite" (to ask you to solve a puzzle for me and to tell me what sort of blunder I committed; 106, 65). As Peter Brooks comments on these words, "[Balzac's] ambitious young men may not be brooding intellectuals, but they are theorists of their destinies, and quickly come to understand that the realization of *vouloir/pouvoir* depends on a certain social *savoir*."[8] The boudoirs Rastignac visits, Balzac tells us quite explicitly, are above all sites of learning (105, 65).

In *Illusions perdues,* however, Balzac offers a rewriting of *Le Père Goriot* in which this commitment to learning begins to dissolve. Once again, he presents us with a young provincial man with some talent and endless ambition and with a society woman who is to serve as his ticket to social success and as something of a mentor. Like Rastignac, Lucien de Rubempré doesn't quite understand the etiquette of Parisian high society and is bound to produce a series of social blunders: he will dress atrociously and shout loudly every time he recognizes an acquaintance at the opera. Like Rastignac, Lucien will request the help of an aristocratic protectress (174, 159), and he will begin to understand "les impitoyables lois du monde" (the inexorable laws of the world; 85, 63). No doubt these are the same laws Balzac had in mind when in *Le Père Goriot* he spoke of "une haute jurisprudence sociale qui, bien apprise et bien pratiquée, mène à tout" (an advanced social jurisprudence which, when learned and well practices, opens every door; 106, 64). There are further remnants of this language of knowledge or of lack of thereof in *Illusions perdues:* at the opera, Lucien looks "comme un étranger qui ne savait pas la langue" (like a foreigner who does not speak the language; 192, 177), and he is fully aware that there is an abyss between him and the world he is trying to penetrate (184, 168). And, to his credit, he will soon master some of the art of appearance.

But we should not fail to note a certain progression here—for Julien Sorel, the integrated problems of selfhood and knowledge; for Rastignac, the understanding that he will need to learn the laws of the world; and, for Lucien, as we shall soon see, only traces of both. In other words, Julien believes he must work on constantly reshaping himself, Rastignac believes he must learn, and Lucien retains some of the same rhetoric of knowledge, but both his and Balzac's interest seem to lie elsewhere. In *Illusions perdues* we find only remnants of the discourse that permeated *Le Père Goriot:* if Mme de Beauséant was asked for a solution to a puzzle—"le mot d'une énigme"—Lucien's mentor, Louise de Bargeton, is only asked for help. In *Illusions perdues* the interest in knowledge as a condition of success is largely displaced, as Balzac makes it clear that his exploration this time will go beyond the learning of manners and codes.

*Illusions perdues* eschews the interest in knowledge in order to explore the immensely seductive proposition that the key to social mobility lies not in a meticulous learning process, but in the single bold gesture of self-invention. This alternative theory of social advancement is introduced by Louise early in the novel. As she puts it while persuading Lucien to take up the name de Rubempré, "Plus tôt il se fera, plus vite il sera sanctionné" (The sooner it is done, the sooner it will be sanctioned; 81, 59). He only needs to take the distinguished name—his real last name is Chardon (thistle)—and further conversions will ensue automatically. At least in Louise's seductive description of this process, only a few decisive alchemical moves will make all the difference: Lucien will take the new name, they will go to Paris, and Louise will introduce him to the Marquise d'Espard's circle. And then Lucien simply needs to be put in the spotlight, and he will be recognized for all that he is.

> Vous ne sauriez croire combien il est utile à un jeune talent d'être mis en lumière par la haute société. Je vous ferai recevoir chez madame d'Espard; personne n'a facilement l'entrée de son salon, où vous trouverez tous les grands personnages, les ministres, les ambassadeurs, les orateurs de la Chambre, les pairs les plus influents, des gens riches ou célèbres. Il faudrait être bien maladroit pour ne pas exciter leur intérêt, quand on est beau, jeune et plein de génie. Les grands talents n'ont pas de petitesse, ils vous prêteront leur appui. Quand on vous saura haut placé, vos œuvres acquerront une immense valeur. (160)

(You cannot imagine how helpful it is to young talent to be placed in the limelight of high society! I will get an introduction for you to Mme d'Espard; no one has ever found it easy to get an entrée into her drawing room, where you will meet all the great: ministers, ambassadors, orators of the Chamber, the most influential peers, wealthy and famous people of every kind. You could scarcely fail to arouse their interest, handsome as you are, and young, and talented. Men of genius are not petty-minded; they will give you what help they can. When you are known to be highly placed, your works will acquire immense prestige.) (143)

This understanding of social mobility is, however, quickly challenged by the Marquise d'Espard herself. Having arrived in Paris, and having joined the Marquise d'Espard's opera party, Lucien is dismissed as an imposter the moment his hostess realizes that he has no legitimate claim to the name de Rubempré. As she tells Louise, "Attendez donc que le fils d'un apothicaire soit réellement célèbre avant de vous y intéresser" (You must wait until the son of a chemist is really a celebrity before you take him up; 197, 184). One cannot just call himself de Rubempré and expect to be treated as such.

Or perhaps one can. While it is easy to dismiss all this as a provincial fantasy from which both Louise and Lucien are cruelly awakened as soon as they arrive in Paris, the fact of the matter is that some version of the theory according to which identity and social status can be changed through one radical gesture will linger throughout the novel. The power of this apparent illusion lies in the fact that it is a collective fantasy rather than a simple manifestation of the hero's naïveté. In part, the understanding of upward mobility as something like instant creation ex nihilo can be attributed to the exceptionally influential example of the Corsican lieutenant who spoke bad French but nonetheless managed to become the ruler of France and much of Europe. As Vautrin tells Lucien at the end of *Illusions perdues,* "C'est le défaut des Français dans votre époque. Ils ont été gâtés tous par l'exemple de Napoléon" (It is the great fault of Frenchmen of your generation. You have all been spoiled by the example of Napoleon; 628, 659). However, Napoleon's unprecedented rise was only part of a much larger debate about the sources of political legitimacy and social privilege. In Vautrin's words:

> Les Français ont inventé, en 1793, une souveraineté populaire qui s'est terminée par un empereur absolu. Voilà pour votre histoire nationale.... Sans-culotte en 1793, Napoléon chausse la couronne de fer en 1804. Les féroces amants de *l'Egalité ou la Mort* de 1792, deviennent, dès 1806, complices d'une aristocratie légitimée par Louis XVIII. (629–30)

> (The French in 1789 invented the idea of popular sovereignty, and it ended in the absolute rule of an Emperor.... Napoleon was a sans-culotte in 1793, and donned the iron crown in 1804. The fierce fanatics of Equality or Death in 1792, in 1806 conspired with the Legitimist aristocracy for the restoration of Louis XVIII.) (660–61)

By the 1830s, following decades of political upheaval, France had become a country with several intermingled and competing elites: on the one hand, the ancient nobles, whose members could often trace their privileges deep into the Middle Ages, and, on the other, the Napoleonic aristocracy, populated by plebeians recently ennobled by a man who usurped the French throne, declaring himself no less than an emperor even though his claims to noble heritage were slim at best. Lucien's ambition to reinvent himself as the heir to the noble name of de Rubempré therefore speaks to one of the central ideological anxieties of Restoration France: Who has the legitimate right to call themselves noble and, consequently, who can claim the social and economic privileges associated with the noble status?

For the Marquise d'Espard, who is scandalized to discover that Lucien is simply "a Chardon" who had usurped the name of his mother's noble family, the answer to such questions is quite simple:

> Au roi seul appartient le droit de conférer, par une ordonnance, le nom des Rubempré au fils d'une demoiselle de cette maison; et si elle s'est mésalliée, la faveur serait énorme, et pour l'obtenir, il faut une immense fortune, des services rendus, de très hautes protections. (198)

> (Only the King has the right to confer, by a special ordinance, the name of Rubempré on the son of a daughter of that family; if she made a misalliance,

it would be an enormous favor, and it would cost an enormous sum to obtain it, or services rendered, or the most powerful influence.) (184)

The Marquise's legitimist view is in line both with the actual legal provisions during the Restoration that explicitly treated the usurpation of noble titles as a criminal offense, and with the fundamental principles that traditionally governed the institution of nobility. As Édouard de Barthélemy wrote in 1858, "Il était de règle absolue que nul ne pouvait acquérir un titre héréditaire autrement que par lettres patentes qui devant être enregistrées dans un des cours souveraines" (It was an absolute rule that a hereditary title can be obtained only through the letters of patent recorded in one of the sovereign courts).[9] From a legitimist perspective, the right to ennoble is a central royal prerogative. In fact, the power to do so at will provides grounds for the definition of sovereignty: a sovereign is one who can ennoble.[10]

What Lucien desires is, therefore, both ideologically unwelcome and illegal. It is not, however, impossible, for the reality was much murkier than the legitimist discourse would admit. The paradox shaping early and mid-century France was that the concept of the elite was still defined in aristocratic terms—to be someone was to be noble—while the very idea of aristocracy was put under extreme pressure by a series of dramatic political changes since the revolution of 1789. The 1789 Declaration of the Rights of Man and the Citizen eliminated aristocratic privileges, establishing the legal equality of all citizens. This was followed by a formal abolition of hereditary nobility and by the mass persecution of nobles during the Reign of Terror. Under Napoleon, however, the tide had turned. He had presided over a gradual "drift towards monarchical hierarchy" beginning with the creation of the Légion d'honneur in 1802 and culminating in the establishment of his own imperial nobility in 1808, although without violating the principle of equality before the law.[11] Several further twists ensued. When the old nobility was reinstated during the First Restoration in 1814, the new monarchical order recognized the Napoleonic titles. However, when Napoleon briefly returned to power during the Hundred Days, he was less generous and immediately disestablished the old nobility. Finally, when Napoleon was definitely ousted in 1815, the provisions of the First Restoration were back in force, recognizing both the old and the new nobility. For nearly a quarter of a century, an institution meant to embody continuity and stability of the social order was repeatedly disestablished, reestablished, and reconfigured every few years.

While, strictly speaking, the Marquise d'Espard is correct to argue that under the provisions of the Charter of 1814 the right to ennoble belongs to the king alone, recent historical developments have severely complicated the social status of the aristocracy. The ambivalence is captured in the language of the charter itself: "La noblesse ancienne reprend ses titres. La nouvelle conserve les siens. Le Roi fait des nobles à volonté; mais il ne leur accorde que des rangs et des honneurs, sans aucune exemption des charges et des devoirs de la société" (The old nobility takes back its titles. The new keeps theirs. The King creates nobles at will; but he doesn't accord them anything beyond ranks and honors, without any exemption from the burdens and duties of society).[12] The rhetoric of the charter sums up the complexities associated with any claim to legitimate power in a country that went through seven constitutions between 1791 and 1814. The text struggles with both the revolutionary and Napoleonic legacies as it simultaneously accepts the equality of all citizens and the existence of the imperial nobility. Paradoxically, in order to advance its own legitimist agenda, the Restoration must recognize the ultimate gesture of illegitimacy and equate the status of the old nobility with that of the imperial nobility created by Napoleon. The very document that affirms the related institutions of royal sovereignty and hereditary nobility goes on to admit that both can be effectively usurped. It is ultimately an act of post hoc legitimation of both Napoleon's invention of the new nobility and of his self-invention as a constitutional monarch. As one hostile pamphletist of the period observes, "L'archi-roturier Buonaparte a-t-il pu donner ce qu'il n'avait pas lui-même?" (Can the arch-commoner Bonaparte give what he himself doesn't have?)[13] Apparently, he can.

If Lucien takes for granted self-invention ex nihilo—usurpation, if you will—it is because the political legacy of the thirty years preceding his appearance on the stage of Parisian high society has radically destabilized the notion of legitimacy. The great lesson of the Napoleonic years is the one about the power of performativity: you are who you say you are. This lesson is so widespread that even die-hard legitimists who try to counter it cannot quite shake off the thought that one can acquire social identity simply by enacting it. The Marquise d'Espard is quick to reject Lucien's attempt to pass as a legitimate member of the aristocracy precisely because she knows that his claims are not entirely implausible. In the caustic words of Germaine de Staël, "After the restoration, we met in all directions with counts and barons created by Bonaparte, by the court, and sometimes by themselves."[14]

There are few better examples of this mechanism than that of the Baron du Châtelet, who will be the first to introduce Lucien to the world of aristocratic salons. In a sense, du Châtelet is self-invention embodied. Born simply Sixte Châtelet, and without any actual aristocratic pedigree, he has added the particle *du*, which indicates nobility, before his last name during the early days of the empire. Soon he started to rise through the ranks of imperial bureaucracy, receiving from Napoleon the title of Baron. After the fall of the empire, we find him in a self-imposed exile, but he is soon back to become a part of the Parisian high society that Lucien seeks to penetrate. More than that, by the end of *Illusions perdues* the Napoleonic Baron is made a Duke by a royal patent. No doubt, Châtelet is meant to embody a paradigmatic destiny: a usurper-turned-Baron by the greater usurper Bonaparte who is turned Count under the restored monarchy. And if du Châtelet can do it, why shouldn't Lucien?

Torn between contradictory assumptions about social mobility, the novel cannot grant Lucien's fantasy of self-ennoblement, but it cannot conclusively dismiss it either. Even after the Marquise d'Espard's stern rejection of Lucien, *Illusions perdues* will refuse to fully let go of the notion that upward mobility may function as something akin to alchemical transmutation. In fact, toward the end of the novel, after he has already been crushed in Paris, Lucien will once again express his commitment to this project, when he is invited to rejoin Louise de Bargeton's circle. His plan is astonishingly simple: he will get a superior outfit, enter the circle as a man of fashion, behave like a man of fashion, and thus become one. In other words, he will triumph by making an appearance (595, 622). And this plan (to the extent to which it *is* a plan) comes remarkably close to success, and is only derailed by local intrigues aimed at bringing down his friend David Séchard (613, 642).

Is self-invention possible? Is it possible to acquire social status through an alchemical process that miraculously turns nothing into something? To answer such questions, Balzac will have to rewrite Lucien's story in *Splendeurs*. However, before doing so he will go on to examine a different set of assumptions about social mobility: If Lucien cannot rise through the fantasy of ennoblement, perhaps he can do so through the nascent capitalist economy?

## Enter Capitalism: Balzac and the Economics of Destruction

Swiftly exiled from the aristocratic universe embodied in the Marquise d'Espard, Lucien will have to find a less glamorous path to success: instead of reinventing himself as M. de Rubempré, he will have to toil his way through the competing underworlds of Parisian writers and journalists. The stark choice he is presented with—between the world of the Cénacle, the literary circle headed by Daniel d'Arthez, and the world of journalism epitomized in Etienne Lousteau—offers itself as the novel's true dilemma, at least for a moment: it is a choice between an economically disinterested commitment to art and an ethically disinterested commitment to journalism, between a world that adamantly refuses to take part in any form of exchange characteristic of capitalist economy, and a world that seems to offer a plethora of exchange models. Lucien, of course, is quick to pick the latter, and it is then and there that *Illusions perdues* turns more properly into an anatomy of capitalism. Significantly, however, the results of Balzac's economic inquiry are as convoluted and disturbing as the results of his inquiry into the status of aristocracy: in *Illusions perdues* capitalism functions as a self-destructive economy.

At least since Georg Lukács, critics have lamented the commodification of all ideological content in *Illusions Perdues*.[15] The problem, we are told, is that everything is for sale. As Christopher Prendergast writes, echoing this Lukacsian sentiment, "The organizing theme of the novel" is "the pervasive corruption of literature as it is increasingly subjected to the values of the cash nexus."[16] Even Balzac's hero knows that "il y a des impôts sur tout, on y vend tout, on y fabrique tout, même le succès" (Everything is taxed, everything is for sale, everything is manufactured, even success; 390, 396). Etienne Lousteau is the master and the principal guide through this economy: "A ce métier de spadassin des idées et des réputations industrielles, littéraires et dramatiques, je gagne cinquante écus par mois, je puis vendre un roman cinq cents francs, et je commence à passer pour un homme redoutable" (I make fifty crowns a month as a hired gangster, trading in commercial, literary, and theatrical reputations; I could get five hundred francs for a novel, and I am beginning to have a reputation of being a man to be reckoned with; 259–60, 251–52). Being a journalist, Lousteau is in a position to sell free copies of books he gets from publishers and free tickets he gets from the theaters fearing bad reviews. In fact, he is often directly paid by publishers simply not to attack a forthcoming book (259, 251), and he hopes that this influence as "un homme redoutable" will enable him to climb the social ladder of journalism, and perhaps beyond.

In some ways, Lukács was obviously right in concluding that Balzac's novel portrays the moment in the development of capitalism in which all relations are turned into a version of the stock exchange.[17] What his analysis—along with numerous subsequent readings that argue that *Illusions perdues* embodies the triumph of capitalism—misses is that the novel seems completely unable to imagine economic exchange as a value-creating process. Lucien's unsuccessful attempts to cash in on his literary works underscore this impossibility. He first uses his journalistic influence to blackmail the publisher Dauriat into buying his collection of sonnets, the *Marguerites*. And although the money is very real (he is paid three thousand francs in cash) the transaction is fundamentally flawed: Dauriat has purchased the rights to the manuscript precisely in order *not* to publish it, thus sabotaging Lucien's literary career. Unlike the *Marguerites*, Lucien's novel, *L'Archer de Charles IX,* is bought by publishers genuinely interested in publishing it, yet of such poor credit that their checks are impossible to cash. For the five thousand francs worth of checks, Lucien is first offered three thousand, and then, after traversing the whole of Paris on his way from one creditor to another, only fifteen hundred.

The problems Lucien experiences with checks are indicative of the novel's larger concern with the nature of monetary and social transactions. What forms of exchange are possible and how do they function? Is it at all possible to gain something through exchanges? As my examples demonstrate, the commodification of intellectual and creative activity is by no means the final lesson of *Illusions perdues*. The most striking feature of the process of commodification Lukács describes is that it fails to produce a viable economy. The ostensible reduction of all relations to financial ones generates an economy of destruction whose ability to create value is doubtful at best. If the novel is about subjecting intellectual activity to the logic of the cash nexus, why is it that turning one's intellectual and creative efforts into cash is so difficult? In other words, the problem is not, as one would infer from the Lukácsian tradition of interpreting *Illusions perdues*, that Lucien sells his soul. The problem is that he can't.

This difficulty arises from the fact that in *Illusions perdues* Balzac treats capitalism not as a profit-driven economic system, but as a form of a primitive exchange economy. Commodities are exchanged in a demanding game of social positioning in which the straightforward acquisition of wealth plays only a secondary role. As Claude Lévi-Strauss explains in *The Elementary Structures of Kinship*,

> Goods are not only economic commodities, but vehicles and instruments for realities of another order, such as power, influence, sympathy, status and emotion; and the skillful game of exchange (in which there is often no more real transfer than in a game of chess, in which the players do not give each other the pieces that they move alternatively forward on the chessboard but merely seek to provoke a counter-move), consists in a complex totality of conscious or unconscious maneuvers in order to gain security and to guard oneself against risks brought about by alliances and by rivalries.[18]

Within such a system, exchange can function not as a value-creating mechanism, but as an instrument of social and economic warfare. For Lévi-Strauss, one crucial form of such warfare is the practice of potlatch, in which generosity in gifting becomes a hostile act. Its aim is "to surpass the rival in generosity, to crush him if possible with future obligations which it is hoped it cannot meet, so as to take from him his prerogatives, tiles, rank, authority, and prestige."[19] In a more extreme form, such warfare can lead rivals to fully espouse the principle of negative reciprocity and engage in a straightforward trading of injuries, a practice both destructive and self-destructive: one is prepared to destroy or hurt the opponent, even if it also means hurting oneself.[20] In this context, blackmail constitutes a particularly interesting example of negative reciprocity: one is forced to give something away simply in order not to be retaliated against.

The economy Lousteau describes to Lucien is entirely governed by the law of negative reciprocity. As a journalist, he is given free copies of books and free tickets to the theater solely due to the fear of retaliation. Lucien's own problems with Dauriat offer an equally good example of this principle: he has attacked a book published by Dauriat in retaliation for the fact that the publisher hasn't even read the poems Lucien offered him, and Dauriat will now retaliate by buying Lucien's manuscript precisely in order to arrest his literary career. In exchange, writes Georg Simmel, "the sum of all values is greater afterward than it was before, and this implies that each party gives the other more than he had himself possessed."[21] In the models of exchange represented in *Illusions perdues,* the sum of values might actually be smaller. Thus we end at the opposite end of Simmel's definition of exchange: exchange is a fundamental form of destruction, as one does not make a sacrifice in order to gain something, but, rather, in order not to lose, or even simply in order to hurt the rival.

There is, however, no doubt that participants in this economy of destruction see themselves as social climbers, just as they see their access to the means of destruction as a source of social power. Once again, Lousteau to Lucien:

> Dans trois jours, si nous réussissons, vous pouvez, avec trente bons mots imprimés à raison de trois par jour, faire maudire la vie à un homme; vous pouvez vous créer des rentes de plaisir chez toutes les actrices de vos théâtres, vous pouvez faire tomber une bonne pièce et faire courir tout Paris à une mauvaise. (300)

(Three days from now, if we are successful, you will be in a position to make any man's life a misery to him, just by publishing a series of thirty jokes against him, at the rate of three a day; and you will be able to take your percentage of amusement from all the actresses in your theatres; you will be able to ruin a good play and send all Paris to see a bad one.) (297)

The power Lucien gains is primarily the power to destroy, or to draw a gain for himself under the sheer threat of destruction. As Lousteau notes, once Lucien claims this position of power, publishing his novel will cease to be a problem, as publishers will be happy to accept it, fearing retaliation. One form of extortion or another is the modus operandi of journalism: straightforward blackmail implying a threat to reveal an inconvenient truth, or a form of protection racket involving the promise that the victim will not be attacked. It is no coincidence that Balzac takes the time to explain the meaning of "chantage" ("blackmail"), a new word Lucien doesn't know, and "une invention de la presse anglaise, importée récemment en France" (an invention of the English press, recently imported into France; 421, 430). Being introduced only in 1836, the word is, indeed, new, and *Illusions perdues* is regularly listed as one of the first instances of its usage.[22]

However, while Lousteau seems to understand very well how to engage in racketeering, extortion, and blackmail, he fails to perceive the reversibility that is inscribed in this economy. First, extortion always implies the threat of inflicting some form of damage, usually by diminishing the economic capital of the victim. The victim then engages in exchange not by attempting to create value, but by struggling not to lose any. Although the blackmailer, of course, does gain something, this gain is temporary, as the means of blackmail are at the disposal of different parties and the blackmailer can quickly turn into the blackmailed. Not only do the publishers have considerable leverage over the journalists who are usually aspiring writers, but the journalistic world is divided between the liberals and the royalists, who both have equal access to the means of public defamation. Lucien discovers this the hard way. Once he has switched to the royalist side, he is presented with the ultimatum to choose between publicly attacking his friend d'Arthez or seeing his lover Coralie's career suffer: if Lucien doesn't destroy d'Arthez, his new royalist friends will leave Coralie to be destroyed by the liberal press without lending her any support (450–51, 462–63).

The distribution of power in *Illusions perdues* is such that it creates a vicious circle of retribution. Since the blackmailer can always become the blackmailed, the whole economy is an extremely efficient mechanism of arresting reputations and hindering social climbing. In fact, one might say that the world of journalism works through a successful exchange of hindrances and obstructions. Paris thus becomes the capital of paralysis. Paradoxically, Lucien is trying to propel himself into the higher spheres of society through an economy of destruction. The real scandal of Lucien's journalistic episode is therefore not that he enters a world predicated on economic value instead of intellectual honesty; the scandal is that this is a flawed economy.

Toward the end of the novel the two models of social climbing—blackmail and ennoblement—are brought together to inflict the final wounds. Lucien has tried to use what he had learned in the world of journalism in order to regain access to high society: he has applied the power of tarnishing reputations to du Châtelet and Louise, hoping that this will give him some leverage over his victims (425, 434). But, according to the principle of negative reciprocity, Lucien's attack prompts an immediate act of reprisal. He is lured into stopping the attacks and turning to the royalist side under the assumption that he will finally get the noble patent, which proves to be another empty promise.

*Illusions perdues* is not a novel about selling one's soul to the ruthless economy of nascent capitalism. It is about the impossibility of doing so. Perhaps we should not be surprised that after the Parisian catastrophe Lucien will go back to the original notion of self-invention: he will put on his clothes and reenter Louise's circle, hoping to radically alter his social position. And why wouldn't he? The original plan proves no worse than everything else he has tried: self-invention, it turns out, is no more chimerical than elaborate planning. This final desperate gesture testifies as much to the power of the fantasy of self-invention as it does to the failure of all else. Self-invention cannot be entirely discredited, as there is nothing that can replace it: it lurks as the novel's great unfulfilled promise, and it is not possible to simply dismiss it.

Lucien de Rubempré's attempt to conquer Paris ends with a very clear defeat and with no clear lessons: the fantasy of aristocratic self-invention has crumbled, and so has the attempt to master the economy of journalism and publishing. Perhaps a bit more luck was needed, a bit more structure. Perhaps it is the hero's fault? Were we not repeatedly told that he is beyond help? The ending of *Illusions perdues* gives Lucien what he was denied in the beginning: the possibility of an apprenticeship. The great failure of education ends with the sudden introduction of Vautrin, *La Comédie*'s greatest villain, who will serve as something like a tutor ex machina, offering the hero a remedial course in the laws of society. With Vautrin, the discourse of learning will be back in full force. For the tutor, Lucien is a tabula rasa (628, 659), and Vautrin will remind him how important it is to acquire experience (628, 660) and introduce him to an "instruction sommaire" (intensive course of instruction; 634, 665).

Now that all else has failed, Lucien is offered a proper pact with the devil (633, 665). If he cannot navigate the world on his own, he might be able to do so with the guidance of Vautrin, now in the guise of a Spanish priest, Abbé Carlos Herrera. The paradox of this solution is that it introduces Vautrin as an agent of order, however perverse that might seem: he restores the logic of self-fashioning as a process, imposes discipline, and insists that success will require rigor, self-control, and learning. The haphazard struggles of an autodidact will be replaced by a rigorous and structured process. Is it possible that Vautrin is the bildungsroman's last hope?

## The Scene of Rewriting: Toward a Diabolic Self-Fashioning

More than anything else, the beginning of *Splendeurs et misères des courtisanes* is a radical rewriting of the initial situation of *Illusions perdues*. The novel begins at the opera, the scene of Lucien's initial Parisian fiasco, where he was abandoned by Louise de Bargeton and the Marquise d'Espard. At the beginning of *Splendeurs,* however, he has already gained a protector: the novel begins at a masked ball, and Vautrin is immediately seen with his watchful eye on Lucien, hiding behind a domino mask, and following his protégé through the crowd (38, 18). In addition to acquiring a protector, Lucien has been granted the noble name of de Rubempré by a royal ordinance (40, 19) and is now regarded, in the words of one socialite, as "un jeune homme du plus grand mérite, et si bien appuyé que je me croirais très heureux de pouvoir renouer connaissance avec lui" (a young man of the greatest merit, and so well backed that I should be exceptionally glad to renew my acquaintance with him; 43, 22). *Splendeurs* therefore offers a new dealing of cards and performs something like an exercise in the possible worlds theory: What if the propositions which were not true in the world of *Illusions perdues* ("Lucien is a de Rubempré" and "Lucien has a protector") were true? At the beginning of *Splendeurs* Lucien *is* what he only *pretended* to be in *Illusions perdues*.

But, beyond these basic propositions, it seems that *Splendeurs* is also keen to introduce the same set of problems *Illusions perdues* has swept under the rug and then allowed to resurface only with Vautrin's sudden appearance at the end of the novel. In many ways *Splendeurs* returns us to the point where Stendhal's Julien Sorel left the French bildungsroman: knowledge, discipline, planning, secrecy, rigorous work on the self. Vautrin's plan goes something like this: Lucien, who is now allowed to call himself de Rubempré, will court the daughter of the Duc de Grandlieu in order to fortify his position within the Parisian aristocracy, and this project will be funded by using Esther Gobseck, Lucien's lover, as a tool to extract money from the wealthy banker Baron Nucingen. This thoroughness means that the project will take considerable time: Lucien's entire adventure in *Illusions perdues* takes barely eighteen months; in *Splendeurs*, it will take six years.[23]

Vautrin has introduced method and rigor in order to discipline both Lucien de Rubempré and the bildungsroman plot. As he has promised at the end of *Illusions perdues,* the project of transforming Lucien will be based on the principle of secrecy, in an attempt to augment the failed strategies Lucien was employing throughout the first of the two novels. For Vautrin, secrecy is the condition of control: he will hide his own identity, Lucien's relationship with Esther, and the sources of Lucien's money. And yet the fundamental principle of control also proves to be the fundamental weakness of Vautrin's project. Not only will it turn out that secrets are impossible to keep, but the insistence on secrecy will collide with the principles that we know well from *Illusions perdues:* those of legitimacy and negative reciprocity.

In *Splendeurs,* it is true, Lucien has his family name back, but he is quickly treated to another unpleasant lesson about entering the world of aristocracy. In *Illusions perdues* he has been told that the noble name can be conferred on him only by the king; in *Splendeurs* he will learn that even a royal ordinance will not suffice, as it turns out that attaining a sufficient level of legitimacy by the standards of Parisian nobility is effectively impossible. Even with the name de Rubempré, he will still have to account for himself.

> Non seulement la position de Lucien n'était pas assez nette, et ces mots: "De quoi vit-il?" que chacun avait sur les lèvres à mesure qu'il s'élevait, demandaient une réponse; mais encore la curiosité bienveillante comme la curiosité malicieuse allaient d'investigations en investigations, et trouvaient plus d'un défaut à la cuirasse de cet ambitieux. (130)

> (Not only was Lucien's situation insufficiently clear, and the words: "What does he live on?" which everybody asked as he rose in the world, still in need of a reply; but also benevolent curiosity, as much as that of the malicious, proceeded from investigation to investigation, and discovered more than one chink in the ambitious young man's armour.) (98)

This is yet another reminder of the sense of unease that the idea of nobility as an empty signifier generates: Lucien will not be allowed to wear his name as a sign that masks his identity and the sources of his fortune. It turns out that the aristocratic fear of illegitimacy runs deeper than even the Marquise d'Espard has suggested. In order to marry into a noted aristocratic family, the hero is required to have more than name and wealth; he is asked to purchase back his family land, and to do so with money from appropriate sources. This means that he will have to pretend that the hundreds of thousands of francs, which were made by exploiting Nucingen's passion for Esther, come from the business of his friend David

Séchard, whom he left behind in the provinces. Lucien will have to create the fiction of a legitimate business enterprise so that he can buy his family land and become what his name suggests: a landed aristocrat in possession of the Rubempré estate.

The paradox is, of course, that Lucien is barred from using illegitimate means to attain the land that will serve the fiction that he is the legitimate heir to the Rubempré estate. This requirement reveals the nobility's longing for the illusion of historical continuity and confirms the power of performativity: the appearance of continuity will create continuity. The underlying assumption is that if Lucien takes back the land, the three decades during which the titles were abolished and the land taken will be forgotten, along with the fact that he was not born de Rubempré. And if Lucien is asked to retake his ancestral land in order to finalize the fiction of legitimacy, is he not fulfilling the central ideological ambition of the Restoration?

But there are further unpleasant surprises, and further specters of the forces Vautrin wanted to leave behind in *Illusions perdues*. As Lucien and Vautrin scramble to gather a million Francs in order to purchase the Rubempré estate, they are discovered and blackmailed. The mechanism is very close to the one Lousteau has described in *Illusions perdues:* not "la bourse ou la vie" (your money or your life) but "la bourse ou l'honneur" (your money or your character; 423, 432–33). As Corentin, the spy hired by Nucingen, tells Lucien in *Splendeurs:*

> Vous êtes entre les mains d'un homme qui a le pouvoir, la volonté, la facilité de prouver au duc de Grandlieu que la terre de Rubempré sera payée avec le prix qu'un sot vous a donné de votre maîtresse, mademoiselle Esther.... Les manœuvres extrêmement habiles employées contre le baron de Nucingen seront mises à jour.... Donnez une somme de cent mille francs et vous aurez la paix ... Ceci ne me regarde en rien. Je suis le chargé d'affaires de ceux qui se livrent à ce *chantage,* voilà tout. (286–87)

(You are in the hands of a man with the power, the will, the ability to prove to the Duc de Grandlieu that the Rubempré estate with the price a fool gave you for your mistress, Mademoiselle Esther.... The extremely clever maneuvers used against Baron Nucingen will be brought to light. . . . Give me a sum of a hundred thousand francs and you will be left in peace. This does not concern me personally. I am acting on behalf of those who have planned this *blackmail,* that is all.) (236)

Once the blackmail is refused, the blackmailer acts on the threat, exposing Lucien to the Duc de Grandlieu and prompting both a further investigation into Lucien's affairs (297–98, 245–46) and further rounds of reprisals. Just like Lucien in *Illusions perdues,* Vautrin ends up caught in the logic of lex talionis, retaliating against those who thwart his plans not with the aim to limit the damage, but to inflict pain on his enemies (332–33, 277).

With the return of the law of negative reciprocity we also witness the erosion of the principle of secrecy on which Vautrin's entire project rests. As he struggles to hide the unsavory sources of Lucien's wealth, he has to counter the efforts of Nucingen's spies and of the Duc de Grandlieu's investigative committee, but to no avail. Whereas Lucien failed to make his way through the intricate web of economic and ideological suppositions in *Illusions perdues,* the elaborate plans of his mentor will fare no better. Vautrin's attempts to advance Lucien's career through an elaborate conspiracy will crumble as the novel increasingly transforms into an extensive police inquiry into his dealings, until both the mentor and his protégé are arrested, and the latter breaks down under questioning. "Et dire," laments Vautrin, "que notre sort dépend d'un regard, d'une rougeur de Lucien devant ce Camusot, qui voit tout, qui ne manque pas de la finesse des juges!" (And to think that our whole fortune depends on a glance, on Lucien blushing in front of this Camusot, who sees everything, who isn't lacking in the subtlety of judges!; 499, 426–27). Once exposed, Lucien kills himself in prison.

Significantly, *Splendeurs* will use its seven hundred pages only to offer a failure just as stunning as that in *Illusions perdues* and, one might add, a further disorganization of the bildungsroman's narrative strategies. After years of extensive guidance by Vautrin, Lucien has gone through with the suicide he had already planned at the end of *Illusions. Splendeurs* has simply postponed the inevitable. Balzac has pushed his hero through two different plots in order to master the laws of social mobility, but with the same disastrous result. In *Illusions perdues* he has attempted to disassociate selfhood, knowledge, and social advancement by exploring the notion of social identity as an instant invention. In *Splendeurs* he has in some ways reverted to Stendhal's understanding of social mobility as a disciplined process in an attempt to satisfy the Restoration's thirst for legitimacy. This thirst, however, cannot be satisfied, and, besides, the techniques that Vautrin and Lucien used have proven to be far too implicated in the destructive economy that, as we have seen in *Illusions perdues*, functions much better as a tool for paralyzing than as a tool for advancing social mobility. If *Splendeurs* were to bring structure, planning, and order to the processes of self-fashioning and upward social movement, they have clearly failed to do so: meticulous planning fails just as miserably as no planning at all. In Balzac, even the pact with the devil cannot guarantee success.

If *Illusions perdues* ends in the failure of the protagonist, *Splendeurs* ends with a much more telling failure of plotting. The great revelation of the novel's ending is not that Lucien de Rubempré cannot be disciplined, but rather that the genre refuses discipline. As Christopher Prendergast observes, what is astonishing is that the plot slips beyond not Lucien's but Vautrin's control: "From the moment of Esther's suicide, the plot of *Splendeurs* runs riot, largely in the form of a series of messages and letters that cross, conflict, arrive too late, or cannot be transmitted; the communicative circuits get blocked, seize up, go wild."[24] But, as scholars of French realism have known for a long time, the apparent triumph of contingency reads equally well as the triumph of the state.[25] In the midst of this confusion, Vautrin has abdicated as a tutor in social relations in order to assume the role of a policeman, while the bildungsroman plot has entirely given way to the police inquiry and related intrigues that continue well after Lucien de Rubempré's death. D. A. Miller, whose influential reading of the novel has the great virtue of linking the increased interest in the performance of state functions at the end of *Splendeurs* with the question of novelistic form, comments that "clearing the ground not just for the routinized exercise of policing functions, but also for their routinized representation, Balzac's novel of disillusionment is appropriately concluded at the end of the Vautrin trilogy, but only because it there asks to be completed in a quite different genre which will nonetheless precisely honor its request: the *roman policier*."[26] But the novel's escape *into* the *roman policier* is also an escape *from* the bildungsroman, and it seems to me equally justified to ask not only why the novel turns to the police, but also why it turns away from education.

Parallel to Lucien's death and Vautrin's change of career is the end of the Restoration. If Vautrin has managed to survive this change it is because he was prepared to take a new role, rightly recognizing that he was no longer needed in his previous function as the shady facilitator of social mobility: the problem he sought to solve was no longer there, as the coordinates of the world he was trying to navigate had changed. Among other provisions introduced under the liberal government of Louis-Philippe was *La loi modificative de code penal,* which suppressed the part of Article 259 that prohibited the usurpation of titles.[27] It will take another coup d'état and another usurper—Napoleon III—to make usurpation illegal again in 1858. Balzac, who died in 1850, will not live to see the usurpation of titles recriminalized under the Second Empire. The fact that usurpation was decriminalized in 1830 signals a larger ideological shift with respect to the social role of nobility: the titles no longer had quite the same significance they had enjoyed under the Bourbons.

Indeed, French lawmakers at the time recognized as much. During an 1835 debate in the Chambre des pairs, the Comte de Montlosier argued: "Ces titres de noblesse qu'on avait énoncés dans la Charte on les a effacés dans le Code criminal. . . . En conséquence, peau a peau, tout ce qui s'apelle noblesse est effacé" (These titles of nobility that were anounced in the Charter were erased in the Penal Code. . . . Consequently, bit by bit, everything that we call nobility is being effaced).[28] Those on the opposite side of the political spectrum were very happy to concur that the status of nobility became much more precarious within the legal framework established in 1830. As Alexandre Glais-Bizoin argued in the Chambre des députés, the position of nobility was severely undermined by the fact that the Charter of 1830 insists in its first article that all Frenchmen are equal. When reminded that other articles of the charter grant the king the right to award titles and stipulate that the old nobility takes back its titles, he responded: "J'ajouterai que l'article est inutile et qu'il est en contradiction avec un loi de 1832, par laquelle vous avez déclaré qu'il était permis a tout Français de prendre une titre, sauf a porter peine de sa vanité, c'est-a-dire le ridicule" (I will add that the article is pointless and in contradiction with an 1832 law by which you allowed all Frenchmen to take a title solely in order to flatter their vanity, that is, in order to ridicule it).[29] Glais-Bizoin correctly sensed, in his cynical interpretation of the law, that under the new regime the institution of nobility was significantly weakened without being formally abolished.

Why would the government of Louis-Philippe allow such a change? The new monarchy was still embroiled in many of the old debates about the social and legal status of aristocracy, and it, too, suffered from a legitimacy deficit. As one historian notes, "Whatever its historical exemplars, there can be no doubt that the July Monarchy was of illegitimate birth, anxious about its own origins."[30] However, the Orleanist monarchy and the Restoration regime relied on fundamentally different concepts of political legitimacy. As François Furet points out, "One glaring difference separates the Charter of 1814 from that of 1830: the second was no longer 'granted' by the king, it was contractually accepted by him as a condition of his accession."[31] Because the Restoration was informed by the legitimist ideology that emphasized the inherited rights of the king and the nobility, it had to regard the usurpation of noble titles as a threat to its very existence and hence had no choice but to criminalize it. To put it differently, the Restoration had to maintain the improbable fantasy of continuity with the ancien régime, and of uninterrupted succession, and was consequently particularly sensitive to the implication that noble titles can be taken rather than given. The July Monarchy was much less troubled by these issues, as it rested on the idea of popular sovereignty. And, while being a monarchy, no matter how bourgeois, it certainly maintained some interest in the traditional forms of legitimation of royal power, the refusal of the new regime to prosecute usurpation—indeed, its willingness to completely decriminalize it—indicates that usurpation had lost much of its ideological significance: self-invention was no longer seen as the crucial ideological threat. And, although self-ennoblement had by no means disappeared under the Orleanist regime (in fact, it escalated, demonstrating the continuing attraction of the noble aura), the tension between legitimacy and usurpation could no longer be articulated in quite the same way.[32] There was a certain degree of performativity that this regime could afford to live with, just enough for the central problem of *Illusions perdues* and *Splendeurs* to be made obsolete.[33]

It is no wonder, then, that for Balzac the drama of social climbing has very clear temporal boundaries: it starts in the early years of the Restoration and ends with its demise. The Balzacian bildungsroman served as a tool for exploring a socioeconomic and ideological configuration that generated a particular kind of tension between self and society—a configuration that disappeared or was at least seriously altered under the July Monarchy. With the end of the Restoration, the story of Lucien de Rubempré must also come to an end, as it has become anachronistic: the ideological pressures surrounding the question of legitimacy, pressures that simultaneously invoked and censured the dream of self-invention, have started to dissolve.

Is this the end of the bildungsroman, then? Of course it is: one of many. If we were to lament the death of the bildungsroman genre, we would be condemned to grieve continuously. Contrary to the familiar Bakhtinian definition of the novel as a genre always in the process of becoming, the bildungsroman can be defined as a genre that always finds new ways to break down.

# 2

# THE GREAT EVASION

Dickensian Bildungsroman and the Logic of Dependency

In Balzac, as we have seen in chapter 1, the ruthless parvenu is invited to take center stage as the true, if troubled, hero of modernity. In Dickens, he is reduced to the grotesque caricature that is Uriah Heep, the repulsive antagonist in *David Copperfield*. In Balzac, the bildungsroman protagonist is driven by an urge to embrace the rapaciousness of developing capitalism; in Dickens, he is taught that he can achieve a worthwhile existence only by avoiding it. As a form, the Dickensian bildungsroman explores ways of sheltering the hero from the very forces Balzac so readily unleashes on his young provincials. In place of the intense struggle to penetrate the higher orders of society and attempts to understand and manipulate economic processes, Dickens installs a set of narrative mechanisms whose main purpose is to contain the socioeconomic pressures of capitalist modernity and guide his heroes to the safety of a respectable existence. The brazen pursuit of success and fame has given way to the rescue of neglected children: both the shameless parvenu and his scheming mentor withdraw to make space for a thoroughly pacified bildungsroman hero and for the benevolent forces that will save him. The bildungsroman therefore mutates into a tale of rescue, repeatedly rehearsing different scenarios in which external factors—variously understood as state bureaucracy, caring benefactors, malevolent conspirators, or simply the bizarre imagination of strangers—demonstrate the power to shape the hero's fate.[1]

The curious obsession of the Dickensian bildungsroman with acts of rescue stems from a distinctly Victorian anxiety about the nature of personal agency and individual responsibility: thoroughly shaped by a version of liberal individualism that had found its popular embodiment in the idea of self-help, early and mid-nineteenth-century social thought was strongly invested in the concept of personal responsibility and extremely reluctant to acknowledge the role of external circumstances in shaping one's life path. As Edwin Paxton Hood argues, "A man must act: whether he is necessitated to labour for his maintenance; or is freed by fortune from all apprehension, and from all constrained exertion; yet he must act."[2] In stark contrast to this dominant moral doctrine, Dickens's bildungsromans persistently query the limits of autonomous action and advance an understanding of agency that decisively favors external intervention over individual choice. By focusing on neglected children placed in the care of brutal guardians, anonymous benefactors, and ruthless criminals, *Oliver Twist, David Copperfield,* and *Great Expectations* all examine the proposition that one's place in the world—and sometimes even mere survival—is determined not by active efforts toward self-realization but by the care and terror exercised by various guardians.

The power of these external forces to shape the social identity of the hero is forcefully asserted through the acts of naming that occur in each of Dickens's bildungsromans. "The bestowal of the name," writes Nathan Miller, "is in itself an act of supreme importance, as it betokens the starting-point of the individual's life in the group."[3] In Dickens, those who control the hero's name also have the ability to control his life. Oliver Twist is named through an arbitrary act of state bureaucracy embodied in Mr. Bumble: "We name our fondlins in alphabetical order. The last was S,—Swubble, I named him. This was a T,—Twist, I named *him*. The next one as comes will be Unwin, and the next Vilkins. I have got the names ready made till the end of the alphabet, and all the way through it again, when we come to Z."[4] Bumble's quasi-divine power to assign names in accordance with the impersonal logic of the alphabetical order serves to underscore Oliver's status as a passive object in the hands of a bureaucratic mechanism that has the prerogative to dispose with him in whatever way it sees fit.[5] "'By the bye,' said Mr. Bumble, 'you don't know anybody who wants a boy, do you? A porochial 'prentis, who is at present a deadweight; a millstone, as I may say, round the porochial throat? Liberal terms, Mr. Sowerberry, liberal terms?'" (27).

In Dickens's subsequent bildungsromans the act of naming will continue to signal dependency, custodianship, and belonging. The hero of *David Copperfield* is named—or, rather, renamed—by his great-aunt Betsey Trotwood when he escapes the life in the bottling factory to which his stepfather, Murdstone, has condemned him. "'I have been thinking, do you know Mr. Dick, that I may call him Trotwood?'—'Certainly, certainly, call him Trotwood, certainly,' said Mr. Dick."[6] In a gesture that marks the reversal of David's fortune and the establishment of his dependence on a new guardian, the aunt's surname will become the hero's first name, inscribed onto all of David's clothing "with an indelible marking-ink" (184). The change of name also marks a new beginning of the bildungsroman plot, as David will now be able to attain a new identity, along with social prospects that were unavailable while he was subject to his stepfather's tyrannical rule: "Thus, I began my new life, in a new name, and with everything new around me" (184).

In an even more literal sense, naming will signal the beginning of life in *Great Expectations*. Famously unable to pronounce his own full name, the hero of Dickens's penultimate completed novel names himself Pip. The novel, nonetheless, goes on to quickly challenge the status of self-naming as a gesture that generates a fully autochthonous identity. Pip's transformation from a common boy into a gentleman, promised by the anonymous benefactor, will take place only if he accepts never to change his name: "You are to understand, first, that it is the request of the person from whom I take my instructions that you always bear the name of Pip. You will have no objection, I dare say, to your great expectations being encumbered with that easy condition."[7] Instead of being a sign of autonomy, Pip's name becomes a contractual obligation. The terms are agreed upon, the contractual relationship is established, and Pip embarks on a life path envisioned *for* him. Great expectations are something to be given and accepted: they are a ready-made future Pip is to agree to, and to which he will have to sacrifice his full name. In each of the three novels, to control the hero's name is to exercise a certain kind of parental or pseudoparental prerogative as well as to demonstrate power over the hero's fate, and sometimes over his subjectivity. The moments of naming, renaming, and—in Pip's case—of surrendering one's name to the mysterious benefactor mark the establishment of the relation of dependency that is the central feature of the Dickensian bildungsroman.

With precision worthy of Vladimir Propp's *Morphology of the Folktale,* Dickens's novels fill the structural roles of villains and helpers, locating the center of narrative tension not in the relationship between the hero and the world but in the encounter between the hero's adversaries and his benefactors. Oliver Twist is threatened by the brutal parish bureaucracy exemplified in Mr. Bumble, as well as by the criminal underground of Fagin, Sikes, and Monks, who are all strongly invested in corrupting—if not physically destroying—him, until he is rescued through the benevolent interventions of Mr. Brownlow and Rose Maylie's circle. David Copperfield is saved from the terror and neglect of Edward Murdstone and his equally tyrannical sister, Jane, through the involvement of surrogate mothers like his nurse, Peggotty, and, in particular, his munificent if eccentric aunt Betsey. *Great Expectations,* of course, complicates the clearcut distinction between guardianship and terror, but its focus on the identity of Pip's benefactor reveals a remarkable continuity in the central preoccupations of the Dickensian bildungsroman: repeatedly returning to the question of external forces that direct the hero and define his social position, Dickens's novels obsessively examine the meaning of dependency and guardianship.[8]

This shift of focus has profound effects on the structure of Dickens's bildungsromans. In *Oliver Twist* the problem of individual development is completely suppressed by the story of Oliver's rescue. In *David Copperfield,* in which a bildungsroman does materialize, the narrative nonetheless remains focused on the power of both benevolent and hostile agents to shape David's future. So much so, in fact, that the conventional preoccupations of the bildungsroman—work on the self, formal education, artistic development, professional aspirations—are largely hollowed out: we know that David achieves the ideal of bourgeois respectability through a fulfilling marriage and literary success, but neither his emotional maturation nor his literary career manage to wrestle the narrative focus away from the story of his rescue by Betsey Trotwood. Finally, *Great Expectations* repeats many of the same evasive moves: although Pip leaves "for London and greatness" (144), the novel's outcome depends far more on the identity of the mysterious benefactor than on the hero's ability to navigate the vicissitudes of the metropolis. Throughout this chapter I will explore the variety of containment strategies that Dickens uses to redirect the focus of the bildungsroman away from the process of willful self-making.[9]

## The Power of Benevolence: Dickens and the Rhetoric of Self-Reliance

Almost without exception, both Victorian legislators and contributors to the enormous body of mid-nineteenth-century self-help literature subscribed to an understanding of the human condition that went particularly far in privileging individual responsibility over the force of external circumstances. As numerous volumes on self-cultivation, self-education, self-training, self-culture, and self-formation testify, the prevailing moral philosophy has relied on the concept of individual agency to such an extent that it left very little space for any exemptions to the principle of personal moral responsibility. As Edwin Paxton Hood argues, "All the education that has ever been in the world, has been the result of self-determination, self-training, and self-reliance."[10] Significantly, the argument in favor of self-reliance would routinely transform into an argument against external assistance. In the words of Samuel Smiles, the best-known Victorian popularizer of the widespread doctrine of self-help, "Whatever is done *for* men or classes, to a certain extent takes away the stimulus and necessity of doing for themselves; and where men are subjected to over-guidance and over government, the inevitable tendency is to render them comparatively helpless."[11] This view of outside help as inherently inimical to one's ability to act as a moral agent also explains much of early Victorian resistance to charity: if you are helped you will not help yourself. And while in theory this influential moral doctrine allowed for the existence of the truly helpless—as exemplified, for instance, by the concept of the "deserving poor"—in reality both social commentators and legislators tended to espouse an exceptionally restrictive understanding of helplessness and to demand absolute accountability of just about anyone.[12]

There are few better examples of this attitude than the 1823 Report of the Charity Commission, in which the commissioners launched an extraordinary attack on Anthony Highmore's book *Pietas Londinensis*. A survey of London charities, the book was an attempt to draw public attention to the value of various benevolent institutions, among them a London maternity hospital. According to Highmore, before the Queen's Lying-In Hospital was established, poor patients from Bayswater had to walk so far to access medical care that it was not uncommon for women to give birth on the street while on their way to get help.[13] And while Highmore considered the establishment of a maternity hospital an unambiguously positive development, the commissioners took a vastly different view of the issue: "We agree with Mr. Highmore that nothing can be more shocking than that women should be running about in such a state, totally unprovided; but we should ask him whether the occurrence of such events is not entirely due to the existence of Lying-in hospitals. If there were no such receptacles women would be left to their own prudence, and might, perhaps, reflect upon the inconveniences that necessarily attend a state of pregnancy, and guide against them before-hand."[14] Significantly, *Oliver Twist* opens with a brutal parodic assault on the moral philosophy that considers imprudence to be the key effect of outside help. The description of Oliver's birth at the beginning of the novel not only recalls the language of self-help manuals, commending the newborn hero for taking matters into his own hands, but explicitly repeats the argument about the detrimental effects of outside help:

> The fact is, that there was considerable difficulty in inducing Oliver to take upon himself the office of respiration,—a troublesome practice, but one which custom has rendered necessary to our easy existence; and for some time he lay gasping on a little flock mattress, rather unequally poised between this world and the next: the balance being decidedly in favour of the latter. Now, if, during this brief period, Oliver had been surrounded by careful grandmothers, anxious aunts, experienced nurses, and doctors of profound wisdom, he would most inevitably and indubitably have been killed in no time. There being nobody by, however, but a pauper old

woman, who was rendered rather misty by an unwonted allowance of beer; and a parish surgeon who did such matters by contract; Oliver and Nature fought out the point between them. (2–3)

If, as the authors of the Charity Report believed, the absence of medical assistance promoted individual responsibility, then it is precisely the lack of proper care that forced the newborn Oliver to embrace the spirit of self-reliance and fight for his life: Oliver survives only because he has been left to his own devices. Of course, the very structure of the novel's plot demonstrates precisely the opposite, systematically undermining the extreme version of the self-reliance argument that Dickens was parodying in this passage. Oliver's fate is fundamentally dependent on the intervention of various caring figures, and it is only because he finds a surrogate parent in Mr. Brownlow that he can hope for a life worth living. Much in the same way, David Copperfield's future hinges on the willingness of his great-aunt to take him in. In Dickens, the role of "anxious aunts" in rescuing his bildungsroman heroes cannot be overestimated: in the face of so much insistence on self-reliance and the detrimental effects of what is deemed to be unwarranted help, he set out to explore an alternative vision of agency that fully acknowledged the reality of external circumstances.

In pursuing this path, Dickens also develops a competing moral vision: if it is impossible to control one's own standing in the world, then providing help and care is not simply a naïve and detrimental exercise in sentimentality, but a pressing social imperative. In the words of Hugo Reid, who offers one of the most compelling Victorian versions of this argument, "The world is not all composed of 'clever pushing fellows who get on,' and 'never-do-wells' who don't deserve to get on. The great majority of ordinary plodders who remain where they have been set, rise by good fortune they have done nothing to deserve,—or sink by the pressure of forces they could neither foresee nor withstand."[15] This position closely anticipates the critique of liberal moral rationalism in the work of contemporary care ethicists: "The liberal portrayal of the self-sufficient individual enables the privileged to falsely imagine that dependencies hardly exist, and when they are obvious, to suppose they can be dealt with as private preferences, as when parents provide for their infants. The illusion that society is composed of free, equal, independent individuals who can choose to be associated with one another or not obscures the reality that social cooperation is required as a precondition of autonomy."[16] If some form of dependency is a key aspect of the human condition, what is needed is a thorough reevaluation of our ethical assumptions: to provide care to those in need is not only justified but has beneficial moral effects for both the receiver and the giver of this care.

The Dickensian bildungsroman is a narrative structure designed precisely to explore the far-reaching consequences of various acts of care and terror. *Oliver Twist, David Copperfield,* and *Great Expectations* are all critically invested in discriminating between caring, neglect, and pseudocare. Both the workhouse bureaucracy in *Oliver Twist* and the Murdstones in *David Copperfield* mistake tyranny for care. While Oliver is persistently exposed to physical violence, David suffers a more subtle form of abuse:

> What would I have given, to have been sent to the hardest school that ever was kept!—to have been taught something, anyhow, anywhere! No such hope dawned upon me. They disliked me; and they sullenly, sternly, steadily, overlooked me. I think Mr. Murdstone's means were straitened at about this time; but it is little to the purpose. He could not bear me; and in putting me from him he tried, as I believe, to put away the notion that I had any claim upon him—and succeeded.
>
> I was not actively ill-used. I was not beaten, or starved; but the wrong that was done to me had no intervals of relenting, and was done in a systematic, passionless manner. Day after day, week after week, month after month, I was coldly neglected. (128)

Both Mr. Bumble, with his refusal of Oliver's request for more food, and Murdstone, with his insistence on "firmness," refuse to acknowledge the very existence of a need, either physical or psychological. Both Oliver and David understand this very well, and both search for guardians who will acknowledge the need to care and to establish a close relationship. "God help me," cries David, "I might have been improved for my whole life, I might have been made another creature perhaps, for life, by a kind word at that season." (40) To become someone else, David will have to acquire a new guardian.

Both Oliver and David approach prospective guardians believing that they will finally be seen for what they are—innocent victims in need of rescue. "Don't turn me out of doors to wander the streets again," Oliver pleads with Mr. Brownlow. "Don't send me back to the wretched place I came from. Have mercy upon the poor boy, sir!" (104). David will face Betsey Trotwood with a very similar plea: "I am David Copperfield, of Blunderstone, in Suffolk—where you came, on the night when I was born, and saw my dear mama. I have been very unhappy since she died. I have been slighted, and taught nothing, and thrown upon myself, and put to work not fit for me. It made me run away to you. I was robbed at first setting out, and have walked all the way, and have never slept in a bed since I began the journey" (163). Although such professions of innocence and helplessness will not go untested—Brownlow entrusts Oliver with money and books (a test he fails, because he is abducted by Fagin), while Betsey Trotwood defers her judgment on David's fate until she consults the Murdstones—what the benevolent figures in these novels decisively refuse to do is to operate under the *assumption of guilt*. The reactions of Mr. Brownlow and Betsey Trotwood are rooted in what contemporary care ethicist Nell Noddings calls the "desire to respond positively to need."[17]

The association of need and guilt is the modus operandi of both malevolent characters in Dickens's novels and of the prevailing moral philosophy: if you are in dire need of assistance you must have brought this need on yourself, most likely through some form of moral defect. Contrary to this, benevolent figures have an intuitively different response to need, even if they express some reservations. As Mr. Brownlow tells Oliver, "You say you are an orphan, without a friend in the world; all the inquiries I have been able to make, confirm the statement. Let me hear your story; where you come from; who brought you up; and how you got into the company in which I found you. Speak the truth, and you shall not be friendless while I live" (104). Later in the novel, when Oliver is caught after being forced to take part in a break-in, Rose Maylie will afford him the same benefit of the doubt: "Aunt, dear aunt, for mercy's sake, think of this, before you let them drag this sick child to a prison, which in any case must be the grave of all his chances of amendment. Oh! as you love me, and know that I have never felt the want of parents in your goodness and affection, but that I might have done so, and might have been equally helpless and unprotected with this poor child, have pity upon him before it is too late!" (231) In both cases, it is the initial emotional impulse that should be trusted as the primary guide toward a proper moral judgment.

In accepting the primacy of emotional response over rational judgment, Dickens undermines several key aspects of the pervasive ethical rationalism. Because the dominant moral doctrine tended to conflate the need for assistance and moral corruption, it generally responded to pleas for help in one of two ways: it either charged those in need with helping themselves or it offered assistance in the form of paternalist intervention that will guide the corrupt and the deluded toward moral reform. Dickens is careful to avoid both of these paths: while the very structure of his fictional worlds challenges the notion of self-reliance, he is also extremely skeptical of any attempt to assert the position of moral superiority over those in need and tends to equate paternalist intervention with terror and abuse.[18] In both *Oliver Twist* and *David Copperfield* he distinguishes systematically between benevolent acceptance and paternalist attempts at control and coercion.

As Nell Noddings points out, to care is to open oneself to the needs of the other, not to shape the other according to one's own aspirations, nor to project one's own needs and fantasies into the other: "When my caring is directed to living things, I must consider their natures, ways of life, needs, desires. And although I can never accomplish it entirely, I try to apprehend the reality of the other."[19] The narrative logic of Dickens's bildungsromans reveals an analogous ethical vision: empathizing with others is vital, but actively tampering with selves is decisively dangerous. In *David Copperfield*, to be shaped by another is to be exposed to a violent and terrorizing action that will rob you of individuality and humanity if it doesn't kill you first. Self-fashioning is not a part of a process of social apprenticeship, but a mechanism of exercising dominance over the weak. Edward Murdstone's attempt to form Clara Copperfield at the beginning of the novel serves to underscore this point. "I knew as well," comments David, "that he could mold her pliant nature into any form he chose, as I know, now, that he did it" (39). By the time David comes back from the school to which he was sent, his mother has already fallen victim to the tyranny of the Murdstones: "[Murdstone] is better able to judge of it than I am; for I very well know that I am a weak, light, girlish creature, and that he is a firm, grave, serious man . . . he takes great pains with me; and I ought to be very thankful to him, and very submissive to him even in my thoughts; and when I am not, Peggotty, I worry and condemn myself, and feel doubtful of my own heart, and don't know what to do" (98). David's own great fallacy is that he will reproduce this domineering relationship with his child-wife, Dora, even if in somewhat less authoritarian terms: "What other course was left to take? To 'form her mind'? This was a common phrase of words which had a fair and promising sound, and I resolved to form Dora's mind. I began immediately. When Dora was very childish, and I would have infinitely preferred to humour her, I tried to be grave—and disconcerted her, and myself too" (592). The formation is not only a failure but, more important, it offers a terrifying echo of Murdstone's words: "Yes, I had a satisfaction in the thought of marrying an inexperienced and artless person, and forming her character, and infusing into it some amount of that firmness and decision of which it stood in need" (43). The lessons David Copperfield is to learn will be concerned precisely with the limits of formative domination: "I found myself in the condition of a schoolmaster, a trap, a pitfall; of always playing spider to Dora's fly, and always pouncing out of my hole to her infinite disturbance" (593). Shaping others is the work of the Murdstones of this world, and the hero should have known better, especially given the fact that he has escaped such formative efforts.

When Betsey Trotwood decides to take David out of Murdstone's hands, she does so precisely on the grounds of saving the boy from the fate that has befallen his mother: "'Mr. Murdstone,' she said, shaking her finger at him, 'you were a tyrant to the simple baby, and you broke her heart. She was a loving baby—I know that; I knew it, years before you ever saw her—and through the best part of her weakness you gave her the wounds she died of'" (182). Since shaping means domination, the rescuers in both

*Oliver Twist* and *David Copperfield* offer the heroes benevolence and the promise of a respectable future, but never have the ambition of engineering the heroes' selves. Both Mr. Brownlow and Betsey Trotwood are really facilitators of self-realization. The distinction is far-reaching and reflects Dickens's ambivalent attitude toward the ambition of the privileged and purportedly morally superior upper classes to discipline and shape the less fortunate. To engage in extensive formative work on others, as Murdstone does with Clara Copperfield, is to slip into an authoritarian intervention.

One of the significant consequences of Dickens's fear of tyrannical formation is that the question of self-fashioning—so central to much of the bildungsroman tradition—is displaced. For the heroes of Goethe, Balzac, Stendhal, Eliot, Hardy, and Joyce, the intensive work on the self constitutes the natural course of events, even if in some instances it ends in utter failure. During this formative process, bildungsroman heroes will often put themselves at the disposal of mentors who will shape and discipline them: Wilhelm Meister submits to the guidance of the Society of the Tower, Lucien de Rubempré is shaped by Vautrin, and Daniel Deronda follows Mordecai Cohen. Dickens, however, is far too wary of the detrimental consequences of subjection to allow dominant mentors to step in. In fact, Dickens's commitment to a version of moral sentimentalism that simultaneously hails benevolent intervention and rejects paternalist tyranny puts some very curious demands on the bildungsroman plot. The hero is lifted from his previous position defined by poverty and suffering by external forces that act as agents of care. As a consequence, active search for one's place in the world is displaced, marginalized, and sometimes completely suspended. Perhaps the advocates of self-help were not completely wrong: once the hero is saved, the questions of his education and profession lose much of their relevance.

In *Oliver Twist*—which, of Dickens's bildungsromans, most explicitly explores victimhood and helplessness—such questions are barely asked. Agency exists in the novel primarily as resistance. As J. Hillis Miller writes, "Oliver wills to live, and therefore resists violently all attempts of the world to crush him or bury him or make him into a thief. But at the center of this fierce will, there is passivity, the passivity of expectation, of 'great expectations.'"[20] Oliver, of course, asks for more food (12), stands up for himself in the face of Noah Claypole's bullying (44), and escapes to London to seek his fortune (54). But he is also auctioned by the parish, taken by the Artful Dodger to Fagin, then kidnapped by Nancy and Sikes, and sought by Brownlow, who even offers a reward if the boy is found. Beyond the broadly defined struggle between the disreputable and reputable worlds, there are very few details as to what Oliver will become: the secret of his future is replaced with the secret of his origin, which will eventually attract most of the plot's energies.

Oliver's adoption by Brownlow contains only a vague and unspecified promise of education (439), met, on the other side, by Fagin's attempt to shape Oliver into a criminal. But Brownlow's education of Oliver is never described, and Fagin's attempt to turn him into a criminal fails spectacularly precisely because Oliver cannot be shaped (205). In Steven Marcus's colorful description, "He is active in the way that a ball batted back and forth between opposing sides is active: he is moved through space."[21] Because Oliver's self cannot be fashioned, the battle over his future soon turns into a struggle for sheer physical control over the boy. Oliver is, as Dickens scholars have been noting for a long time, unchangeable, and a bildungsroman describing his development or education would be superfluous.[22] Dickens's narrator admits as much as he sketches a bildungsroman that could have been written:

> How Mr. Brownlow went on, from day to day, filling the mind of his adopted child with stores of knowledge, and becoming attached to him, more and more, as his nature developed itself, and showed the thriving seeds of all he wished him to become—how he traced in him new traits of his early friend, that awakened in his own bosom old remembrances, melancholy and yet sweet and soothing—how the two orphans, tried by adversity, remembered its lessons in mercy to others, and mutual love, and fervent thanks to Him who had protected and preserved them—these are all matters which need not to be told. (439)

They need not to be told because everything is already settled. With Mr. Brownlow's adoption of Oliver (437), the respectable world has triumphed. After a series of false protectors, Oliver has found a proper guardian. He is reclaimed, his fate is sealed, and it will suffice to vaguely gesture toward his future. Development and education can find their way into the novel only as an afterthought.

**The Great Evasion**

In *Oliver Twist,* the fascination with rescuing the hero will simply preclude the possibility of a novel of education. Oliver is adopted and the novel ends. A decade later, in *David Copperfield,* the novel will continue for another five hundred pages after David changes hands, but it is difficult to escape the impression that the moment in which Betsey Trotwood responds to David's plea to "befriend and protect" him in the face of the Murdstones (181) and in which she takes over as his guardian, constitutes the real peripeteia. This reversal is, in fact, the condition of the bildungsroman to come: only under the benevolent eye of his new protectress can David hope to become someone. And even though *David Copperfield* is far more interested in moral growth and psychological development than *Oliver Twist,* the change in guardianship continues to command a curiously prominent place within the novel's narrative logic. This focus on the act of rescue further marginalizes the more common preoccupations of the bildungsroman: in significant ways, the question of the hero's further development—of becoming, to use the Bakhtinian term—will seem almost as obsolete as it was in *Oliver Twist.*

Although David's adoption by Aunt Betsey entails the promise of "another beginning" (184), allowing him to become "a new boy in more senses than one" (193), the process of his development, including formal schooling, is largely hidden from the reader. As David's education in Dr. Strong's school takes off, the narrative rapidly accelerates: "A blank, through which the warriors of poetry and history march on in stately hosts that seem to have no end—and what comes next! *I* am the head-boy, now; and look down on the line of boys below me, with a condescending interest in such of them as bring to my mind the boy I was myself, when I first came there" (229). A blank, indeed. Once again, the Dickensian education is contentless and will simply serve as an indicator that the hero has achieved the proper status—"well educated, well dressed, and with plenty of money in my pocket" (243). This triumph is a fait accompli, already inscribed in Betsey Trotwood's defeat of the Murdstones, and it is no surprise that David will step into the world with no distinct desires: "I suppose the opening prospect confused me. I know that my juvenile experiences went for little or nothing then; and that life was more like a great fairy story, which I was just about to begin to read, than anything else" (233). David is not only confused or unsure; he is devoid of any vision of the future. Facing his prospects with no ideas of his own, he is sent on a journey, an "expedition" (235) to see the world.

In many ways this is the oldest trick in the book, especially if the book is a bildungsroman: to truly enter a process of education (or disillusionment, for that matter) you must step into the world. Wilhelm Meister, Lucien de Rubempré, Jane Eyre, Lucy Snowe, Roderick Hudson, Jude Fawley—all these bildungsroman heroes and heroines will embark on a voyage toward self-realization, however miserably such a voyage might end for some of them. Yet in *David Copperfield* the great journey toward self-understanding is really a trip to David's childhood maid, Peggotty (234)—a trip from one surrogate mother to the next, from one caregiver to another. The journey involves a brief stop in London, but the detour only reinforces the sense that David's world is limited. In London he goes to the theater to see *Julius Caesar,* but Dickens allows his hero to enjoy the metropolis for no more than a few passages before finding a way to evacuate him. David has barely had the time to express his fascination with the performance when Steerforth, a childhood friend, walks in and drags the hero and the story back to the predetermined path to Peggotty (243).

It is not terribly surprising that after this journey David has no better vision of his life path than before it started: "My aunt and I had held many grave deliberations on the calling to which I should be devoted. For a year or more I had endeavoured to find a satisfactory answer to her often-repeated question, 'What I would like to be?' But I had no particular liking, that I could discover, for anything" (233). Because of this indecisiveness, a profession will have to be suggested by the aunt, who thinks that David should become a proctor.

> "What *is* a proctor, Steerforth?" said I.
> "Why, he is a sort of monkish attorney," replied Steerforth. "He is, to some faded courts held in Doctors' Commons,—a lazy old nook near St. Paul's Churchyard—what solicitors are to the courts of law and equity. He is a functionary whose existence, in the natural course of things, would have terminated about two hundred years ago. I can tell you best what he is, by telling you what Doctors' Commons is. It's a little out-of-the-way place, where they administer what is called ecclesiastical law, and play all kinds of tricks with obsolete old monsters of acts of Parliament, which three-fourths of the world know nothing about, and the other fourth supposes to have been dug up, in a fossil state, in the days of the Edwards." (292)

Once David gets the opportunity to examine Doctors' Commons, he will only add that he is "very well satisfied with the dreamy nature of this retreat" (301). A little out-of-the-way place and a dreamy retreat, in other words, the most obscure and obsolete of bureaucratic positions: such are the aspirations of Victorian England's indispensable bildungsroman hero. If the bildungsroman is habitually seen as the genre that explores the encounter with capitalist modernity, one must begin to wonder whether *David Copperfield* refuses such an encounter.

In fact, David makes it something of a habit to turn the situations that offer the opportunity to extend his world into venues for returning to the past. When invited to a dinner party—the quintessential moment of entering the social world in work by realist writers like Balzac or Tolstoy—he shows very little interest in what he finds there. Writing about the French realist tradition, Bakhtin has famously described the bourgeois drawing room as the site of the great encounter between the private and the public: "The interweaving of petty, private intrigues with political and financial intrigues, the interpenetration of state with boudoir secrets, of historical sequences with the everyday and biographical sequences."[23] On the opportunities such spaces offer, David has this to say: "There were other guests—all iced for the occasion, as it struck me, like the wine. But, there was one who attracted my attention before he came in, on account of my hearing him announced as Mr. Traddles! My mind flew back to the Salem House; and could it be Tommy, I thought, who used to draw the skeletons!" (317–18) In *David Copperfield,* meeting old friends unmistakably displaces new prospects.

Among the most important victims of this evasive movement is David's literary career. Despite various attempts to read *David Copperfield* as a representative instance of mid-Victorian interest in authorship as vocation, it is difficult to escape the fact that in the novel itself, literary profession is referenced rather than described or analyzed.[24] "I labored hard at my book," reports David Copperfield, "without allowing it to interfere with the punctual discharge of my newspaper duties; and it came out and was very successful" (588). It is very difficult to extract from this sentence David's (and Dickens's) understanding of literary production, much less the ethical or economic views on which such an understanding might be based. One wonders, in fact, whether scattered references to hard work reflect any theory of profession, or, indeed, any interest in the literary profession.

The scandal of *David Copperfield* is precisely that the profession has a name but no content. David's authorship emerges suddenly in chapter 43, after some five hundred pages of text, and, save for the fact that he has been working hard and doing well, it will remain a mystery. The status of the artistic profession in *David Copperfield* is essentially without precedent among the major European bildungsromans: we are introduced to the aesthetic theories of Goethe's Wilhelm Meister and Joyce's Stephen Dedalus, we read the poems of Lucien de Rubempré in Balzac's *Illusions perdues,* we even learn about the unsuccessful literary and artistic projects of Frédéric Moreau in Flaubert's *L'Éducation sentimentale.* We also witness the creative crises of James's Roderick Hudson, not to mention those of Thomas Mann's Adrian Leverkühn. With David Copperfield, we know nothing: no titles, no aesthetic ideas, no literary preoccupations, except for a handful of references that suggest that David's penchant for storytelling can be traced to his schooldays and that his writing arises from personal experience (see, e.g., 80 and 699). As Alexander Welsh notes,

"So slightly does the narrator of his own life touch upon his career that as readers we are a little taken aback and we have to remind ourselves that this is a novel about a novelist."[25] Nor is Dickens more interested in the practical side of a literary career that occupies such a prominent place in a novel like Balzac's *Illusions perdues:* equally remote from the forces of the market and from internal development, "profession" in David Copperfield is an empty space.

Having discarded so many of the usual preoccupations of the bildungsroman—education, profession, art, and the journey to the metropolis—*David Copperfield* nonetheless gestures toward something resembling moral development. Near the end of the book, having realized that his "undisciplined heart" has trapped him in an intellectually and emotionally unfulfilling marriage to Dora, David looks for a way out (595). As we have seen, his first impulse is to reshape Dora in accordance with his own desires. However, the attempt to "form her mind" brings David perilously close to the kind of tyranny Murdstone previously exerted over his mother and is soon abandoned: "It remained for me to adapt myself to Dora; to share with her what I could, and be happy; to bear on my own shoulders what I must, and be happy still" (595). This moment, in which David comes to terms with the inadequacy of his marriage to Dora, abandoning the futile ambition to shape another human being into a projection of his own desires, certainly points toward maturation: instead of simply remaking his child-wife as he wishes, he will have to live with the consequences of his choices and make the most out of the life he has.[26] And yet David will not have to suffer those consequences for very long: having been exposed as an inadequate wife, Dora quickly dies, opening the way for David to showcase his emotional growth by marrying the far more mature Agnes Wickfield. As Barbara Hardy points out, "Dickens is really only approaching, and then retreating from the idea of showing the disenchanted life. . . . He is touching on a marvelous subject for the psychological novel, but only touching on it. He chose to summarize, to evade, and then cut the knot with Dora's death."[27] The supposed attainment of maturity takes its place next to a series of evasive moves through which the narrative has already tried to suppress both the encounter with the outside world and the exploration of the hero's psychology. As we have seen, *David Copperfield* has demonstrated a profound lack of interest in artistic and intellectual development; it has refused to articulate the problem of professional ambition (unless a vague desire to be educated and avoid manual labor counts as ambition); it has offered us a hero with no plans for the future and with no unrealistic youthful projects; and it has finally denied us a psychological drama.

What is left is a hero trapped in a circular movement within a predefined circle of friends and relatives—Aunt Betsey, Peggotty, Mr. Micawber, Steerforth. In fact, except for Dora and her father, Mr. Spenlow, who appear in chapter 23, practically all of the novel's chief characters are introduced to us by chapter 15. David's work as a parliamentary reporter and author, and his trip to the Continent late in the novel, introduce no new characters: the world of *David Copperfield* consists almost exclusively of relatives, childhood friends, and teachers. In other words, the world of the novel refuses to extend and simply stops expanding once David grows up. The hero may have matured, but one wonders whether he has faced the world at all.[28] The interpretation according to which *David Copperfield* chronicles the education of the protagonist's "undisciplined heart" has gained considerable traction precisely because a reading that would like to insist that the novel tracks some form of growth has very little else to cling to.

And yet *David Copperfield*'s complex and elaborate flight from the world and from the exploration of self-fashioning reveals the profound stability of the novel's emotional and ethical coordinates. Agnes is not just an intellectually formidable figure; unlike the hapless child-wife Dora, she is also capable of responding to David's most pressing desire, the desire to be cared for and protected: "I had always felt my weakness, in comparison with her constancy and fortitude; and now I felt it more and more" (700). She takes up the role of David's "guide and best support" (738) and rescues him from the misery of his continental tour by expressing encouragement. His response clearly outlines this dependency: "I wrote to her before I slept. I told her that I had been in sore need of her help; that without her I was not, and I never had been, what she thought me; but that she inspired me to be that, and I would try" (699). The renewed commitment to Agnes reinvigorates David's literary career, and he goes on to produce yet another work of fiction with no known content and no known name: "After some rest and change, I fell to work, in my old ardent way, on a new fancy, which took strong possession of me. As I advanced in the execution of this task, I felt it more and more, and roused my utmost energies to do it well" (699). For David, to have Agnes next to him is to accept once again the status of "the cared–for," and to complete his pantheon of guardians by finally finding the one who can fully participate in his intellectual and emotional life.

At the end of the novel, we find David surrounded with protective figures: Agnes, Betsey Trotwood, and Peggotty (748). In the final chapters, he has slipped into "fame and fortune" (741), into a vague state of prosperity, as if this was a natural effect of the benevolence that surrounded him. As Carol Gilligan writes, "The ideal of care is thus an activity of relationship, of seeing and responding to need, taking care of the world by sustaining the web of connection so that no one is left alone."[29] But such an ideal is extremely difficult to maintain outside familial relations and domestic space, and *David Copperfield* will have to limit the hero's relations to those with whom care is traditionally associated: a maid, a great-aunt, and a wife.[30] As the novel draws to an end, the circle of care has closed, obliterating in the process all other realities of life, external and internal.

## Fatal Extraction

Yet not everyone is ushered in the fantasy of care. At the end of *Great Expectations,* even in the purportedly more optimistic version of the ending suggested to Dickens by Edward Bulwer-Lytton, we find Pip and Estella at the site of the burned-down Satis House. What is left behind by Miss Havisham is, appropriately, a wasteland. At this site of Estella's tyrannical education, the place where she was "brought up by Miss Havisham to wreak revenge on all the male sex" (179), life can continue only after the lessons have been forgotten, or, rather, superseded by the agony of her later life: "Now, when suffering has been stronger than all other teaching, and has taught me to understand what your heart used to be. I have been bent and broken, but—I hope—into a better shape. Be as considerate and good to me as you were, and tell me we are friends" (478). Even at the very end, when Pip and Estella seemingly step into a new life, we feel that we have witnessed a scene of mourning rather than of promise.

In *Great Expectations* Dickens has altered the key propositions of the bildungsroman plot in a way that forecloses the possibility of a comforting conclusion, which he previously offered in *Oliver Twist* and *David Copperfield*. As we have seen, in both of these novels care is administered by surrogate parents who rescue the heroes and secure for them a promise of respectable life. In both novels, parental care and upward mobility are firmly aligned. *Great Expectations,* however, dissolves this crucial alignment, replacing well-intentioned benefactors with frightening puppet-masters.[31] While the power to elevate the hero out of poverty and ignorance is granted to the grotesque figures of Miss Havisham (in the case of Estella) and Magwitch (in Pip's case), the other key attributes of the benevolent guardian—the willingness to care for and protect the helpless hero—are transferred to the thoroughly disempowered figure of Joe Gargery, Pip's poor and illiterate surrogate father. As the novel constantly reminds us, upward mobility and care are firmly opposed.

One of the consequences of this realignment is that in *Great Expectations* social mobility becomes tied precisely to the kind of formative domination Dickens's earlier bildungsromans rejected. Rather than responding to need, both Miss Havisham and Magwitch act as diabolic demiurges and aspire to be the engineers of human souls. In that respect, they recall Edward Murdstone's attempt to form his wife "into any form he chose" (39). However, while in *David Copperfield* Dickens robs Murdstone of the opportunity to shape David into submission, in *Great Expectations* he explores to the fullest the devastating consequences of subject-engineering. In different ways, both Magwitch's ambition to "own a gentleman" and Miss Havisham's formative efforts directed at Estella have dehumanizing effects. Pip's entry into the world of Satis House, perceived by Pip and everyone around him as the first step in his movement upward, is really the moment in which he is turned into a useful instrument in the sinister attempt to turn Estella into a figure of vengeance and hatred, utterly devoid of empathy. As Miss Havisham announces, "With my teachings, and with this figure of myself always before her, a warning to back and point my lessons, I stole her heart away, and put ice in its place" (395). Significantly, both Pip and Estella self-consciously acknowledge their status as mechanical puppets. Whereas Pip comes to the realization that he was "a model with a mechanical heart to practise on when no other practice was at hand" (319), Estella finally recognizes that she has been engineered to fit Miss Havisham's desires: "I must be taken as I have been made. The success is not mine, the failure is not mine, but the two together make me" (302).

In *Great Expectations,* the opposition between care and terror is brought to such an extreme that Joe Gargery, the central figure of caring in the novel, literally cannot communicate with Miss Havisham: "I could hardly have imagined dear old Joe looking so unlike himself or so like some extraordinary bird; standing as he did speechless, with his tuft of feathers ruffled, and his mouth open as if he wanted a worm" (98). Utterly dumbfounded by the appearance of Satis House, Joe answers all of Miss Havisham's questions by talking to Pip and fully recovers only after they have left (99–100). And while Joe is, of course, famously inarticulate, we should nonetheless appreciate the allegorical potential of this scene—between his caring innocence and Miss Havisham's project of subject-engineering, there can be no communication.

The irony of Pip's position is precisely that in *Great Expectations* care is associated with poverty and ignorance while the promise of social mobility lies elsewhere. In this novel, mobility is indistinguishable from the breakdown of the caring relation. As Vincent Pecora writes, "Pip's native guilt, inculcated by his resentful sister, is multiplied many times over as he comes to realize how far his 'expectations' as an heir to Miss Havisham have almost destroyed the one relationship in his life that suggests genuine kinship and fellow-feeling—his friendship with the illiterate blacksmith and abandoned father-figure, Joe."[32] To this Dickens adds further layers of irony: Pip has been altered—for the worse, he suggests—by serving as a puppet to Miss Havisham, only to discover that his life was managed by a figure far more sinister. With the discovery that the mysterious benefactor is not the grotesque old woman but Magwitch, the transported convict, the prospect of becoming a gentleman is invalidated both practically and symbolically.

Toward the end, the novel will nonetheless seek to ameliorate this state of affairs, by allowing for the assumption that the unlikely benefactor is not simply a madman with a "fixed idea" (339) and the owner of a gentleman (317), but rather a hunted man in need of rescue. In fact, the attempt to save Magwitch from the certain death he faces in England as an escaped convict will be by far Pip's most significant undertaking. And if the monstrous convict can be humanized, there must be a lesson there: "For now, my repugnance to him had all melted away; and in the hunted, wounded, shackled creature who held my hand in his, I only saw a man who had meant to be my benefactor, and who had felt affectionately, gratefully, and generously, towards me with great constancy through a series of years. I only saw in him a much better man than I had been to Joe." (441). Following this reversal, the novel offers a proliferation of gestures of care: Pip nurses his ailing benefactor and, after Magwitch's death, simultaneously falls into poverty and illness, only to be attended by Joe: "I was slow to gain strength, but I did slowly and surely become less weak, and Joe stayed with me, and I fancied I was little Pip again. For the tenderness of Joe was so beautifully proportioned to my need, that I was like a child in his hands" (461). This regression seems to turn the novel into something akin to a morality play: between forces of mobility and care, Pip chooses the former, only to lose everything and recognize the value of care.

This realization, however, comes too late to avert the dismal ending. Meddling with selves has already gone too far with Miss Havisham's toying with Pip and Estella, and with Pip's initially mysterious social elevation. The prospect of creating the circle of care such as the one at the end of *David Copperfield* will be denied Pip. After his defeat in London, he attempts to go back home and marry his childhood friend Biddy, who throughout the novel represented the obvious alternative to Estella: "Biddy was never insulting, or capricious, or Biddy to-day and somebody else to-morrow; she would have derived only pain, and no pleasure, from giving me pain; she would far rather have wounded her own breast than mine" (128). Biddy has, however, already married Joe. This is yet another of Dickens's ironic reversals: the two caring figures rejected by Pip have come together in a kind of union he can never hope to achieve, and they have even named their son Pip, symbolically displacing the novel's hero as the object of care.

Given such an outcome, it is easy to argue that *Great Expectations,* with its somber ending and grotesque benefactors, indicates a fundamental shift in Dickens's understanding of benevolent intervention. The novel has offered a new dealing of cards, a redistribution of narrative propositions that results in a scenario directly opposed to that of his earlier bildungsromans.[33] And yet the emergence of benefactors as grotesque monomaniacs doesn't undermine the commitment to benevolent intervention but rather reemphasizes the vital relationship between mobility and ethics: for Dickens, upward mobility makes sense only within the ethical context of care. Pip therefore fails not because Dickens's assumptions about social mobility and permissible forms of benevolent intervention have changed, but because they have not. If the prospect of social mobility now seems ironized and defeated, it is only because Dickens has always accepted it only conditionally, as a corollary of care. From the perspective of moral sentimentalism, once the relationship between mobility and care is dissolved, upward mobility is delegitimized: relieved of the accompanying ethical attributes, social advancement will become an instance of destructive uprooting, a fatal extraction.

*Great Expectations* shares with *Oliver Twist* and *David Copperfield* both a set of ethical assumptions and the impulse to look away from the more common preoccupations of the bildungsroman. Here, the bildungsroman dissolves into a Gothic tale. In a novel like *Oliver Twist,* the bildungsroman is turned into a site of rescue. Yet both gestures are equally successful in turning the plot's focus away from the mechanisms of socialization. In *Great Expectations,* as Pip arrives in London, Herbert Pocket steps in as his guide in acquiring proper manners and in learning the ways of the metropolis. Yet this education is almost as elusive as the books of David Copperfield: we are informed that it takes place, but it has very little content. Herbert's course in etiquette occupies only a marginal position in a conversation that focuses on the mystifying life of Miss Havisham (177–80). Like Dickens's previous bildungsromans,

*Great Expectations* places social advancement under the auspices of an external authority, and it is only natural that the novel moves sharply away from the mechanisms that govern active pursuit of social position, and from the work on the self that usually follows such a pursuit. The mystery surrounding Miss Havisham, that MacGuffin of *Great Expectations,* successfully marginalizes the instruction in the ways of the metropolis.

# 3

# CHARLOTTE BRONTË AND THE GOVERNESS AS A LIBERAL SUBJECT

In the final pages of George Eliot's *Middlemarch* (1871–72), the narrator works unusually hard to persuade us that all will be well with Dorothea Brooke. Unlike Maggie Tulliver, whose every impulse is thoroughly stifled even before she meets an early death in *The Mill on the Floss* (1860), and unlike Gwendolen Harleth, who is left abandoned and confused at the end of *Daniel Deronda* (1876), the heroine of *Middlemarch* is treated to what appears to be a reasonably favorable ending. Following the death of her first husband—the singularly unappealing Edward Casaubon—Dorothea will find a much more suitable partner in Will Ladislaw. While the heroine's second marriage comes at a cost, as she will have to forgo both her social position and any claim to Casaubon's property, the financial losses seem to be amply compensated by Will and Dorothea's mutual devotion and a shared sense of purpose in advancing the larger cause of social reform. As the narrator tells us, "They were bound to each other by a love stronger than any impulses which could have marred it."[1] And yet, in spite of the conciliatory tones that dominate the final pages of *Middlemarch,* even such a promising union as this one cannot help but turn into an exercise in disempowerment. Although Eliot insists that "Dorothea could have liked nothing better" than to provide Will with "wifely help" (793), such rhetorical assurances cannot avert the obvious conclusion that the heroine's own reformist ambitions can be carried out only vicariously, with her existence "absorbed into the life of another" (793). At the end of her own novel, Dorothea is relegated to a supporting role.

The ending of *Middlemarch,* with its struggle to portray the frustration of Dorothea's desires as a source of contentment rather than anguish, forcefully illustrates some of the central difficulties in the debate about the female bildungsroman. On the one hand, given the constraints imposed on Victorian womanhood, the vicarious path to self-fulfillment that Eliot offers to Dorothea might as well be seen as a kind of triumph: because she inhabits a world that severely limits her access to vocational and geographic mobility, a world in which every socially desirable outcome of female development involves some form of submission to patriarchal authority, Dorothea should perhaps count her blessings for having found Will. On the other hand, we may well wonder what remains of the bildungsroman when the options available to its protagonists are as limited as they undeniably were for Victorian women. The heroes of the male bildungsroman may routinely fail to conquer the world, but they are at least invited to try. In fact, as I have shown in the first two chapters of this book, one of the bildungsroman's favorite narrative mechanisms is to promise its heroes some grand prize—wealth, fame, noble title, gentleman status—and then renege on the promise. But such a promise, however illusory, is never extended to women. Reflecting on the fate of the female bildungsroman protagonist in the nineteenth century, Susan Fraiman writes, "Her finding of friends, her picking of work are both subsumed by the single, all-determining 'choice' of a husband, and even this (turning down a Mr. Collins, seeing through the blandishments of a Wickham) is mostly a negative prerogative."[2] And if the protagonist is prevented from freely engaging the world, is there still a bildungsroman?

Perhaps there is not. As Felicia Bonaparte rather bluntly argues in a response to Fraiman, "It is regrettable that women were not in the past able to engage in those actions novelists of Bildungsromane liked or needed to write about, and I certainly hope the future will correct this gross injustice."[3] Bonaparte's argument, like the similar dismissal offered by Franco Moretti some years later, hinges on the assumption that the bildungsroman demands a certain kind of plot that was simply unavailable to women: "Wide cultural formation, professional mobility, full social freedom—for a long time, the west European middle-class male held a virtual monopoly on these, which made him a sort of structural *sine qua non* of the genre. Without him, and without the social privileges he enjoyed, the Bildungsroman was difficult to write because it was difficult to imagine."[4] And because such privileges did not extend to women, the absence of the female bildungsroman, at least in the nineteenth century, is merely an unfortunate reality that we will have to learn to live with.[5]

Such an argument, however, faces some serious limitations, historical as well as theoretical. The historical difficulty is, of course, that the key authors of the nineteenth-century English novel, including Austen, Eliot, Gaskell, and the Brontës, were obsessively producing narratives of female development. The theoretical difficulty is that the bildungsroman is defined not merely through a set of actions available to the protagonist—going to a metropolis, traveling abroad, choosing a profession, trying to rise through the ranks—but also through a certain dynamics between self and society, a dynamics that demands that the developmental process unfold through a complex negotiation between individual desires and societal pressures. Once this broader understanding is introduced, the question is no longer whether there is such a thing as a female bildungsroman, but, rather, how exactly gender inflects the genre's thematic scope and formal structures. In the introduction to *The Voyage In,* the pioneering 1983 collection that inaugurated the debate about the female bildungsroman, Elizabeth Abel, Marianne Hirsch, and Elizabeth Langland ask, "What psychological and social forces obstruct maturity for women? What are the prevailing patterns of women's development in fiction? How does gender qualify literary representations of development?"[6] The answer the editors provide is that the constraints imposed on female development in the nineteenth century gave rise to a distinct form of the bildungsroman, one that supplanted the traditional definitions of the genre by emphasizing circularity in place of linear development, and inward growth in place of socialization: "Male protagonists struggle to find a hospitable context in which to realize their aspirations, female protagonists must frequently struggle to voice any aspirations whatsoever. For a woman, social options are often so narrow that they preclude explorations of her milieu."[7] However, while such a theorization is certainly preferable to the outright dismissal of the female bildungsroman, it is not without its problems. To define the narrative of female development in purely negative terms—which is to say simply in terms of what women cannot do—is to underestimate the complexity of its relationship to the bildungsroman's generic demands. As Fraiman observes, "Those theories of female developmental fiction that recuperate a wholly different plot of spiritual growth and domestic relationship remain, in my view, too obligingly within the given contours of 'women's culture,' neglecting the troubling appeal and predominance of the *Bildungsroman* for female figures."[8] And if we refuse both the facile rejection of the female bildungsroman and the attempts to imagine it as a mere reverse image of the "conventional" bildungsroman, what might be a way forward?

In my view, we should first recognize that social constraints exert pressure on the structure of the bildungsroman in a nonlinear way. As we have seen in chapter 2, the stunned agency of the Dickensian hero emerges precisely from a social context that categorically demands that men actively engage the world. Conversely, while the lack of access to occupational and geographic mobility certainly does limit the thematic scope of the female bildungsroman—in the words of one Victorian commentator, "Young women cannot emigrate as their brothers do"—this narrowing does not merely turn the female bildungsroman into a narrative of passive involution, but produces a series of complex and often contradictory formal effects.[9] The female bildungsroman, as we shall see in a moment, simultaneously amplifies the tension between socialization and self-fulfillment, seeks to appropriate for its heroine some of the characteristic prerogatives of male development, and pivots toward the logic of compromise usually stressed by traditional theories of the genre.[10]

The restrictions placed on female development in the nineteenth century tend to throw the clash of inward desires and outward circumstances into sharp relief, pressuring the heroine to confront the realities of her position with unusual force. In *Middlemarch,* Dorothea Brooke must come to terms with the fact that her marriage to Edward Casaubon will not be the sublime exercise in intellectual growth she had hoped for, and that the man who was supposed to be the "guide who would take her along the grandest path" (30) is really a talentless, pedantic, and cruel "elaborator of small explanations," as Will Ladislaw calls him (199). Maggie Tulliver in *The Mill on the Floss* and Gwendolen Harleth in *Daniel Deronda* will similarly have to wrestle with the fact that they are denied both economic security and emotional fulfillment: whereas Maggie struggles, not quite successfully, to persuade herself that her every worldly desire is illegitimate, Gwendolen stumbles through *Daniel Deronda* dazzled and confused by the loss of social status, the catastrophe of her marriage to Grandcourt, and Deronda's rejection.

At the same time, precisely because the opposition between what is possible and what is desired is so stark, the female bildungsroman seems to be particularly interested in compromise. Unlike the male hero who generally hopes, however misguidedly, to move up in the world, the bildungsroman heroine is often equally worried about downward mobility. Her social position is dependent not on her own labor, but on inheritance or her husband's wealth, both of which can be withdrawn—family fortune can dissipate, leaving the heroine less well off than she had hoped to be (as is the case with Gwendolen Harleth); inheritance can bypass women and go straight to male relatives (as in Austen's *Pride and Prejudice*); and husbands can bequeath their property as they see fit (as Dorothea finds out in *Middlemarch*). Because the threat of losing current status is one of its central economic concerns, and because this can usually be averted only through marriage, the nineteenth-century female bildungsroman generally focuses on negotiating the emotional, ethical, and financial aspects of matrimony. In doing so, it also has a pronounced tendency to seek a compromise between economic security and emotional fulfillment. The central twist of the marriage plot—the rapprochement between the heroine and the man she initially detests—results from precisely such negotiations: Elizabeth Bennet can marry Mr. Darcy, conveniently averting a life of poverty, but only after she has been persuaded of his worthiness, and Lucy Snowe can accept Paul Emanuel only when she is sure that he is not the mendacious Jesuit she thought him to be.

Finally, in its most radical form, the female bildungsroman functions as a device to appropriate for its protagonist a greater degree of individual agency than the social context of Victorian England would normally allow. After all, Brontë's Lucy Snowe *does* emigrate. And, in contrast to the notoriously passive Dickensian bildungsroman heroes, both Lucy and Jane Eyre seem not only remarkably resourceful but obsessed with the value of individual agency: whereas Dickens largely uses the bildungsroman to recluse his young men from the mechanisms of social mobility to which they *do* have access, Brontë uses the same form to try to endow her heroines with an unlikely degree of self-reliance.

As this brief discussion demonstrates, narratives of female development maintain a complex relationship to the process of socialization, simultaneously trying to navigate the strict limits imposed on female development and seeking plausible mechanisms to look beyond those limits. As I will demonstrate in the pages that follow, the female bildungsroman is perhaps best understood not in opposition to the male version of the genre (which, as we have seen, is plagued with issues of its own), but rather as a kind that introduces an added layer of complexity to the exploration of individual development. Because the position of the bildungsroman heroine is generally more constrained than that of the male hero, the already difficult negotiations between desires and circumstances are put under additional strain. The difficulty faced by male heroes is that they struggle to navigate the process of socialization under the disorienting conditions of modernity; the difficulty faced by the heroine is that she first has to struggle to gain access to this process. In other words, the female bildungsroman follows the development of a modern subject, but one with limited access to the privileges of modernity. Consequently, it simultaneously examines the forms of specifically female disempowerment and engages in complex narrative maneuvering in order to appropriate for its heroines an amplified sense of agency. Of course, like its male counterpart, it produces troubling results both when it crushes its protagonists and when it finds a way to rescue them. As the examples of Dorothea Brooke, Elizabeth Bennet, Jane Eyre, and Lucy Snowe all demonstrate, the female bildungsroman is often a form that strives to engineer a tolerable compromise for its young women, but the terms of such compromise remain contested to such a degree that one sometimes wonders whether what is achieved should be seen as reconciliation or surrender.[11]

In the pages that follow I wish to explore this dynamics by focusing primarily on the work of Charlotte Brontë, a writer unique both in her readiness to use the bildungsroman form in order to imagine female development in terms usually reserved for men and in her readiness to engineer unlikely compromises. The nature of Brontë's project becomes fully apparent when her heroines are contrasted with Dickens's heroes. While David Copperfield seeks refuge from the vicissitudes of modern capitalism in the "tranquillity and peace" (720) of an obscure bureaucratic position, Jane Eyre threads the opposite path, seeking access to the forms of mobility routinely denied to Victorian women. As she puts it in one of her iconic formulations, "It is in vain to say human beings ought to be satisfied with tranquillity: they must have action; and they will make it if they cannot find it."[12] While Dickens's bildungsroman heroes persistently refer to their own helplessness and ask to be rescued, Jane evinces what can only be described as a kinetic obsession.[13] As both her rhetoric and her actions make clear, from Jane's perspective it is free movement that secures her status as a self-governing subject. On the one hand, she invariably articulates her desires by appealing to a symmetrical rhetorical structure in which movement is equated with vitality and in which inertia is indistinguishable from death. On the other, she not only engages in a series of audacious demonstrations of mobility when she successively abandons Lowood, Thornfield, and Moor House, but she vigorously resists even apparently trivial attempts to encroach on her freedom of movement. As she refuses St. John Rivers's attempts to direct her life, the defense of physical and moral autonomy become indistinguishable: "I perceived soon that Mr. Rivers had placed a chair behind me, and was gently attempting to make me sit down on it. He also advised me to be composed: I scorned the insinuation of helplessness and distraction, shook off his hand, and began to walk about" (308).

In novel after novel, Dickens works to subvert the key claims of liberal individualism by portraying his young men not as self-reliant agents committed to an active work on the self, but as passive beings inescapably shaped by forces over which they had no control. And while he uses the bildungsroman form in order to relieve the male hero of the demand for self-reliance, Brontë follows the opposite path, trying to construct a narrative within which it would be possible for a young woman to take on attributes of an autonomous, self-determined subject. Of course, critics have long recognized that Brontë's books can be productively read in terms of power struggle between the female protagonist and the forces that seek to subdue her.¹⁴ Both Terry Eagleton and Nancy Armstrong have explored the significance of the heroine's domination in Brontë's novels, while Susan Lanser has persuasively interpreted *Jane Eyre* as an attempt to assert the authority of Jane's (and Charlotte's) perspective.¹⁵ She argues, "The form of *Jane Eyre* involves the imposition of the self-authorizing and totalizing voice I have associated with the Romantic hero upon a very different and particularly female genre."¹⁶ However, while Brontë's interest in empowering Jane is beyond doubt, what makes her project both unique and uniquely difficult is that she wanted to have the rebellion of her heroines legitimized.

The difficulty with this project was, of course, that within the confines of Victorian domestic ideology female self-assertion and respectability were difficult to reconcile. After all, young women were not meant to be liberal subjects. Brontë was therefore facing a unique challenge: How was she to break up this monopoly and claim for her heroines a significant degree of autonomy and self-determination without turning them into rebels prepared to step fully outside of the established social order? How to empower the socially marginalized figure of the impoverished gentlewoman just enough to open up for her the possibility of professional and sexual fulfillment while trying to keep her within the confines of middle-class respectability?¹⁷ The complexity of these questions is apparent in the fact that, like Balzac and Dickens, Brontë had to return to the bildungsroman form on several occasions, each time renegotiating the relationship between passivity and action and between submission and self-assertion. In this chapter I explore *Jane Eyre* and *Villette* as variations of a precarious balancing act in which Brontë struggled to imagine a socially sanctioned vision of feminine self-realization.

## The Governess in the Attic

In many ways, the figure of the governess was the natural starting point for Brontë's exploration of the possibilities of female agency, not just for obvious biographical reasons, but also because of the unique position that this figure occupied in the Victorian social imagination. As novels, memoirs, newspaper articles, and firsthand accounts included in various instruction manuals all testify, in mid-Victorian England the figure of the governess offered a key site for reflection on female disempowerment: as a gentlewoman devoid of the economic capital that would grant her the prospect of independence or respectable marriage, yet still bound by the demands of middle-class respectability, she is condemned to a position synonymous with the breakdown of social and familial ties and very difficult to reconcile—in Victorian England, at least—with professional and emotional fulfillment.

Not unlike one of Dickens's orphans, the governess constructed by these narratives was condemned to exclusion, dependency, and passivity. It is therefore not surprising that Lady Blessington's *The Governess* (1839) mirrors if not the thematic scope than certainly much of the power dynamics of *Oliver Twist*. Clara Mordaunt, the heroine of *The Governess*, is treated to a full range of Dickensian misfortunes: following the bankruptcy and death of her father, she is left in the care of a poor, elderly aunt and finally compelled to make a living as a governess. Mistreated by a series of insufferable mistresses—women who are vicious, grotesque, and sometimes simply insecure—she moves from one impossible situation to another, continuously presumed guilty of every crime from minor indiscretions to adultery and theft. When Clara is finally exonerated, she is quickly treated to a highly respectable husband and an immense fortune she inherits from a hereto-unknown relative. As in Dickens, however, her good fortune seems largely dependent on the emergence of a benevolent stranger, a caregiver prepared to adopt the heroine and defend her innocence in the face of naysayers. In *The Governess,* the role that Dickens awards to Mr. Brownlow in *Oliver Twist* is played by the well-meaning elderly Quaker Abraham Jacob:

> Remember, maiden, that henceforth I consider thee as my child; yeah, verily, I will be unto thee as father.... Thou hast suffered enough by the unkindness to which thou hast been exposed; thy fame, thy life itself, might have been the sacrifice; but now I assert over thine actions the right of a parent, and my home shall be thine, until thy husband. I announce to thee,

before those kind friends, that I will render thee independent from any future exertions on thy part to earn thy subsistence, and will never again hear on thy going out as a governess.[18]

Blessington's novel unmistakably captures a series of tropes that will dominate the construction of the governess in the popular discourse over the next half a century. Invariably, the governess is a figure of loss: a victim of a sudden disaster, she loses her family, home, possessions, and the promise of a respectable future she was taught to expect. From Madame Bureaud Riofrey's *Memoires of a Governess* (1841) to Eliot's *Daniel Deronda,* becoming a governess is imagined as a traumatic instance of sudden and unexpected downward social movement. About Gwendolen Harleth George Eliot writes, "For a lady to become a governess—to 'take a situation'—was to descend in life and to be treated at best with a compassionate patronage."[19] As Eliot's reflections suggest, the most disturbing aspect of becoming a governess was that it implied an irreversible loss of social status: to "take a situation" was to become trapped in a state both deeply ambivalent and effectively inescapable.

As numerous Victorian commentators have pointed out, the governess fell between the classes, trapped in a space "above the kitchen, below the drawing room."[20] While her genteel background simultaneously kept her above the position of a servant and robbed her of the class solidarity servants extended to each other, her status as a dependent employee precluded her from claiming full citizenship of the family drawing room. One of the consequences of this indeterminate state was that the governess lacked access to the mechanisms that would allow her to alter her social position. With no alternative occupations available and no property, without a clear position within the social hierarchy and hence not enough social capital to attract the prospect of a respectable marriage, she was condemned to linger in what Harriet Martineau describes as the state of "enforced celibacy."[21] The governess is precluded from participating in the ideal of the Victorian middle-class family and is condemned to the status of a perpetual dependent, lingering in the corner of the bourgeois drawing room, "mixed up with the family, one among them, but not of them."²² In the final instance, to become a governess is to be trapped in a paralyzing existential condition.

As we have seen, Lady Blessington's Clara Mourdant breaks away from this state of paralysis with the help of some very Dickensian narrative witchcraft. What Blessington offers is, in the final instance, a fairy-tale solution to the problem of the governess's social standing: with the help of a benevolent outsider, Clara is miraculously lifted from a state of poverty and abuse, married off to a man both modest and exceedingly rich, and, finally, given a large inheritance of her own. Through these interventions, she is returned to the state of affluence from which she has fallen, liberated from the prison-house of a governess's life, and allowed to reclaim the role of a wife.

As Mary Poovey has shown in great detail, *Jane Eyre* raises many of the common Victorian concerns about the governess as a socially ambivalent figure.²³ Jane's initial position in the Rochester household forcefully embodies the understanding of the governess as a second-class gentlewoman, privy to the events of the drawing room, but not allowed to participate in them: in chapter 17, while Adèle chats with Blanche Ingram and her party, Jane sits next to the window, as a half-hidden listener (148). However, while Brontë was all too aware of the limitations the governess faced, she also saw her as a particularly useful vehicle for the exploration of social mobility. Because she is not properly integrated into a family, Jane can legitimately leave the household in search of other opportunities in a way in which neither a daughter of the house nor a wife could. In a perverse way, for Brontë, the governess embodies both paralysis and independence: while she can hardly hope to fundamentally alter her social standing, Jane can at least go and suffer somewhere else.

Whether this is actually a plausible account of the governess's position is beside the point. By imagining her protagonists as the one kind of female figure that simultaneously has a foot in the genteel world, maintains a degree of geographic mobility, and is free from familial bonds, Brontë seeks to endow her heroines with a higher degree of social freedom. In this respect, the comparison with governess narratives is again instructive. As we have seen, in Blessington's *The Governess* the dependent and impoverished heroine is liberated from her unfortunate position solely through the benevolence of external actors. For Brontë, such a simple rescue is out of the question. While not entirely averse to some of the narrative mechanisms Blessington resorts to—Jane Eyre is also a recipient of a significant inheritance from a newly discovered relative—Brontë strenuously resists the temptation to provide her heroines with a miraculous escape. In both *Jane Eyre* and *Villette* her project centers on imagining a process through which the socially marginalized female figure might be able to negotiate her way to independence and self-fulfillment. Jane Eyre in particular sees herself as the kind of liberal subject described a decade later by John Stuart Mill. What Jane desires for herself is what Mill describes as the "liberty of tastes and pursuits; of framing the plan of our life to suit our own character; of doing as we like, subject to such consequences as may follow."[24] When she rejects St. John's proposal, she does so precisely on the grounds that marriage to him would force her into a life that is contrary to her nature: "I daily wished more to please him: but to do so, I felt daily more and more that I must disown half my nature, stifle half my faculties, wrest my tastes from their original bent, force myself to the adoption of pursuits for which I had no natural vocation" (308). Like Mill, Brontë's heroine posits sovereign command over one's fate as a necessary condition of meaningful existence.

Such sovereign command is, however, neither a sufficient goal in itself, nor easily accessible to Jane, who is doubly disempowered as a woman and as a governess. If she was simply to claim for herself the privileges of self-determination, she would invariably end up outside of the social order—a proposition that, as we shall see, Jane repeatedly rejects. Brontë is therefore forced to construct a narrative that honors Jane's claim to the privileges of a liberal subject while simultaneously securing her place within the confines imposed by Victorian domestic ideology. As Terry Eagleton observes, "Where Charlotte Brontë differs most from Emily is precisely in this impulse to negotiate passionate self-fulfillment on terms which preserve the social and moral conventions intact."[25] While certainly interested in endowing Jane with a set of properties inimical to her social position—mobility in place of paralysis, resistance to authority in place of submission, an active pursuit of inward desires in place of passive suffering—Brontë also wants her heroine to be validated within the limits of a value system in which a respectable marriage continues to occupy a central position. This dual demand—to empower the governess and have her engineer her own rescue while also having this newly empowered figure legitimized—turns Brontë's bildungsromans into sites of particularly challenging negotiations. What these negotiations entail is an attempt to produce a narrative space within which the young heroine can perform powerful rebellious gestures, try to fulfill her desires, and attain an unprecedented level of independence, while simultaneously keeping these transgressive acts within such confines that will allow her to be reintegrated back into the role of a wife. Jane therefore treads carefully the narrow passage between the Scylla of self-effacement and the Charybdis of unrestrained self-indulgence, rejecting the unconditional surrender to the forces of patriarchal oppression, yet nonetheless embracing the institutional framework of a middle-class marriage.[26]

## A Proper Bildungsroman

If in the more conventional governess narratives (and in Dickens's novels, for that matter) escaping abuse and attaining a tolerable level of prosperity usually function as a narrative end in itself, Brontë uses the precarious social standing of her heroine in order to initiate a complex process of self-definition. In each of her successive homes, Jane tries to reconcile the social role she plays with carefully crafted self-understanding, and when she fails to achieve this goal, she leaves. One after the other she refuses the roles of an unwanted alien (Gateshead Hall), a sexless inmate (Lowood Institution), Rochester's mistress (Thornfield Hall), and a submissive wife to St. John (Moor House) in order to attain for herself the fantasy of marriage with Rochester once that union becomes socially acceptable (Ferndean Manor).[27]

In rejecting each of these roles, she is also trying to overcome the sense of incompleteness and isolation each of them carries. As she muses after rejecting Rochester's offer to move to France as his mistress, "Whether is it better, I ask, to be a slave in a fool's paradise at Marseilles—fevered with delusive bliss one hour—suffocating with the bitterest tears of remorse and shame the next—or to be a village schoolmistress, free and honest, in a breezy mountain nook in the healthy heart of England?" (308) This is in many ways the novel's central question: If Jane is not simply in search of a better situation or greener pastures, but rather on a quest to integrate the realities of life with the prospect of emotional, professional, and moral fulfillment, how does she realize such desires without being condemned to the role of a social outcast?

By the time she decides to leave Rochester, Jane has already started to answer this question through a simultaneous rejection of frivolity and asceticism. This positioning is played out during her return to Gateshead to visit her dying Aunt Reed. What she discovers there, in addition to the fact that she has a living uncle in Madeira, is that her cousins Eliza and Georgiana have come to embody two opposing yet equally unacceptable principles. While Georgiana's life seems steeped in frivolity and devoid of all intellectual and moral content, Eliza has adopted a doctrine of radical renunciation already foreshadowed in the ascetic figure of Helen Burns: "Here were two natures rendered, the one intolerably acrid, the other despicably savourless for the want of it. Feeling without judgment is a washy draught indeed; but judgment untempered by feeling is too bitter and husky a morsel for human deglutition" (202). The solution offered to her once Rochester's marriage to Bertha Mason is revealed would imply precisely the kind of misbalance she recognized in her two cousins: within Jane's ethical universe, to accept the role of Rochester's mistress would be to succumb to feeling, reject judgment, and suffer the inevitable consequences.

Having been offered a life she found emotionally fulfilling but ethically and socially untenable, Jane reverts to a state of isolation and disappears into the wilderness (295), only to discover Moor House as a site where she can try to establish the kind of balance between emotional and social imperatives she was denied at Thornfield. The intellectual communion with Diana and Mary Rivers seems particularly conducive to this goal, given what Jane describes as the "perfect congeniality of tastes, sentiments, and principles" (298). The subsequent revelation of the familial links between Jane and the Rivers family, already prefigured in her strong affinity with the two sisters, allows her to reconcile her emotional desires with what she takes to be an ethically justified course of action.

The decision to share her inheritance with them unites feeling and judgment. While she believes it is just to lift her relatives from poverty, there is also a different kind of motive in play: "'With me,' said I, 'it is fully as much a matter of feeling as of conscience: I must indulge my feelings; I so seldom have had an opportunity of doing so'" (330). Having unexpectedly attained economic independence, she can now opt for a life with Diana and Mary, reestablishing a quasi-familial unit.

But this, of course, is a false solution, and not just because of her lingering desire for Rochester. The real limitation of life in Moor House is that it suffers from a misbalance of its own under the domineering shadow of St. John's religious zeal. After Helen Burns and Eliza Reed, once again Jane is faced with a doctrine of renunciation. However, while Helen and Eliza make no explicit claims on Jane herself, St. John's asceticism demands a sacrifice in the form of Jane's life. In many ways St. John epitomizes the opposite solution to the problem of desire from what Jane herself has been struggling to achieve. He too articulates the desire for a more active life that Jane has been pronouncing throughout the novel (308), but for St. John such desires are errors rejected and left in the past. The same logic is reflected in his rejection of Rosamond Oliver: despite loving her "wildly" (318), and despite the fact that their marriage would face no practical obstacles—she is a wealthy heiress, and he is a clergyman from an old and respected family—he proposes to Jane instead. This decision is motivated by a principle much harsher than the common demand of Victorian ethics to elevate duties above personal desires. In saying no to Rochester, Jane has rejected an emotionally fulfilling but socially problematic relationship. St. John is faced with no such choice. What he rejects is the prospect of a marriage both emotionally fulfilling and socially welcome. As Eagleton notes, the issue with St. John is that "he presses the orthodox view that duty must conquer feeling to a parodic extreme."[28] Whereas he works to squash desire even when it doesn't entail a serious moral conflict, Jane works to accommodate it if she possibly can. Unsurprisingly, for her the former position is equated with death. In the final instance, the Indian sun, which she fears she cannot bear, really stands for the rejection of life itself (352).

Significantly, in *Jane Eyre* both the radical rejection of desire and utter indulgence are associated with either death or exile. Helen Burns's early death seems inseparable from the harsh ascetic doctrine to which she subscribed. John Reed's excesses end in suicide, while Bertha Mason, whose madness is intertwined with sexual rapacity, kills herself by jumping from the top of Thornfield Hall. Both extremes tend to be geographically displaced, most obviously in the case of Bertha, whose madness is associated with her origin in the West Indies. However, the ethical geography of *Jane Eyre* is not rooted simply in the colonial imagination. Jane's destination as Rochester's mistress was meant to be Marseilles (306), while Eliza goes away to be, as Jane bluntly puts it, "walled up alive in a French convent" (206). Like Eliza's path to France, St. John's journey to India is yet another form of self-denial that effectively extinguishes life.

In suggesting that Jane come with him, St. John has introduced her to a proposition radical enough that she is willing to reconsider all alternative paths: "God did not give me my life to throw away; and to do as you wish me would, I begin to think, be almost equivalent to committing suicide. Moreover, before I definitively resolve in quitting England, I will know for certain whether I cannot be of greater use by remaining in it than by leaving it" (352–53). Having rejected a series of problematic social roles that implied either radical self-denial or indefensible self-indulgence, and having rejected, in a manner so illustrative of Brontë's xenophobia, the foreign lands associated with those roles, Jane wants to explore the improbable but intensely attractive prospect of living a full life in England. The great reversal that the ending of *Jane Eyre* offers is that something resembling a fulfilling existence might be possible after all: following the death of Bertha Mason, a union with Rochester is not only tenable, but constitutes the most effective way for Jane to reconcile her desires to an ethically and socially acceptable existence.

This reversal, of course, comes at a cost that many readers have deemed too high. While Jane refuses to be exiled either to Marseilles (as Rochester's mistress) or to India (as St. John's wife), her emphatic insistence on the happiness of life with Rochester seems undermined by the fact that their union takes place in the seclusion of Ferndean, in a different kind of exile, where she becomes his fellow outcast.²⁹ Moreover, despite the forceful rejection of St. John's proposal, Jane, the female narrator of her own life, surrenders the novel's final words to the man whose path of worldly renunciation she has refused to follow (385). In the final instance, this novel, which seemed rife with subversive impulses, seems prepared to fold back into the arms of patriarchy. As Parama Roy suggests, "Jane ends up rather too well-adjusted and well-endowed for Brontë to carry through her radical convictions to the end. Brontë gives her assent to camouflaged and insidious forms of patriarchalism in other ways as well. . . . She thus yields a furtive assent to the authoritative word of her culture, in matters socioeconomic as well as religious."³⁰ But there is nothing furtive in Jane's assent. While Roy is certainly right in criticizing earlier feminist interpretations for their "desire to read *Jane Eyre* as a coherent, unambiguous feminist (and non-racist) discourse," her own sense of dissatisfaction with the novel stems from a misunderstanding regarding Brontë's relationship to Victorian middle-class ideology.³¹ However tempting such a reading might be, the liberatory impulses that permeate *Jane Eyre* do not entail the ambition to overturn the entire edifice of Victorian social relations, including both clear class distinctions and colonial expansion. Instead, they consist in Jane's desire to carve a new kind of place for herself within that edifice.

The crucial element of this project is to redefine marriage itself. As we have seen in the brief discussion of *Middlemarch* at the beginning of this chapter, Victorian marriage was difficult to dissociate from a sense of submission and from the glaring asymmetry in the roles assumed by husband and wife. In fact, despite Eliot's desire to circumvent these issues by portraying the marriage of Will and Dorothea as a particularly fortunate union, her heroines are generally aware that marriage entails the wife's submission. This is apparent not only in Dorothea's misguided reflections on her first marriage as a state of a "voluntary submission to a guide who would take her along the grandest path" (30), but also in Gwendolen Harleth's remarkably clear-eyed vision of what her marriage with Grandcourt would entail in *Daniel Deronda*: "Her observation of matrimony had inclined her to think it rather a dreary state in which a woman could not do what she liked, had more children than were desirable, was consequently dull, and became irrevocably immersed in humdrum. Of course marriage was social promotion; she could not look forward to a single life; but promotions have sometimes to be taken with bitter herbs—a peerage will not quite do instead of leadership to the man who meant to lead; and this delicate-limbed sylph of twenty meant to lead" (31). What becomes increasingly obvious—and that to a significant degree drives Gwendolen's reluctance to marry Grandcourt—is that whatever power she might attain would be, at best, the power to clandestinely control her master (114–15). In case of the Victorian marriage, empowerment and surrender are often difficult to disentangle.

Three decades before the publication of *Daniel Deronda,* Brontë was struggling with the same issue. As we have seen, Jane Eyre has rejected not only the role of Rochester's mistress, but also that of a "useful tool" (354) in St. John's missionary expedition, the very embodiment of marriage as submission. When she finally does marry Rochester, she does so believing that their union is established on grounds different from anything else she has been proposed before: "To be together is for us to be at once as free as in solitude, as gay as in company. We talk, I believe, all day long: to talk to each other is but a more animated and an audible thinking. All my confidence is bestowed on him; all his confidence is devoted to me; we are precisely suited in character—perfect concord is the result" (384). Brontë's wording in this description of marital happiness once again approaches the central claims of Mill's liberalism. Mill's *The Subjection of Women,* published some two decades after *Jane Eyre,* argues that the legal subordination of women to men is a strange and untenable remnant of premodern social organization. While institutions such as slavery and absolute monarchy which were based on little beyond "the law of force" have disappeared, the subjection of women somehow persists "as an isolated fact in modern social institutions,[32] a solitary breach of what has become their fundamental law, a single relic of an old world of thought and practice exploded in everything else."[33] Mill was particularly concerned about the effects of subordination on marital life: "It often happens that there is the most complete unity of feeling and community of interests as to all external things, yet the one has as little admission into the internal life of the other as if they were common acquaintance. Even with true affection, authority on the one side and subordination on the other prevent perfect confidence. Though nothing may be intentionally withheld, much is not shown."[34] In other words, not only mutual devotion, but also the ability to share the inner life of the other partner, is impossible without the condition of equality. As the shared rhetoric of *Jane Eyre* and *The Subjection of Women* shows, what Brontë is trying to suggest at the end of the novel is precisely a union predicated on the balance of power that Mill has in mind. However, because the novel cannot hypothesize equality before the law, it tries to achieve equality by other means—by disempowering Rochester and by empowering Jane.

It goes without saying that this is a problematic equilibrium. As both Eagleton and Fraiman observe, the power Jane acquires by caring for the mutilated Rochester remains curiously mixed with subservience.[35] In Fraiman's words, "This role as interminable caretaker bears an uncanny resemblance to the maternal role women conventionally play in relation to men and servants in relation to masters."[36] In a way, Jane, like Dorothea Brooke after her, is reduced to providing "wifely help." And yet the fact that the balance offered by the ending of *Jane Eyre* seems unsatisfactory is precisely what reveals the novel's kinship with the so-called classical bildungsroman. Among more than a dozen novels I analyze in this book, *Jane Eyre* is perhaps the easiest one to reconcile with the description of the bildungsroman offered by the genre's most influential early theorists, such as Dilthey and Lukács.[37] In Lukács's view, the key condition that the bildungsroman must fulfill is "that a reconciliation between interiority and reality, although problematic, is nevertheless possible; that it has to be sought in hard struggles and dangerous adventures, yet is ultimately possible to achieve"—in other words, to not get quite what you wanted, and to be happy with it.[38] Jane's partial surrender, the fact that her desires have been fulfilled only in a substantially qualified form, the deep ambivalence of the novel's conclusion, with its benevolent nod toward the dying St. John and its uneasy balance between socialization and exile—all of this points precisely to the logic of "problematic" compromise that Lukács had in mind.

The fact that *Jane Eyre* falls relatively comfortably within the parameters of the classical bildungsroman does not, however, constitute sufficient cause to reevaluate the usefulness of that category. If anything, it helps to show how precarious and historically contingent the fantasy of reconciliation really is. Paradoxically, it is precisely because of the limits imposed on female socialization in Victorian England—the very limits that many critics think of as inimical to the concept of the bildungsroman—that Jane Eyre is forced through such complex negotiations between her desires and the realities of her socioeconomic position. The delicate balance she achieves is an anomaly not only with respect to the female bildungsroman but also to the genre as a whole. Just how precarious this balance is should be apparent from the difficulties Brontë encounters when she tries to reproduce a similar balancing act in *Villette*.

## Lucy Snowe and the Forms of Self-Denial

*Villette* abandons the teleological thrust of *Jane Eyre*—so much so, in fact, that it literally elides both the beginning and the end of Lucy Snowe's narrative. The familial disaster that sets Lucy's story in motion and the outcome of Paul Emanuel's journey are both withheld from the reader. This sharp contrast has led the very critics who elevated Jane Eyre to the pedestal of a feminist heroine to read *Villette* as a text that capitulates in the face of patriarchy, surrendering back the limited space of feminine agency won by Brontë's earlier novel. In Sandra M. Gilbert and Susan Gubar's reading, *Villette* emerges as nothing less than "perhaps the most moving and terrifying narrative of female deprivation ever written."[39] If *Jane Eyre* can be read as a narrative of empowerment, however precarious and constrained, *Villette*, it appears, offers no such opportunity. The novel's formal complexities have further helped to solidify the perception of *Villette* as a site of crisis, with the psychological crisis of Lucy Snowe extending into a crisis of narrative authority and, finally, of novelistic form. Lucy's psychological stability is under persistent threat and her voice as a narrator is so unreliable that the coherence of the novel as a whole seems to be brought into question. "In *Villette*," writes John Hughes, "the narrator follows bewildering, perverse, or obscure antinarrative principles that raise the shock and intensity of narrative alienation or disappointment to a new level."[40]

*Villette*, however, is not simply an exercise in opacity, but a rewriting of *Jane Eyre*. As my first two chapters have demonstrated, the redeployment of the bildungsroman form in several successive (*David Copperfield* and *Great Expectations*) or even concurrent variations (*Illusions perdues* and *Splendeurs et misères des courtisanes*) indicates an attempt to redistribute the narrative and ideological propositions of the original story. Dickens's *Great Expectations* rethinks the relationship between care and terror articulated in *David Copperfield*, while Balzac's *Splendeurs* reexamines the contradictions of Lucien de Rubempré's quest for success that were already apparent in *Illusions perdues*. Brontë repeats the same gesture, returning to the tension between submission and self-realization she had begun to explore in *Jane Eyre*. Whereas *Jane Eyre* is a novel that struggles to reconcile desire with social norms, *Villette* is trying an even more difficult negotiation: how to renounce desire and accept an inherently limited existence, while maintaining moral autonomy and the status of a free subject.

*Villette*, like *Jane Eyre* six years earlier, introduces a young heroine of respectable background who suffers a family disaster, is flung into poverty and isolation, and forced to take up the role of a caregiver. Both novels use the figure of the governess—Lucy begins as a nursery governess at Mme Beck's—to explore the state of homelessness and the tension it generates between self-realization and submission.[41] Finally, both texts tie together closure and loss. Jane becomes Mrs. Rochester, but only after she has found Rochester crippled and in self-imposed exile; in a mirror image of *Jane Eyre*, Lucy achieves professional triumph, but the promise of marital union seems hollow.[42] And yet, if the ending of *Jane Eyre* at least allows to be read as a victory, however fragile that victory may have been, *Villette* seems to foreclose such a reading, not just because of the apparent death of Paul Emanuel, but because of the overall structure of its world, simultaneously opaque and despondent, oppressive and saturated with acts of surveillance that have attracted so much critical attention.

In *Villette* Brontë offers a version of *Jane Eyre*'s plot in which she is eager to disallow, or at the very least complicate, the sometimes blunt celebration of female agency we find in the earlier novel. In *Jane Eyre*, domination is rejected at every junction, from Gateshead to Moor House.

Even Jane's marriage to Rochester, which otherwise could be read as an act of submission to the authority of the husband, is carefully crafted as a union of equals precipitated precisely by Jane's newly found independence. *Villette* offers no such clarity, not only on the level of the plot's outcome, but, more significantly, on the level of the protagonist's desires. We know that Jane Eyre desires movement and independence. What Lucy Snowe desires is a much more demanding question.

In *Villette,* Brontë recreates the state of exception with which *Jane Eyre* begins: Lucy, too is an outcast, an "anomalous" being.[43] But Lucy, unlike Jane, has a prelapsarian past to narrate, a past that offers significant clues to her psychology. The novel spends the first three chapters—some forty pages—reflecting on her summer in Bretton, where she first observes Polly and Graham. To a degree, this beginning is a matter of narrative expediency, as it helps establish Polly as Lucy's counterpart and prepares the quasi-familial reunion with the Brettons in Villette. But the Bretton chapters also suggest something more consequential: Lucy's status as "a mere looker on at life" (197) is not simply a consequence of her isolation in Mme Beck's *Pensionnat,* but a role willingly embraced before circumstances have transformed her into an outcast.[44]

Forced to take up the role of Miss Marchmont's maid, Lucy muses that the old woman at least "gave me the originality of her character to study" (50). This, of course, is not very persuasive: she has to settle for observing the character of a bedridden old woman because she has little else to hope for. However, her previous character study—her observation of Polly—was an amusement of choice, rather than a predicament (38). Condemned to a life in Mrs. Marchmont's room, Lucy is almost resigned: "I forgot that there were fields, woods, rivers, seas, an ever-changing sky outside the steam-dimmed lattice of this sick chamber; I was almost content to forget it" (50). Jane Eyre doesn't forget such things: "I traced the white road winding round the base of one mountain, and vanishing in a gorge between two: how I longed to follow it further!" (*Jane Eyre,* 72). Furthermore, having followed the road from Lowood to Thornfield, she almost immediately looks to the next horizon (93). My point, however, is not that Lucy is simply a weaker heroine, but that she is a different kind of heroine, because Brontë has undertaken to explore a different set of propositions.

*Villette* establishes a much more ambiguous relationship between activity and passivity, desire and submission. In *Jane Eyre,* the crippling state of homelessness is coupled with a heroine who refuses to submit to various forms of authority, and for whom mobility is the most fundamental inward desire. Lucy Snowe, however, vacillates between protestations of passivity and audacious gestures. For her, passivity is intermittently a natural and comforting state of affairs and a crippling condition. She is a remarkably mobile figure—"a rising character," (442) as she describes herself—but more often than not her actions and her desires are oddly decoupled.

If *Jane Eyre* equates action with a search for a fuller existence, in *Villette* action is quite often a mere condition of survival, an unwanted necessity. As Lucy admits to herself, "It seemed I must be stimulated into action. I must be goaded, driven, stung, forced to energy" (50). She is "unfurnished with either experience or advice to tell me how to act, and yet—to act obliged" (61). In a climactic moment, as she breaks down in a London inn—"Whence did I come? Whither should I go? What should I do?"—Lucy admits to herself that she "*could* go forward" (62–63, emphasis original). The emphasized conditional seems crucial here: what she expresses is not determination—not "I must go forward"—but a recognition of necessity.

Corollary to this attitude toward action is Lucy's valuation of passivity. However oppressive the life with Miss Marchmont may have been, Lucy claims that she was ready to spend another twenty years as her maid (50). And when Mme Beck offers her the role of the English teacher, she is prepared to pass on the opportunity and is literally dragged by Mme Beck from the nursery to the schoolroom: "Inadventurous, unstirred by impulses of practical ambition, I was capable of sitting twenty years teaching infants the hornbook, turning silk dresses and making children's frocks" (105). When forced by necessity she is more than capable of resolution, of "forming a project"; she can cross the English Channel, she can be a teacher in an unfamiliar country, she can be an actress in Paul Emanuel's play, but once the pressures subside she immediately withdraws back to her shell (see, e.g., 197).

Significantly, however, this withdrawal is never articulated in religious terms, and should be carefully distinguished from the various forms of religious renunciation that appear elsewhere in Victorian fiction. As I have argued, Jane Eyre defines her position precisely against such acts of renunciation, including Helen Burns's "doctrine of endurance" (47). As Helen tells the bewildered Jane, "It is weak and silly to say you *cannot bear* what it is your fate to be required to bear" (47, emphasis original). Another mid-Victorian heroine, Eliot's Maggie Tulliver in *The Mill on the Floss,* will attempt to follow a similar path. Struggling to cope with the devastating aftermath of her father's bankruptcy and illness, she finds an answer in the teachings of Thomas à Kempis: "It flashed through her like the suddenly apprehended solution of a problem, that all the miseries of her young life had come from fixing her heart on her own pleasure, as if that were the central necessity of the universe" (237). Like Helen Burns, Maggie finds an answer in espousing self-effacement: "pleasure" here really stands for the self, for her existence as an autonomous being. Denied every form of self-realization, intellectual as well as emotional, she espouses a doctrine that proclaims any interest in self-realization a sin, thus persuading herself that her socially imposed deprivation is a morally preferable state that she should embrace. The novel, however, offers a dissenting view of Maggie's condition. As Philip Wakem tells her, "You are shutting yourself up in a narrow, self-delusive fanaticism, which is only a way of escaping pain by starving into dulness all the highest powers of your nature.... You are not resigned; you are only trying to stupefy yourself" (266–67). What Philip (along with Eliot's narrator) recognizes under the mask of religiosity is an inadequate defense mechanism: Maggie is trying to subdue the pain of being denied a worthwhile existence by persuading herself that she is renouncing earthly life in the name of a higher principle.

*Villette,* however, is free of such delusions, despite its heroine's despondency, passivity, readiness to settle for a limited existence, and desire to "escape occasional great agonies by submitting to a whole life of privation and small pains" (50). This impulse bears only superficial similarity to the one that guides Maggie Tulliver. When Philip Wakem tries to give

Maggie a copy of Sir Walter Scott's *The Pirate*, she refuses on the grounds that it will reawaken all her dormant desires: "It would make me long to see and know many things; it would make me long for a full life" (249). After appearing in a play during Mme Beck's "fête" Lucy follows the same line of reasoning as she decides never to take up acting again: "A keen relish for dramatic expression had revealed itself as part of my nature; to cherish and exercise this new-found faculty might gift me with a world of delight, but it would not do for a mere looker-on at life: the strength and longing must be put by" (197). And yet in Lucy's case self-control does not lead to a religiously sanctioned self-negation. Her isolation is a reality to be reckoned with and perhaps inescapable, but certainly not a just or divinely sanctioned state of affairs. As she puts it in a sharp rebuke to the kind of reasoning that Maggie Tulliver will later espouse, "Of course I did not blame myself for suffering: I thank God I had a truer sense of justice than to fall into any imbecile extravagance of self-accusation" (383). Lucy Snowe may see herself as "a hermit" (382) or a caged animal (383); she may be tortured by loneliness and prepared to subdue her desires in order to preserve sanity (151–52); but she is fiercely protective of her moral and intellectual independence. In that respect, there is very little difference between her and Jane Eyre.

A comparison with the ethical reasoning of Eliot's Maggie Tulliver and Brontë's own Helen Burns is again instructive. While coated in the language of Christian forgiveness, Helen's doctrine of self-negation really entails a denial of moral autonomy. When she refuses to acknowledge the cruelty of the punishment she is forced to endure, she really suggests that it is pointless to contemplate the ethical justification of others' actions toward us (*Jane Eyre*, 49). As James Buzard puts it, the problem is that Helen "turns forbearance into utter passivity."[45] In *The Mill on the Floss*, Maggie Tulliver repeats a very similar gesture. When she accepts the doctrine of self-denial, her capitulation is complete: she has not only acknowledged that her desires cannot be realized in the world, but has also accepted to condemn those desires. She has effectively—though temporarily and, in the final instance, unsuccessfully—agreed to submit to the will of others and surrender her interiority. Lucy Snowe accepts no such surrender. Whereas Maggie responds to outside pressures by extending the worldly defeat onto her inward self, Lucy divides her existence in two in an attempt to safeguard her inner self, opting to "hold two lives—the life of thought, and that of reality" (105). As Marianne Thormählen points out, the writings of the Brontës (and this is certainly true of Charlotte) are driven by a "commitment to the freedom of the individual to pursue truth and goodness unencumbered by restraints imposed by earthly institutions and their human representatives."[46] For Lucy, despite acts of suppression and withdrawal, the defense of autonomy remains a vital goal.

Of course, Lucy Snowe holds one strategic advantage over Maggie Tulliver: she is in a position to reject the demands of the outside world on grounds other than "selfish" desire for self-preservation. Like Eliot's other heroines, Maggie Tulliver is continuously pressured to submit to the burden of familial and communal obligations. In the case of Lucy Snowe, however, the only outside context is the Catholic world of Labassecour, which has no legitimate claim on her. In the context of Brontë's powerful anti-Catholicism, Lucy's desire for self-preservation is conveniently aligned with the defense of true religion against the oppressive mechanisms of "Romanism."[47] This, in turn, legitimizes Lucy's acts of self-assertion. *Villette* therefore generates a unique situation for the bildungsroman heroine. Lucy can negotiate with the forms of domination she is exposed to on wholly different terms, because, from the novel's point of view, these forms are inherently illegitimate. The question is, then, how to exist as a dependent, a passive inmate of the Pensionnat, and yet preserve moral agency and individual dignity?

### The Fat Children of Catholicism

If Jane Eyre's positioning against the forms of existence she finds unacceptable plays out through her rejection of a variety of living embodiments of frivolity and asceticism, in *Villette* a similar positioning is enacted through Lucy's responses to art, including her own performance in Paul Emanuel's play, her ambiguous response to Vashti, and her unambiguous rejection of the painting of Cleopatra. And while both Lucy's own theatrical performance and the performance of Vashti are usually interpreted as liberating experiences, the paintings she observes at the gallery have routinely been read as complicit with patriarchy.[48] This opposition is certainly reinforced by Lucy's own comparison of Cleopatra with Vashti's diabolic performance: the former is for her little more than a ridiculously opulent mass of naked flesh, while the latter, although alternately captivating and terrifying, is a genuinely transgressive figure (370–71). "For Lucy," Sally Shuttleworth writes, "Vashti on stage transcends socially imposed sex-roles; she is neither woman nor man, but a devil, a literal embodiment of inner passion."[49] Whereas Cleopatra portrays what seems an absurdly sexualized vision of the female body, and the four scenes that constitute "La vie d'une femme" seem just as absurd in their forced and insincere asceticism, "cold and vapid as ghosts" (288), Vashti embodies a version of female existence that escapes both the sexualizing male gaze and the attempt to confine women to a narrow domestic space.

However, both the terms in which Lucy rejects Cleopatra and the lessons she draws from Vashti demand further scrutiny. Cleopatra in particular embodies not just a generic male gaze, but a culturally specific and distinctly Catholic vision of femininity. In *Villette,* sensuality and the surrender to bodily appetites are firmly aligned with Catholicism. An early description of Mme Beck's Pensionnat forcefully captures this connection:

> A strange, frolicsome, noisy little world was this school: great pains were taken to hide chains with flowers: a subtle essence of Romanism pervaded every arrangement: large sensual indulgence (so to speak) was permitted by way of counterpoise to jealous spiritual restraint.... There, as elsewhere, the CHURCH strove to bring up her children robust in body, feeble in soul, fat, ruddy, hale, joyous, ignorant, unthinking, unquestioning. "Eat, drink, and live!" she says. "Look after your bodies; leave your souls to me. I hold their cure—guide their course: I guarantee their final fate." (177)

This rant against the fat children of Catholicism clearly anticipates a later fit of rage in which Lucy assails "Paul Peter Rubens" [*sic!*] along with "the army of his fat women" (371). Similarly, her objection to Cleopatra is not that the woman in the painting is being objectified, but that her body expresses the same characteristically Catholic "sensual indulgence" she has witnessed at Mme Beck's. She estimates the painted woman's body weight at "fourteen to sixteen stone" (between two hundred and two hundred and twenty pounds), concluding that she must be "very well fed" (285). Moreover, this Cleopatra was clearly "strong enough to do the work of two plain cooks," and hence "she ought to have been standing, or at least sitting bolt upright," instead of lying seminaked among a mess of pots and pans (285). This corrosive, mocking description reveals something more than what most critics describe as Lucy's resistance to an oppressive, male-constructed vision of women's role: it reveals a resistance to the baroque vision of femininity that epitomizes the sins of Catholicism.

The alternative set of images to which Paul Emanuel despotically directs her offers a series of clear antipodes to Cleopatra. "La vie d'une femme" reduces female existence to succession of conventional roles: a devout young girl, a bride, a young mother, a widow (288). As with Cleopatra, critics have interpreted Lucy's rejection of these representations as sign of her resistance to yet another suffocating, male-imposed vision of femininity.[50] And yet these women are not just another face of male oppression; they are also another face of Catholicism. This is particularly the case with the paintings of the maid and the bride: "The first represented a 'Jeune Fille,' coming out of a church-door, a missal in her hand, her dress very prim, her eyes cast down, her mouth pursed up—the image of a most villainous little precocious she-hypocrite. The second, a 'Mariée,' with a long white veil, kneeling at a prie-dieu in her chamber, holding her hands plastered together, finger to finger, and showing the whites of her eyes in a most exasperating manner" (287–88). It is widely held that "La vie d'une femme" is inspired Fanny Geefs's *Piti Amor Douleur,* which Brontë appears to have seen in Brussels. While the paintings described in *Villette* don't directly correspond to Geefs's triptych, the central figure of the triptych also "shows the whites of her eyes in a most exasperating manner." This upward gaze, symbolically directed toward heaven, is a familiar convention of Catholic religious art, but one that will gain particular prominence in baroque painting. It appears perhaps most consistently in the work of Francisco de Zurbarán, as well as in numerous versions of the assumption of Mary, including a famous 1670 version by Bartolomé Esteban Murillo. That this connection is more than a coincidence should be obvious from the fact that Geefs, an author of numerous religious paintings, painted a copy of Murillo's *Assumption*.[51] However, while in *Piti Amor Douleur* Geefs only gestures toward the characteristic expression of religious devotion—the young woman sits with a sleeping baby in her arms and a dog by her side in a scene suggesting domestic bliss—the painting described in *Villette* explores the convention in the fullest: the young woman is on her knees praying in a state of religious ecstasy.

In rejecting these paintings Lucy Snowe is clearly rejecting an artistic tradition inextricably tied not just to Catholicism, but more specifically to Counter-Reformation.[52] Like the baroque opulence of Cleopatra, the baroque religious ecstasy of the "Mariée" points to the oppressive and ethically suspect aspects of Catholicism. What repels Lucy in these images is not just that the women are subdued and cast in a set of traditional roles, but that these are Catholic women exhibiting the kind of overstated and presumably insincere piety Lucy associates with "Romanism." If the problem with Cleopatra is her overt sensuality, the problem with "La vie d'une femme" is hypocrisy.

The opposition between the two aspects of Catholicism was already articulated in Lucy's description of the Pensionnat—"sensual indulgence" versus "jealous spiritual restraint" (177). The qualities that she attributes to the four painted figures—"insincere, ill-humoured, bloodless, brainless, non-entities" (288)—have appeared before and were applied to the "quite heartless and insincere" (113) aristocratic women of Labassecour. Moreover, the figure of Mademoiselle St. Pierre, one of the teachers at Mme Beck's, demonstrates how the apparently contradictory qualities can be joined: described as a "cold callous epicure," the woman "mortally hated work, and loved what she called pleasure; being an insipid, heartless, brainless dissipation of time" (176). Lucy's judgment on her simultaneously cold and epicurean nature corresponds almost word for word to her later description of the "cold and vapid" (288) paintings. Like Jane

Eyre, who has rejected both the frivolity and asceticism embodied in Eliza and Georgiana Reed, Lucy Snowe rejects an analogous set of qualities embodied in Catholic art and the Catholic women around her.

If Lucy's engagement with painting suggests a rejection of certain models of femininity—a rejection, as I have suggested, more complex and more closely intertwined with her anti-Catholicism than is usually acknowledged—her response to Vashti offers few clear conclusions. While the heroine seems completely overpowered by the diabolical intensity of Vashti's performance, "wild and intense, dangerous, sudden, and flaming" (372), and while both the performance itself and Lucy's response could be interpreted as a release of the repressed female sexual energy, what seems particularly significant to me is the ease with which the novel forecloses the opportunities this chapter has opened.

During her stay in Bretton, when she first encounters Paulina Home, Lucy impatiently observes Polly's separation from her father. She finds the sight unseemly sentimental, "low and long," and famously proclaims that, unlike the sobbing Mrs. Bretton, "I, Lucy Snowe, was calm" (28). When the fire breaks out during Vashti's performance, Lucy is once again conspicuously calm. In the midst of the mass panic, as women and men begin to trample on each other, it appears that only Lucy and Graham Bretton (whom she rediscovers in Villette as Dr. John) have kept their cool: "'Lucy will sit still, I know,' said he, glancing down at me with the same serene goodness, the same repose of firmness that I have seen in him when sitting at his side amid the secure peace of his mother's hearth. Yes, thus adjured, I think I would have sat still under a rocking crag: but, indeed, to sit still in actual circumstances was my instinct; and at the price of my very life, I would not have moved to give him trouble, thwart his will, or make demands on his attention" (374). This passage singlehandedly quenches the unruly impulses of Vashti's performance. It simultaneously articulates Lucy's calm rationality and her desire to submit to Dr. John. The same Dr. John who a minute ago was the object of Lucy's critical gaze because of his seeming inability to empathize with Vashti, suddenly emerges as an embodiment of traditional male virtues, of "comely courage and cordial calm" (374). And, as he pushes forward to rescue the injured

Paulina Home, Dr. John seems firmly in control, whereas Lucy takes up the role of his eager aide. The phrase "Lucy will sit still, I know" is particularly consequential in this context. It suggests that in the midst of the chaotic scene Lucy will be more composed than most, and that she will obey even without explicit command.

Oppressed by the images of unrestrained sensuality and hypocritical modesty (both firmly associated with Catholicism), fascinated by Vashti but nonetheless incapable of being "wicked but strong" (370) like her, what path is open to Lucy? One is clearly the path of outright economic independence that she begins to plot toward the end of the novel. But here, as in *Jane Eyre,* this path is unsatisfactory unless it is somehow reconciled with a larger accommodation of the heroine's interiority. Because in *Villette* the whole burden of patriarchal oppression is displaced onto Catholicism, for Lucy any attempt at self-realization will have to entail a release from the omnipresent threat of "Romanism."

A union with Dr. John could perhaps offer such a release, but that fantasy is reserved for Paulina Home, who increasingly serves as Lucy's double. Paulina's triumph over the insufferably frivolous Ginevra Fanshawe works to validate Lucy's own worldview. Paulina transforms from a weak child into a scrupulous and refined young woman and is rewarded by a fulfilling marriage to Dr. John. Ginevra, with her "flimsy" faculties, her selfishness, and her trivial pursuits is punished by a tumultuous and unhappy union with a Labassecourian officer (691). The religious component is once again vital. During their first encounter, as Lucy is sailing for Labassecour, she is faced with Ginevra's blunt confession: "I have quite forgotten my religion; they call me a Protestant, you know, but really I am not sure whether I am one or not: I don't well know the difference between Romanism and Protestantism" (73). What Ginevra does know is how to apply the lessons of hypocrisy that Lucy sees as inherent to Catholicism. When facing her uncle for the first time after eloping with Comte de Hamal, Ginevra puts on a show as she begs the uncle for forgiveness: "I found myself forced to do a little bit of the melodramatic—go down on my knees, sob, cry, drench three pocket-handkerchiefs" (687). By dropping to her knees, she is literally enacting one of the images from

"La vie d'une femme" that has provoked such disgust in Lucy. The opposition between Paulina and Ginevra once again upholds a sensible, Protestant Englishness over the excesses of the Catholic world of Labassecour.

With the fantasy of an idyllic union displaced onto Dr. John and Paulina, Brontë shuns the opportunity to grant her heroine an easy escape from the oppressive reality of Mme Becks's school. Refusing to stage a miraculous rescue and marry her heroine to a charming and wealthy Englishman, she opts for a complex balance between self-fulfillment and submission. Whereas in *Jane Eyre* she achieves such a balance by granting Jane's desire to marry Rochester only after he has been disempowered and exiled, in *Villette* she tries to engineer a different version of partial, qualified fulfillment by displacing Lucy's sympathies onto Paul Emanuel, the very man who persistently tries to limit her autonomy.

## The Christian Hero

In Lucy's eyes Paul Emanuel undergoes an almost inexplicable transformation. Throughout the novel he is the character most committed to reshaping and disciplining her: Mme Beck, despite her aggressive surveillance, confronts Lucy only once in the novel, and Père Silas, who would gladly convert her to Catholicism, has few opportunities. Paul is therefore the most explicit if sometimes comical voice of Jesuit oppression and the most obvious threat to Lucy's integrity: "I scarcely know any one, Miss Lucy, who needs a friend more absolutely than you; your very faults imperatively require it. You want so much checking, regulating, and keeping down" (526). And yet, in the last third of the novel, this "harsh little man" (483) becomes for Lucy "my professor" (510) and finally "my king" (704).

The seemingly insurmountable distance that Paul Emanuel travels in Lucy's eyes holds important lessons for the analysis of desire and submission in *Villette*. For most of the novel, their encounters consist almost exclusively of scenes of chastisement in which Paul seeks to discipline Lucy: "Mademoiselle, asseyez-vous, et ne bougez pas—entendez-vous?—jusqu'à ce qu'on vienne vous chercher, ou que je vous donne la permission" (Sit down, miss, and don't move—do you hear me? until someone comes to get you or until I give you permission; 287, my translation). He objects to her viewing of Cleopatra and attributes Lucy's audacity to her Protestantism (291), taunts her over the pink dress she wore at the concert (337), and bursts into anger when she mentions that she has "enjoyed the advantage of a little change lately, but not before it had become necessary": "Change necessary! He would recommend me to look at the Catholic 'religieuses,' and study *their* lives. *They* asked no change" (433, emphasis original). Furthermore, he engages in long rants against England that leave Lucy exasperated (493) and insists that "women of intellect" are no more than an unfortunate anomaly (513). Perhaps unsurprisingly, Lucy finally brings her sufferings to an end by sneaking out of Paul's office (518).

The evolution of Paul's and Lucy's relationship clearly entails something of the attraction/repulsion dynamics and power games characteristic of the courtship plot. Most of the time, Lucy finds it easy to resist his attempts to discipline her. She openly rejects the paintings he suggests as "too hideous" to look at (291) and deliberately taunts him when he begins criticizing her dress (481). However, while there is some undeniable playfulness in their rhetorical battles, we are not in a Jane Austen novel, and Paul Emanuel is no Mr. Darcy. Given how oppressed Lucy feels by the Catholic context, and how afraid she is of succumbing to the rhetorical power of Père Silas, it is quite remarkable that she doesn't feel threatened by a man who describes himself as a "lay Jesuit" (531) and persistently tries to convert her. The fact is, however, that she doesn't find Paul Emanuel very persuasive in this role. If in *Jane Eyre* Brontë made the union of Jane and Rochester possible by disempowering Rochester, in *Villette* she makes the union of Paul and Lucy possible by disempowering Paul. As we shall see in a moment, her attraction to his domineering personality is rendered acceptable because he is, it finally turns out, "a lamb" (553) in wolf's clothing.

In *Villette,* the Catholic Church functions as an omnipresent surveillance machinery interested in little else except absolute domination. The Pensionnat, in which everything seems to be exposed to the prying eyes of Mme Beck and Paul Emanuel, is a synecdochic embodiment of the Church's operational principles: secrecy, deception, and cunning. The trouble with Paul, however, is that his better nature betrays him. As Lucy observes, "People said M. Emanuel had been brought up amongst Jesuits. I should more readily have accredited this report had his manoeuvres been better masked. As it was, I doubted it. Never was a more undisguised schemer, a franker, looser intriguer" (433). In spite of his best efforts, he cannot quite play the role of a sinister Jesuit spy. As Lucy puts it after he has abandoned his final attempt to convert her, "All Rome could not put into him bigotry, nor the Propaganda itself make him a real Jesuit. He was born honest, and not false—artless, and not cunning—a freeman, and not a slave" (714).

Because aggressive Catholicism functions as the key power structure in the novel, and a key threat to Lucy's integrity, dissociating Paul Emanuel from the Church turns him from a "pitiless censor" (483) into a fundamentally benevolent presence, and his attempts to subject Lucy to his desires into something far less sinister than it originally appeared. This gesture, however, completely destabilizes the power balance in the novel. As Lucy's revelations near the end of the book make clear, Paul is not just "a good Romanist" (573), but an outright victim of a Catholic conspiracy: molded into submission by the Jesuit hand of Père Silas, his goodness is exploited by a conspiring "junta" (666). Because Brontë has turned him into a victim, willing to sacrifice himself for the unsavory ambitions of others, Paul becomes Lucy's cosufferer, while their commitment to each other becomes an act of rebellion against a common enemy. As Mme Beck tries to send Lucy to bed so that she couldn't meet Paul, Brontë's heroine commits perhaps the most forceful act of resistance in the novel by commanding Mme Beck out of the room: "'No!' I said; 'neither you nor another shall persuade or lead me'" (646). Shortly afterward, Paul rejects Mme Beck's domineering influence in the same exact words. "*Leave me,* I say!" cries Lucy; "*leave me!*" (627, 696, emphasis original) Paul Emanuel demands as he turns Mme Beck out.

The sheer complexity of the narrative mechanisms employed by Brontë in order to approach (and approach only) something resembling a tolerable outcome for Lucy Snowe seems remarkable. As my analysis of Lucy's attitude toward Catholicism shows, Brontë has displaced all forms of oppression—organized surveillance, unrestrained sensuality, brutal self-denial—onto a single alien institution, thus legitimizing Lucy's resistance to each of these pressures. Moreover, by turning Paul Emanuel from the face of Jesuit oppression into its victim, Brontë has attempted, as in *Jane Eyre,* to create a balance of power between the heroine and the male hero. As in *Jane Eyre,* where she had to cripple Rochester in order to negotiate a successful courtship for her heroine, such a balance is easier to achieve by disempowering the man than by empowering the woman. However, while she still attempts to approach the liberal ideal of the marriage of equals, this balance now seems even more difficult to achieve.

Although Paul abandons attempts to convert Lucy, he does so in vaguely patronizing terms, as if in allowing her to remain a Protestant he gives her permission to pursue an eccentric but nonetheless harmless pastime: "Remain a Protestant. My little English Puritan, I love Protestantism in you. I own its severe charm" (713). Moreover, the dream of economic independence can be realized only as Paul's benevolent gift: "You shall live here and have a school; you shall employ yourself while I am away; you shall think of me sometimes" (704). Both gestures indicate that Paul has not transformed from a tyrant into an equal, but rather from a cruel master into a benevolent one. Remarkably, Lucy all but accepts this gentler form of submission.

Paul Emanuel's presumed death constitutes not just a cruel denial of Lucy's marital happiness, but an expression of the novel's uncertainty about the solution it has offered to the problem of female self-realization. If *Jane Eyre* has offered something like a qualified, partial triumph, *Villette* can't bring itself to offer even that much. The tentative equilibrium achieved in the earlier novel seems to have dispersed. And while in some ways the liberatory impulses of the novel are defeated, this defeat ought to be contextualized. The concern with female rather than with male formation has both suppressed and galvanized the bildungsroman plot, and the inadequate conclusion of *Villette* is hardly an outlier within the tradition. As we shall see in the following chapter, toward the end of the nineteenth century the project of male self-fashioning was about to offer exciting new forms of defeat.

# 4

# PORTRAIT OF THE HERO AS AN IDEOLOGUE, CA. 1885–1914

If the work of Charles Dickens is anything to go by, the heroes of mid-nineteenth-century bildungsromans have no political beliefs to speak of. Even David Copperfield—a parliamentary reporter, no less—refuses to discuss politics. What little David chooses to share about his profession is delivered in the dull language of curriculum vitae and focuses exclusively on the technical difficulties of mastering shorthand: "I have tamed that savage stenographic mystery. I make a respectable income by it. I am in high repute for my accomplishment in all pertaining to the art" (535). The content of the parliamentary debates David has witnessed is dismissed as empty clatter and never revealed to the reader, despite the fact that Dickens could easily draw on his own experience as a parliamentary reporter in the early 1830s.[1] And even when clearly intervening in contemporary political debates around poverty and crime—as was the case with *Oliver Twist*—Dickens is very reluctant to directly admit the political discourse into the world of his bildungsromans.

On the other side of the English Channel, such explicit refusal is impossible. Balzac not only gives voice to parliamentary peers, ambassadors, and cabinet ministers, but builds the world of *La Comédie* around the political conflict between liberals and conservatives, between the defenders of the ambivalent Napoleonic legacy and the representatives of the Church and the monarchy. In effect, however, both Dickens and Balzac have a way of dismissing political beliefs as a formative force in their bildungsromans. Whereas Dickens's heroes simply don't think about ideology, Balzac's think about it in strictly pragmatic terms. For Lucien de Rubempré, political persuasion is yet another tool in the conquest of wealth and fame, a tool that he can discard as he sees fit: he will play the role of a liberal republican today, of a conservative monarchist tomorrow, and a liberal again the day after, as long as it will help him to get what he wants. For very different reasons, neither Dickens nor Balzac believe that espousing a set of political beliefs is a vital task for the bildungsroman hero.

In a remarkable contrast to the key texts of mid-century realism, as the nineteenth century drew to a close the bildungsroman was becoming increasingly populated by young ideologues who defined their relationship to the world primarily in terms of political commitments. "Since I began to read and know," admits the eponymous hero of George Eliot's *Daniel Deronda* (1876), "I have always longed for some ideal task, in which I might feel myself the heart and brain of a multitude—some social captainship, which would come to me as a duty, and not be striven for as a personal prize" (642). And while the precise coordinates of this "ideal task" will vary considerably, it is difficult to deny that in the later nineteenth century the bildungsroman hero has, by and large, become a man with a mission. Daniel Deronda espouses the project of Jewish nationalism.[2] James Hyacinth Robinson (*The Princess Casamassima*, 1885–86) and Zola's Étienne Lantier, the young leader of the miners' strike in *Germinal* (1885) are both lured by radical working-class ideologies, while Samuel Butler's Ernest Pontifex (*The Way of All Flesh,* completed in 1884, published posthumously in 1903) goes through life in a perpetual state of ideological upheaval, preaching, in turn, both evangelical Christianity and freethought.

This shift in the bildungsroman's interests came as a result of the massive transformation of European politics in the late nineteenth century. As Julien Benda noted in 1927, "Today there is scarcely a mind in Europe which is not affected—or thinks himself affected—by a racial or class or national passion, and most often by all three."[3] What was at stake was not simply the rise of a particular political ideology, but an unprecedented intensification of ideological activity. In the words of the conservative philosopher Michael Oakeshott, "Contemporary Europe presents the spectator with a remarkable verity of social and political doctrines;

indeed it is improbable that this collection of communities has ever before shown such fertility of invention in this field."⁴ The rapid spread of these new doctrines was made possible by the process of democratization that swept Europe during the final decades of the nineteenth century. With both adult literacy rates and newspaper circulation soaring, and with the franchise greatly extended across Western Europe—both Germany and France introduced universal manhood suffrage—a much broader segment of the population was able to participate in the political process.⁵ Unsurprisingly, this led to the proliferation of political organizations and movements, including a long list of competing socialist parties, various anarchist associations, secular societies, and xenophobic far-right movements. Late nineteenth-century Europe was therefore subjected to two seemingly contradictory but in fact interdependent processes: the rise of mass movements and the intellectualization of politics. In Benda's words,

> Today I notice that every political passion is furnished with a whole network of strongly woven doctrines, the sole object of which is to show the supreme value of its actions from every point of view . . . with what tenacity each passion has built up in every direction the theories apt to satisfy it, with what precision have these theories been adapted to this satisfaction, with what opulence of research, what labour, what profound investigation they have been carried on in all directions. Our age is indeed the age of *the intellectual organization of political hatreds*. (21, emphasis original)

As the intensity of "political passions" soared, they attracted more intellectual energy: in the context of much larger political participation and the proliferation of social groups prepared to defend their collective interests, the imperative of articulating and defending political positions became particularly urgent. What emerged, in the final instance, was a world in which group commitments grew in importance, and in which, to paraphrase Karl Dietrich Bracher, the desire for the intellectual justification of collective aims gained new prominence.⁶

These developments could not fail to impact a genre vitally interested in the process of socialization. As the nineteenth century approached its end, the bildungsroman was increasingly focusing on the struggle for young men's hearts and minds. Its hero could no longer simply strive for success or recognition; rather, he was now forced to define and theorize his existence in relation to an ever-expanding set of political doctrines. This is a development fully anticipated by Fyodor Dostoevsky, whose novels repeatedly explore the problem of ideological justification of acts of violence. In *Crime and Punishment* (1866), Raskolnikov in a way *suffers from ideology:* the moral crisis that follows him through the novel stems from the fact that his conscience cannot accept the theoretical justification his mind has offered for the murders of Alyona and Lizaveta Ivanovna. As he muses toward the end of the novel, "In what way was my idea any more stupid than the other ideas and theories that have swarmed in conflict with one another ever since this world was born?"[7] Evaluating various intellectual frameworks in an attempt to define one's relationship to the world was to become the central activity of bildungsroman heroes, including Eliot's Daniel Deronda, Joyce's Stephen Dedalus, and Thomas Mann's Hans Castorp.

The complexity of this task is visible in the way in which heroes vacillate between competing beliefs and struggle to articulate a coherent position for themselves by drawing on a series of intellectual frameworks—not only political ideologies, but also religious, scientific, and pseudoscientific doctrines. Butler's Ernest Pontifex moves between religious zeal and a commitment to freethought while struggling to assess the implications of the rationalist critique of Christianity. In *Germinal,* Zola's Étienne Lantier struggles to replace a vague sense of indignation prompted by the miserable life of the working classes with an intellectually coherent political program:

> Ce fut l'époque où Étienne entendit les idées qui bourdonnaient dans son crâne. Jusque-là, il n'avait eu que la révolte de l'instinct, au milieu de la sourde fermentation des camarades. Toutes sortes de questions confuses se posaient à lui: pourquoi la misère des uns? pourquoi la richesse des autres? (216)

> (It was at this time that Étienne began to understand the ideas that were buzzing in his brain. Up till then he had only felt an instinctive revolt in

the midst of the inarticulate fermentation among his mates. All sorts of confused questions came before him: Why are some miserable? Why are others rich?) (124)

Having read a variety of anarchist and socialist writings along with some contemporary science, he goes on to construct an idiosyncratic amalgam of Marxism, social Darwinism, and contemporary theories of degeneration. In his eyes, the coming triumph of the proletariat, "vivace, neuf encore" (still new and full of life; 591, 402), over the decadent bourgeoisie constitutes not only a historical but also a biological necessity, exemplifying simultaneously the demise of a degenerate class and the survival of the fittest. A generation later, in Thomas Mann's *The Magic Mountain* (1924), a similarly paradoxical mix of ideological propositions will emerge from the teachings of Leo Naphta, a Jesuit and former Jew who dreams of a "communistic City of God" (577), fusing a conservative Christian critique of political liberalism and Enlightenment rationalism with the commitment to the dictatorship of the proletariat. The unlikely intellectual configurations that emerge in the novels of Zola and Mann testify to the wider shift in the logic of the bildungsroman: the genre has become the site of an intellectual struggle, with many of its protagonists now trying to make their way through the cacophony of doctrines Benda so forcefully describes. In order to step into the world, the bildungsroman hero must first determine what the world is, examining in the process a variety of suppositions, political as well as metaphysical.

As I demonstrate in this chapter through extended readings of James, Butler, and Joyce, this process of intellectualization exercised additional pressure on the bildungsroman form. James's *The Princess Casamassima* occupies an uneasy middle ground between a dynamitard novel and a Balzacian fantasy of social ascent. In Butler's *The Way of All Flesh*, the complex ideological negotiations will turn its hero into an internal immigrant, an intellectual exile maintaining only a very tenuous relationship with the outside world. In Joyce's *Portrait*, the bildungsroman will dissolve into an extended debate about the relationship between individual and collective identity. For the bildungsroman hero, the confrontation with the world becomes a confrontation with its doctrines.

## "You and I Are the Barbarians, You Know"

In 1885 Henry James made an unlikely and—if the early reviews of *The Princess Casamassima* can be trusted—unsuccessful literary excursion into the world of European radical politics. The novel, serialized during 1885 and published in full the following year, exposed James to the critical charge that, having left behind the familiar milieu of polite society described in *The Portrait of a Lady* (1881), he stumbled into the world of London slums that was never his own and that he could not persuasively navigate.[8]

And yet, whatever the flaws of *The Princess Casamassima,* the lack of familiarity with anarchist politics was not one of them. If anything, the novel follows all too closely the British press's dominant attitudes toward emerging social movements. When James's protagonist Hyacinth Robinson declares that "the flood of democracy was rising over the world" (478) he taps directly into the rhetoric often used to describe the rise of mass politics across Europe.[9] As an editorial in the *Times* argued, "In these days theories soon overstep the boundaries of states; dangerous principles are a contraband which quickly pass Custom-house lines or natural boundaries."[10] Among these theories anarchism was perceived as particularly disruptive. As one newspaper commented in 1882, "There is an uneasy feeling all over the Continent that the anarchical movement is quietly and rapidly spreading, that it is becoming more international and secret in its character, and that its weapons are more than ever of the 'dynamitard' type."[11] The fear was well founded: in 1881 Russian anarchists assassinated Czar Alexander II in a bomb plot, while two years later a similar plan by their German counterparts for the assassination of Wilhelm I was foiled. Minor bombings had become a regular occurrence in European capitals, and the British press reported widely on arrests and trials of anarchist conspirators. When James decided to describe the anarchist circle in *The Princess Casamassima* as a decisively international group of conspirators that included not only working-class Londoners, but also a British aristocrat, a London Frenchman, and a German mastermind so mysterious that he is never actually seen in the novel, he was merely reproducing the dominant perception of the movement as a vast international conspiracy.

The odd sense of incongruence, the feeling that something is not quite right, shared by many readers of *The Princess Casamassima,* stems from a different source: the novel complicates the project of self-fashioning by introducing a demanding political commitment as a vital part of the hero's aspirations. If the heroes of mid-century bildungsromans typically desire either unqualified social success (like Lucien de Rubempré) or respectability (like David Copperfield), James's Hyacinth Robinson is torn between social integration and decisive political action, between an aesthetic fascination with the life of the upper classes and the commitment to the anarchist ideology that demands that the object of his fascination be destroyed.

This influx of politics into the bildungsroman destabilizes not only the hero's desires, but also the narrative form. As James wrote in the summer of 1885, "It is absolutely necessary that at this point I should make the future evolution of *Princess Casamassima* more clear to myself. I have never yet engaged in a novel in which, after I have begun to write and send my MS., the details have remained so vague."[12] Whereas Hyacinth Robinson is unsure what kind of hero he wants to be, James was unsure what sort of novel he was writing. In the end, he used the familiar structure of the Balzacian bildungsroman, complete with its poor but ambitious hero who struggles to navigate the metropolis and the aristocratic protectress who will guide him, in order to stage a conflict between the distinct ideological imperative of dismantling the existing social relations in the name of the oppressed, and what is essentially an aestheticist attraction to upper-class life.[13] *The Princess Casamassima* is therefore best understood as parasitical structure transforming from the inside its Balzacian host.

Like so many of Balzac's young parvenus, James's Hyacinth Robinson lingers on the outskirts of the metropolis, condemned to a life of poverty, yet persuaded that he deserves better. Unlike his Balzacian counterparts, however, he wavers between the desire to be initiated into the dazzling world of aristocracy and the imperative of acting in the name of the working classes. "Real success in the world," he muses, "would be to do something with them and for them" (160). The novel therefore portrays two parallel processes of social initiation—one in which Hyacinth is being induced into the anarchist circle around Paul Muniment and one in which he enters the intensely alluring world of Princess Casamassima. In describing the latter process, James reproduces some of the key scenes from *Illusions perdues:*

> Il faisait beau. De belles voitures passaient incessamment sous ses yeux en se dirigeant vers la grande avenue des Champs-Èlysées. Il suivit la foule des promeneurs et vit alors les trois ou quatre mille voitures qui, par une belle journée, affluent en cet endroit le dimanche, et improvisent un Longchamp. Etourdi par le luxe des chevaux, des toilettes et des livrées, il allait toujours, et arriva devant l'Arc-de-Triomphe commencé. (200)

> (It was a fine afternoon. A stream of fine carriages went past him as he made his way towards the Champs-Èlysées. Following the direction of the crowd of strollers, he saw the three or four thousand carriages that turn the Champs-Èlysées into an improvised Longchamp on Sunday afternoons in summer. The splendid horses, the toilettes, and liveries bewildered him; he went further and further, until he reached the Arc de Triomphe, then unfinished.) (186–87)

In his own version of this scene, James turns Hyde Park into the Champs Elysées:

> Sometimes, of a Saturday, in the long evenings of June and July, he made his way into Hyde Park at the hour when the throng of carriages, of riders, of brilliant pedestrians, was thickest.... He wanted to drive in every carriage, to mount on every horse, to feel on his arm the hand of every pretty woman in the place. In the midst of this his sense was vivid that he belonged to the class to whom the upper ten thousand, as they passed, didn't so much as rest their eyes on for a quarter of a second. (164)

And yet, even though he models his hero's encounter with upper-class life on Balzac, James is quick to turn his inquiry in a very different direction. As we have seen in chapter 1, Lucien's guiding impulse is to move upward in the world regardless of the cost. When ignored by the Marquise d'Espard and Louise de Bargeton during the walk on the Champs-Élysées, he promises to make himself a part of this immensely attractive aristocratic universe: "Mon Dieu! pourquoi suis-je ici? mais je triompherai! Je passerai dans cette avenue en calèche à chasseur! j'aurai des marquises d'Espard!" (Oh God, what am I doing here? But I will triumph! I will ride along this avenue in a calèche with a footman! I will possess a Marquise d'Espard; 201–2, 188). In order to achieve this goal, Balzac's hero is happy to momentarily switch political allegiances and allow unfettered ambition to suppress whatever genuine beliefs he had previously held. It takes nothing more than Louise de Bargeton's brief course in the principles of social mobility to fully transform him:

> Elle souleva l'une après l'autre les couches successives de l'Etat Social, et fit compter au poète les échelons qu'il franchissait soudain par cette habile détermination. En un instant, elle fit abjurer à Lucien ses idées populacières sur la chimérique égalité de 1793, elle réveilla chez lui la soif des distinctions que la froide raison de David avait calmée, elle lui montra la haute société comme le seul théâtre sur lequel il devait se tenir. Le haineux libéral devint monarchique *in petto*. Lucien mordit à la pomme du luxe aristocratique et de la gloire. (81)

> (She went through each of the successive social strata and made the poet realise how many rungs higher he would immediately be placed by this able decision. At the same time, she persuaded Lucien to abjure his chimerical notions of popular equality of 1793 and awakened in him that thirst for fame that David's cool reason had calmed; she proved to him that high society was the only stage for his talent. The rabid Liberal became a Monarchist there and then; Lucien bit the apple of aristocratic luxury and glory.) (56)

While Hyacinth Robinson also experiences a crisis of belief prompted by the sight of aristocratic opulence, James uses the shift in Hyacinth's class loyalties in an attempt to generate a serious moral conflict, something Lucien is not really capable of. The distinction between the "miserable many" and the "happier few" (396) is not a gulf to be crossed in a conquest of wealth and fame, but a problem to which Hyacinth struggles to provide an answer. The novel envisions entry into life not as a conflict of political idealism with pragmatic desire for worldly success, but rather as a conflict between the sense of moral repugnance toward the existing social order and an aesthetic attraction to the cultural achievements of the upper classes: Is it worth fighting the cause of equality if the triumph of the poor will entail the destruction of the cultural achievements of contemporary civilization, and, vice versa, is high culture worth the price? As Margaret Scanlan observes, in acknowledging that high culture is fully dependent on the suffering of the masses, Hyacinth anticipates Walter Benjamin's thesis about the relation of civilization to barbarism.[14] Faced with this dilemma, Hyacinth "couldn't (with any respect for his own consistency) work, underground, for the enthronement of the democracy, and continue to enjoy, in however platonic a manner, a spectacle which rested on a hideous social inequality" (165). But if Benjamin argues that the historical materialist "cannot contemplate without horror" the origins of "cultural treasures," James attempts to resolve this problem by positing an aesthetic engagement with the world as a quasi-political alternative to class warfare.[15]

In Hyacinth's eyes the upper class is both the proprietor of high culture and (in this respect he anticipates Proust) a quasi-aesthetic sphere in its own right. The figure of the Princess Casamassima herself— "brilliant, delicate, complicated, but complicated with something divine" (251)—serves as an embodiment of this other, unknown, but immensely attractive reality that offers a release from the life of poverty. In fact, for both protagonists the other class functions as the unknown exotic other. Hyacinth is summoned to the Princess's theater box as a "curious animal" (247) to satisfy her intense desire to learn about the revolution. As Captain Sholto, who first introduced him to the Princess, explains to the hero: "I was looking for anything that would turn up that might take her fancy. Don't you understand that I am always looking? There was a time when I went immensely for illuminated missals, and another when I collected horrible ghost stories (she wanted to cultivate a belief in ghosts), all for her. The day I saw she was turning her attention to the rising democracy

I began to collect little democrats. That's how I collected you" (346). Not that Hyacinth minds being "collected"—their relationship is one of powerful mutual attraction that in the end unwittingly offers aesthetic curiosity as an alternative to political action. Speaking of the masses, the Princess cries: "But I can't leave them alone; they press upon me, they haunt me, they fascinate me. There it is (after all it's very simple): I want to know them, and I want you to help me!" (248). Hyacinth, in turn, feels the same form of attraction to the world *she* represents. As the Princess is explaining to him her personal history ("a wondering bohemian life in a thousand different places"), her newly found commitment to the poor, and disgust with the current state of society, the hero is left bewildered (250). He is not drawn to her because she empathizes with his cause, but because he sees her as an alien life form.

The paradox of her position is that Christina Casamassima simultaneously professes the revolutionary creed and embodies the alluring decadence of the world that the revolutionaries seek to destroy. Indeed, she is the one who offers a particularly incisive view of the social conditions:

> "I determined to see it"—she was speaking still of English society—"to learn for myself what it really is, before we blow it up. I have been here now a year and a half, and, as I tell you, I feel that I have seen. It is the old régime again, the rottenness and the extravagance, bristling with every iniquity, over which the revolution passes like a whirlwind; or perhaps even more a reproduction of Roman society in its decadence, gouty, apoplectic, depraved, gorged, and clogged with wealth and spoils, selfishness and skepticism, and waiting for the onset of the barbarians. You and I are the barbarians, you know." (313)

But Hyacinth is not at all certain that he wants to be a barbarian: while it is her interest in the revolution that brought the Princess to Hyacinth, it is precisely her presence that now draws Hyacinth away from the revolutionary cause: "For my demoralization began from the moment I first met you. Dear Princess, I may have done you good, but you haven't done me much. . . . I may have helped you to understand and enter into the misery of the people (though I protest I don't know much about it), but you have led my imagination into quite another train" (395–96). Even though he has put his life at the disposal of the anarchist leader Hohdhal, Hyacinth's attraction to the Princess and the world she embodies steadily undermines his commitment to the people. As the Princess comments, "I have wondered much—seeing that you cared less and less for the people—how you would reconcile your change of heart with the performance of your engagement ... for I can imagine nothing more terrible than to find yourself face to face with such an engagement, and to feel at the same time that the spirit which prompted it is dead within you" (572). Hyacinth will, then, commit suicide, unable to reconcile contradictory commitments: he cannot go ahead with the terrorist mission in the name of an ideology he no longer espouses, but he is also unable to renege on the promise he had made.

However, while James gestures toward the conclusion that Hyacinth dies faced with the clash of two irreconcilable but equally compelling moral obligations, the novel's ending struggles to bear out such a conclusion. If the case for the revolution is at least fully articulated in the novel—as the Princess explains, present social arrangements are so woefully unjust that they fully warrant violent rebellion—Hyacinth offers no clear political argument against it beyond the suggestion that the world, while cruel and unjust, is also a beautiful sight if one decides to look in the right direction: "He saw the immeasurable misery of the people, and yet he saw all that had been, as it were, rescued and redeemed from it: the treasures, the felicities, the splendours, the successes, of the world" (445). What Hyacinth offers, however, is closer to conformism than to aesthetic redemption. His conclusion is not that art will save the world, but that the inhabitants of the London slums are not worth saving: "The populace of London were scattered upon his path, and he asked himself by what wizardry could they ever be raised to high participations. There were nights in which everyone he met appeared to reek with gin and filth, and he found himself elbowed by figures as foul as lepers" (481; see also 464). By the end of the novel, Hyacinth has resolved the Benjaminian dilemma by persuading himself that the "miserable many" are barely human. He solves for himself the great question of social inequality not by articulating a proper alternative to the radical analysis of class relations offered by the anarchists, but by interiorizing the sense of upper-class superiority.

Unable or unwilling to elaborate a morally compelling case for Hyacinth's choice of indecision and hence unable to mold the rather unglamorous clash between the uncompromising anarchist politics and mere conformism into a decisive moral conflict, toward the end James turns the novel into an increasingly private drama. While suggesting that Hyacinth is facing the choice to kill or be killed, *The Princess Casamassima* increasingly transforms into a Jamesian melodrama of adultery and betrayal: despite the political dilemmas, during the novel's long finale Hyacinth steps off the stage primarily as an abandoned lover. Near the end of the novel, he meets the Princess one last time, even as he feels that their relation has crumbled, and he will leave her in tears, crushed by her rejection. Just as he was once collected as a "curious animal," he is now dismissed with "indifference" and "contempt" (574).

In the final chapter Hyacinth is not pondering contradictory ideological propositions but spying on the Princess alongside the Prince Casamassima, who cannot quite understand whether his estranged wife is plotting a revolution or having an affair with Hyacinth's friend Paul Muniment. As they observe Paul and the Princess entering her house late at night, the Prince's anxiety easily transfers to Hyacinth: "Hyacinth felt his arm seized by the Prince who, hastily, by a strong effort, drew him forward several yards. At this moment a part of the agitation which possessed the unhappy Italian seemed to pass into his own blood; a wave of anxiety rushed through him—anxiety as to the relations of the two persons who have descended from the cab; he had, in short, for several instants, a very exact revelation of the state of feeling of a jealous husband" (519). Over the novel's final hundred pages, the impossibility of sorting out political and class loyalties is increasingly overshadowed by other concerns. The Prince is disgusted by his wife's relations with Paul Muniment; Lady Aurora, the fellow aristocratic revolutionary, is devastated that Paul is interested in the Princess; and Hyacinth on the last day of his life wakes up thinking "that the Princess had done with him" (582). Additionally, the more he feels abandoned by the Princess, the more he revives his interest in the beautiful yet hopelessly banal Millicent Henning. In the final scene before his suicide he sees Millicent accompanied by Captain Sholto and realizes that, with her, as with the Princess, he has been "superseded" (582). This is an accidental revelation that anticipates similar discoveries in *The Golden Bowl* (1904) and *The Ambassadors* (1903), in which Lambert Strether stumbles on Chad and Mme de Vionnet, realizing in an instant the nature of their adulterous relationship. After exchanging glances with Sholto, Hyacinth withdraws, never to be seen again.

Whether he dies as a disenchanted revolutionary or as an abandoned lover is difficult to say. The uneasy relationship between the private and the political, intensified by the accumulation of melodramatic elements at the end of the novel, demonstrates that James felt it was impossible to resolve the conflict between opposing class loyalties in strictly political terms. It will take a different kind of novel (and a different kind of novelist) to fully transform the bildungsroman hero's encounter with the world into an explicit encounter with conflicting ideological positions.

## Science Perverted to Infidelity

*The Princess Casamassima* names very few names. In spite of its transparent ideological context, it makes no mention of Bakunin, Kropotkin, or Marx. It does, however, mention Darwin and Spencer. Speculating on the Princess's motivation to take up the revolutionary cause, Hyacinth concludes that "the force of reaction and revenge might carry her far, make her modern and democratic and heretical *à outrance*—led her to swear by Darwin and Spencer as well as by the Revolutionary spirit" (251). It should come as a surprise to no one that Hyacinth, like Zola's Étienne Lantier, conflates revolutionary political thought and revolutionary changes in the realm of natural sciences. As Susan Budd has shown, from the 1870s onward evolutionary ideas were absorbed into the popular imagination and used to a variety of ideological ends.[16] While a version of social Darwinism was invoked by socialists to bolster the argument about the inevitability of social change as a natural process, from a more conservative perspective it appeared that Darwinism was just one of many disruptive "isms" that formed a joint front to overturn traditional religious beliefs, moral standards, and models of social organization.

In December 1878, the *Pall Mall Gazette* reported on a German scholar's speculations about the political effects of Darwinism: "Does Darwinism make for the aristocratic or democratic principle in politics? Can Darwinism be enlisted in the cause of Socialism? Her Schmidt declares that it cannot. On the contrary, he says, may be called the scientific justification of the idea of aristocracy; or, to put it more plainly, of the right of the stronger to govern the weaker."[17] In the final decades of the nineteenth century, the theory of evolution was increasingly invoked by both the Left and the Right, not to mention numerous attempts to import Darwinism into the methodology of the social sciences. As J. W. Burrow notes, "Contemporaries inevitably assimilated Darwinian evolution to their own contexts of thought and emotional response: defensive, embattled, optimistic, hubristic, polemically materialist, latently or explicitly pantheistic."[18] Although the process of cultural assimilation of Darwinism will gain additional complexity in the coming decades, the initial response was to see the theory of evolution primarily as a challenge to Christianity, naturally affiliated with socialism and freethought. While not everyone would go as far as to believe, with Zola's Étienne, that Darwinism might offer a blueprint for political revolution, Darwinism was nonetheless seen as a gateway drug to more destructive beliefs. Moritz Kaufmann makes the connection in *Contemporary Review:*

> As Socialism in politics tends to Republicanism, as in economics it tends to Communism, so in matters of religion it tends to Atheism. . . . Nor is it very hard to account for this alliance of Socialism and Atheism. It is to a great extent the result of the materialistic tendencies of modern science and mechanical views of the universe entertained by leading scientists. The fact in itself is of some significance, that the same year saw the publication of Mr. Darwin's "Origin of Species" and that of the textbook of social democracy, the work on "Capital" by Karl Marx.[19]

Given that evolution was seen as the paradigmatic expression of widespread spirit of skepticism, and as a vital ally of social movements hostile to organized religion, it is not surprising that, in 1868, a conservative paper launched a scathing attack on Joseph Dalton Hooker, the president of the British Association for the Advancement of Science, and a staunch defender of Darwinism. Under the title "Science Perverted to Infidelity" the author writes: "The infidel theory of Dr. Hooker is no new idea. It is simply that of Dr. Darwin and the learned infidels, skeptics, and rationalists who swarm throughout Christendom.... It results, in the first place, from the deep seated enmity to revealed religion, because such religion places a check on their idle and profane speculations."[20] The complex connection constructed in the public discourse between evolution, antireligious sentiments (embodied primarily in the Secularist movement), and radical ideological projects like socialism and anarchism presented unique challenges to many late nineteenth-century intellectuals' attempts to position themselves ideologically.

When the hero of Butler's *The Way of All Flesh* announces at the end of the novel that "the spirit behind the Church is true, though her letter—true once—is now true no longer," while "the spirit behind the High Priests of Science is as lying as its letter," he is trying to offer an answer to these challenges.[21] By focusing on the relationship between scientific rationalism and religion, *The Way of All Flesh* enacts the question of intellectual and ethical consequences of Darwinism as Ernest Pontifex's personal drama. Ernest has passed through a tumultuous childhood marked by educational failures, a sense of dejection, and an uneasy relationship with his father, an Anglican priest. Uncertain of his choice of profession, he rapidly goes from religious indifference to bigotry and back, lands in prison, experiences a financial disaster, a failed marriage, and a stint as an owner of a tailor shop, only to rise again, thanks to the inheritance he receives from his aunt. And although he is rescued through a very Dickensian inheritance plot, the end of his wanderings is described primarily in intellectual terms. Ernest Pontifex's failures lie not simply in his inability to navigate life, but in his inability to navigate between competing religious and secular teachings, and it is only after he has managed to negotiate his relationship with these ideological projects that Ernest can come to define his relationship with society, however antagonistic.

The process of maturation ends as the hero is able to take an equidistant position toward rival doctrines. For Butler, to attain maturity is above all to attain intellectual independence in the wake of the rise of Darwinism and freethought, and of the religious responses to these secular doctrines. "He has formed no alliances," complains Ernest's publisher, "and has made enemies not only of the religious world but of the literary and scientific brotherhood as well. This will not do nowadays. If a man wishes to get on he must belong to a set, and Mr. Pontifex belongs to no set—not even to a club" (463). Ernest remains committed precisely to opening an intellectual space between powerful contemporary teachings.

The hero's intellectual development includes a series of abrupt shifts, starting with the lackluster Christianity of his father, a Low Church Anglican priest whose chief concern is that the Church of England is drifting back into a union with Rome, through episodes of evangelical zeal and an encounter with the intellectual sophistry of the High Church, until his faith finally crumbles under the pressure of rationalist critique of the Gospels: "He made the New Testament his chief study, going through it in the spirit which Mr. Shaw had desired of him, that is to say as one who wished neither to believe nor disbelieve, but cared only about finding out whether he ought to believe or no" (315). Following this endeavor, he concludes that "whatever else might be true, the story that Christ had died, come to life again, and been carried from earth through clouds into the heavens could not now be accepted by unbiased people" (315). And if the Gospels cannot be trusted, then the whole edifice of Christian faith must crumble (321).

Ernest here repeats a familiar line of rationalist critique of Christianity that was routinely employed by leading freethinkers like Charles Bradlaugh, the founder of the National Secular Society (established in 1865), and G. W. Foote, the founding editor of the *Freethinker* (1881).[22] For Bradlaugh the disproval of Christianity's central arguments was a two-step process in which the dismantling of the Bible's factual claims invariably undermined the ethical value of its teachings.[23] He made the argument explicitly in an 1859 debate: "The questions with which we are dealing, although divided into two parts, hang upon one another, and if it can be taken that I have succeeded in the early part of my position in showing you that the history of Jesus, as narrated in the four gospels is incredible, then you will be obliged to admit at once, without reservation, that his doctrines cannot benefit mankind, because the whole of his teachings hang on belief, and belief in that which is erroneous can never be of benefit to humanity."[24] As we have seen, Ernest Pontifex is happy to concur: his intellectual development shaped by "the wave of skepticism" (232) variously rooted in evolutionary biology and higher criticism, Ernest concludes that the Bible cannot be trusted and hence renounces all "faith in the supernatural element of the Christian religion" (320) in favor of "rationalism pure and simple" (316). Yet for Ernest "rationalism pure and simple" will not do, because he is able to dissolve that crucial connection on which Bradlaugh insists. Unlike Bradlaugh, he is prepared to simultaneously accept evolution as his "article of faith" (412), while still maintaining that "Christian morality at any rate was indisputable" (355). In Ernest's eyes, the epistemological challenges put forward by the joint efforts of contemporary natural science and biblical criticism cannot finally resolve the question of the ethical and metaphysical validity of Christianity's claims.

The readiness to simultaneously dispute the central tenets of Christianity and to refuse the radical implications of attacks on Christian doctrine was central not only to the hero of *The Way of All Flesh,* but also to Butler's own response to these controversies. In 1865, he published *The Evidence for the Resurrection of Jesus Christ, as Given by the Four Evangelists, Critically Examined,* arguing that Christianity's central narrative is little more than a matter of misunderstanding. As Peter Raby writes, Butler "concluded that Jesus had in fact not been dead when his body was handed to Joseph of Arimathea, but later regained consciousness. From the Apostles' sincere belief in the supposed miracle of the Resurrection, everything else in orthodox Christian doctrine followed."[25] The argument pursued is essentially analogous to that advanced simultaneously by freethinkers and revisionist theologians with respect to the historicity of both the Old and the New Testament narratives. In fact, just as Butler was completing his pamphlet in New Zealand, in England and South Africa a controversy was raging over Bishop Colenso's critical reading of the Pentateuch in which he sought to demonstrate "the *unhistorical character*, the *later origin*, and the *compound authorship*, of the five books usually attributed to Moses."[26]

Butler, however, had a prepared answer to challenges of this kind, including his own. "Reason," he writes in his *Note-Books*, "is not the ultimate test of truth nor it is the court of first instance."[27] The supernatural claims of Christianity, most notably its insistence on Christ's miraculous resurrection, may be absurd and frustrating, but hardly constitute sufficient grounds for forsaking religion altogether: "Therefore we ought not to cavil at the visible superstition and absurdity of much on which religion is made to rest, for the unknown can never be satisfactorily rendered into the known. . . . So that the attempt to symbolise the unknown is certain to involve inconsistencies and absurdities of all kinds and it is childish to complain of their existence unless one is prepared to advocate the stifling of all religious sentiment, and this is like trying to stifle hunger and thirst" (346–47). Butler was certainly not prepared to do anything of the sort, as the *Note-Books* repeatedly seek to renegotiate the relationship between science and religion. On science and theology he writes: "We should try to endow neither; we should treat them as we treat conservatism and liberalism, so that they may keep watch upon one another, and letting them go in and out of power with the popular vote concerning them" (340). What is at stake is not so much a project of reconciliation as it is a willingness to subject both to impartial scrutiny.

Butler certainly thought he was doing just that as he was pursuing increasingly bitter attacks against Darwin during the 1870s and 1880s. He strongly felt that Darwin's version of the evolutionary doctrine, unlike the theories of Jean-Baptiste Lamarck and Erasmus Darwin, was turning evolutionary change into a series of random variations, which he could not reconcile with purposeful development. In Butler's view, once devoid of teleology natural selection is reduced to mere chance, and if evolution is a matter of chance, then there is no design behind the process, and if there is no design, there is no God: "Mr. Darwin has told us this on the title-page of the 'Origin of Species.' He there defines it as 'The Preservation of Favoured Races'; 'Favoured' is 'Fortunate,' and 'Fortunate' 'Lucky'; it is plain, therefore, that with Mr. Darwin natural selection comes to 'The Preservation of Lucky Races,' and that he regarded luck as the most important feature in connection with the development even of so apparently purposive an organ as the eye, and as the one, therefore, on which it was most proper to insist. And what is luck but absence of intention or design?"[28] In an even more forceful formulation, Butler finally concludes that "the theory that luck is the main means of organic modification is the most absolute denial of God which it is possible for the human mind to conceive."[29] It is, of course, more than a little paradoxical that an author prepared to deny the reality of resurrection is worried about theological implications of Darwin's theory. Yet Butler's attacks on Darwin and attempts to introduce a rival version of evolutionary theory were a part of his ongoing struggle with spiritual, scientific, and cultural authority, and he strongly believed that Darwinism was a new oppressive orthodoxy.[30] Between competing claims to legitimacy, he was continuously seeking to open up a space for a critical inquiry pursued from the position of intellectual detachment, unobstructed by firm commitments.

This position of dissidence with respect to opposed doctrines and intellectual traditions is precisely what Ernest Pontifex chooses at the end of *The Way of All Flesh:* "In politics he is a Conservative so far as his vote and interests are concerned. In all other respects he is an advanced Radical" (464). As with his relationship with science and religion, what is at stake is not so much a dual commitment as an attempt to attain the position of equidistance. In a marked contrast to *The Princess Casamassima*'s melodramatic finale, the ending of *The Way of All Flesh* appears almost serene, despite the fact that Ernest Pontifex insists that he is an outcast: "For society indeed of all sorts, except of course that of a few intimate friends, he had an unconquerable aversion. 'I always did hate those people,' he said, 'and they always have hated and always will hate me. I am an Ishmael by instinct as much as by accident of circumstances, but if I keep out of society I shall be less vulnerable than Ishmaels generally are'" (438). In the end, this is a powerful rejection of intellectual and social constraints:

between evangelical proselytism and the attempt to embrace and advocate "rationalism pure and simple" (316), Ernest chooses intellectual detachment. And, although it is by no means obvious that this simultaneous distancing from religious dogma and scientific rationalism amounts to sound intellectual independence, the imperative Butler imposes both on himself and on the hero of his bildungsroman testifies to the pressures of the opposing claims to cultural authority in late Victorian England.

The self-imposed exile of Ernest Pontifex indicates not only an appreciation for intellectual autonomy, but also a recognition of the unique social role of a detached intellectual: "There are a lot of things that want saying which no one dares to say, a lot of shams which want attacking, and yet no one attacks them. It seems to me that I can say things which not another man in England except myself will venture to say, and yet which are crying to be said" (438). Conscious withdrawal to the margins is precisely what allows Ernest to practice the oppositional attitude. In the *Representations of the Intellectual,* Edward Said describes the intellectual as "exile and marginal, as amateur, as the author of a language which tries to speak truth to power."[31] Both the hero and the author of *The Way of All Flesh* anticipate twentieth-century theorizations of the role of the intellectual as a deliberate outsider. As the sociologist Ralf Dahrendorf argues, espousing a vision of the intellectual as a version of the royal fool, "The power of the fool lies in his freedom with respect to the hierarchy of the social order, that is, he speaks from outside as well as from inside it. The fool belongs to the social order and yet does not commit himself to it; he can without fear even speak uncomfortable truths about it."[32] Like these contemporary accounts of the role of the intellectual, Butler's version of the bildungsroman hero offers intellectual independence as an answer to the towering social, ideological, and cultural pressures of the late nineteenth century. As we shall see in a moment, Joyce will push the bildungsroman hero even further in the direction of intellectual and literal exile.

## Stephen Dedalus and Nationalism without Nationalism

As Stephen Dedalus steps on the stage of the European bildungsroman in 1914, he brings with him the familiar baggage of unresolved relationships with mass movements, political agendas, and belief systems.[33] Like the novels of Eliot, Butler, Zola, and James, *A Portrait of the Artist as a Young Man* testifies to the profoundly destabilizing effects of the bildungsroman's encounter with contemporary political ideologies. Once again, the hero struggles to negotiate his position with pressures of contradictory commitments: "I will not serve," Stephen famously tells Cranly, "that in which I no longer believe, whether it call itself my home, my fatherland, or my church."[34] Yet as *A Portrait* draws to a close, Stephen appears to offer conflicting formulations of his political stance, leaving the novel's conclusion to hover between the rejection of nationalism and the commitment to nation-building. In many ways, *A Portrait*'s outcome is suspended between Stephen's determination to reject the "nets of nationality, language, and religion" (220) and the promise to "forge the uncreated conscience of his race" (275–76). This double movement between rejection and affirmation—between the tenacious *non serviam* directed at the demands of nationality and religion and an equally resolute announcement of a nationalist mission—testifies, once again, that self-fashioning has become a series of painstaking maneuvers between the conflicting demands of individual and collective identity. The outcome of this maneuvering remains *A Portrait*'s central critical problem.

Stephen's blunt distanciation from the Church and from Irish nationalism has generated significant critical resistance at least since Hugh Kenner declared that "it is high time, in short, to point out that Stephen's flight into adolescent 'freedom' is not meant to be the 'message' of the book."[35] And, since the postcolonial turn in Joyce studies displaced the once-dominant vision of Joyce as an apolitical and internationalist aesthete with a version of Joyce as, above all, a colonial Irish intellectual, it has become common to resolve the apparent tension between Stephen's nationalist and cosmopolitan impulses in favor of the former: the rejection of an aestheticist and cosmopolitan Joyce has naturally led to the rejection of an aestheticist and cosmopolitan Stephen.[36]

On the surface, the argument in favor of an Irish colonial Joyce and, more specifically, in favor of an Irish colonial reading of *A Portrait,* presents itself as a simple demand for appropriate contextualization. As Andrew Gibson writes, "*A Portrait of the Artist as a Young Man* is about the growth to early adulthood of a young Irish intellectual and fledgling artist in Dublin in an extremely specific period of Irish history, approximately 1882–1903, focusing principally on the years 1891–1903. This may seem rather obvious; but the point has sometimes been a little lost in enthusiasm for Joyce's modernity or his modernism."[37] Equally obvious points—that *A Portrait,* although saturated with Catholicism and Irish politics, is a novel written in Pola and Trieste, published in a London literary magazine with the help of an American poet, and written by an author whose intellectual context is decisively international and continental, with powerful links to figures like Gabriele D'Annunzio and Ibsen, not to mention the European epic tradition—leave Gibson unswayed. As he writes in a different venue, "Certainly, he [Joyce] left Ireland for Continental Europe at the age of 22 and, thereafter, never lived in his country of origin again. He saw himself as an exile and increasingly prided himself on his cosmopolitanism. But in the early twentieth century, as in preceding centuries, to be an Irish exile and even a self-exiled Irishman in Europe was to be something much more specific than a European, let alone an internationalist. Joyce did not so much set out to become a modern European genius as he was turned into one."[38] And even if Joyce did turn away from Ireland and toward a wider European cultural context, he did so in response to a decisively Irish cultural situation: "Perhaps," Gibson argues, "the cosmopolitan logic of Joyce's work should be read in relation to an Irish logic. The global Joyce might even be an expression of the Irish one, not a release from him."[39] Finally, writing about Joyce's Catholicism, he concludes: "If the young Joyce was a modern intellectual, he none the less also remained a Catholic intellectual if not a believer. He was a Catholic intellectual because of his background, education and class, because of the culture to which he did not cease to belong, just by virtue of dissenting from it."[40] Gibson is, of course, right to assert that dissent implies a particularly intense relationship with the cultural forms from which one seeks to break free.[41] Yet we should not allow the inherent ambiguities of exile to fully obfuscate the distinction between unwilling belonging and conscious commitment: there is a difference between being born and bred Irish (or Catholic) and willingly espousing the cultural claims of Irish nationalism. Gibson's reading conflates the two, practically co-opting every cosmopolitan impulse back into the prison-house of national culture. In Gibson's hands, local contextualization, in itself a necessary and welcome move, too often becomes an excuse to dismiss both the powerful cosmopolitan impulses of Joyce's work and its decisively international contexts. In the final instance, cosmopolitanism is turned into a symptom to be explained and indeed explained away by the original national context from which Joyce's work emerged.

Other scholars have followed a very similar path in minimizing the implications of Joyce's critique of dominant forms of nationalism, including the Gaelic Revival movement. As Gregory Castle writes, "Joyce challenged the cultural assumptions of the Revival, especially its . . . tendency of idealizing the Irish peasantry and locating cultural authenticity in folklore, legend, and mythology. . . . But it seems to me that we cannot understand the complexity of Joyce's attitude toward Revivalism if we place him outside its influence and lose sight of the fact that Joyce and William Butler Yeats desired the same thing: the creation of an imaginary Irish nation and race."[42] The difficulty with these and other similar critical interventions is that they simultaneously acknowledge and neutralize Joyce's rejection of the Revival, thus incorporating him back into Irish nationalism, perhaps as a capricious and somewhat eccentric nationalist, but a nationalist nonetheless.[43]

Contrary to what has been suggested so often in recent years, our desire to rescue the great Irish writer from being assimilated into English or international modernism has prevented us from seeing that his first novel enacts a systematic repudiation of nationalist tropes. As Eric Hobsbawm observes, commenting on the rise of nationalism in the late nineteenth century, "The basis of 'nationalism' of all kinds was the same: the readiness of people to identify themselves emotionally with 'their' nation and to be politically mobilized as Czechs, Germans, Italians or whatever, a readiness which could be politically exploited."[44] Yet even as he promises to "forge the conscience of his race," Stephen Dedalus proves incapable of an attachment of this kind and consequently rejects the possibility of explicit political mobilization. Significantly, he also rejects essentialist assumptions about ethnic identity and national language. *A Portrait* is therefore not just another bildungsroman in which the process of education is heavily politicized: more than that, it is a novel that thoroughly deconstructs the project of ethnolinguistic nationalism and instead depicts the hero's struggle to imagine an existence unencumbered by what Benda called "the will to group" (2). In the following pages I trace this deconstructive process in detail.

## The Language Question

The demands of the Revival that Stephen fails to espouse—to be "true to his country and help to raise up her language and tradition" (88)— are typical of what Hobsbawm calls the "transformation of nationalism" across Europe. While the sources of ethnolinguistic nationalism can be traced back at least to the primitivist impulses of the German Romantics, the rise of such nationalism as a pervasive collective movement and a decisive political force in the mass society is essentially a late nineteenth-century phenomenon.[45]

Like its many continental counterparts, Irish nationalism had only gradually come to emphasize the identification of ethnicity and a national language. As Hobsbawm points out, "Before the foundation of the Gaelic League (1893), which initially had no political aims, the Irish language was not an issue in the Irish national movement."[46] Yet in the 1890s and 1900s, the possibility of resurrecting Gaelic as a national language had become the central preoccupation of the Irish public. A sustained effort was made not only to increase the number of Gaelic speakers, but also to bring Irish into official use as much as possible, to make it a part of the education system, and, finally, a compulsory subject at the National University. In 1897 the Gaelic League even organized a public competition offering prizes of five pounds for best essays on such topics as "The Influence of Language on Nationality" and "How to Popularize the Irish Language."[47]

Far from being a uniquely Irish development, the Gaelic Revival's focus on national language and folk culture corresponds closely to similar developments across Europe, from Scandinavia to the Balkans.[48] In fact, the proponents of Irish were very much aware of these similarities, invoking the precedents of the "great revival in language, as in the case of Germany, Hungary and Bohemia."[49] In 1904 an appeal for the establishment of the Gaelic Academy was reinforced by invoking the Hungarian experience, as one speaker reported that he has "recently been staying in Hungary, and has returned home full of enthusiasm for the manner in which the Hungarians rescued their language from the oblivion to which it was rapidly tending."[50] Paradoxically, Irish nationalism, which is so often invoked as the indispensable local context of Joyce's writings, follows quite consciously a pattern already developed across Europe.[51]

Like similar nationalist movements across the Continent, in seeking to "restore the Irish language to its proper position," the Gaelic League presupposes a causal connection between the fate of the national language and the historic fate of the nation: "The greatest misfortune that can befall a people is to be deprived of its language. Reason tells us that this instinctive clinging to the language is not a question of sentiment, but, in truth, of life and death. Language, then, is not a mere string of symbols as are figures to a mathematician. It is a living power, influencing the intellect and controlling the thought of man."[52] In the final instance, language bears a privileged relation to national consciousness, and the loss of language inevitably results in national disintegration. A letter to the editor of the *Irish Times* sums up this view:

> Dr. Hyde and his fellow Gaelic Leaguers would never have taken off their coats to fight the up-hill battle they are fighting, on account of mere manner of speech or deportment. They preach from the text, "What shall it profit a man if he gains the whole world and lose his own soul." They have learnt that native speech is the expression of the national soul. They have seen that with the discontinuance of the native speech Ireland's soul has become inert. Following close on the imitation of English speech comes imitation of English thought, until Irish initiative has almost ceased to be.[53]

In *A Portrait* Stephen Dedalus takes a very different view of the language question: "My ancestors threw off their language and took another,

Stephen said. They allowed a handful of foreigners to subject them. Do you fancy I am going to pay in my own life and person debts they made? What for?" (220). Significantly, Stephen takes this view despite acknowledging the foreignness of English. Shortly before renouncing Irish, he finds himself in a minor linguistic dispute with the dean of studies about the words "tundish" and "funnel" (203–4). Although the words are synonyms, Stephen doesn't know what "funnel" means, and the dean, an Englishman, doesn't know the word "tundish," which Stephen uses: "Is that called a tundish in Ireland? asked the dean. I never heard the word in my life" (204). To have his English corrected by an Englishman provokes a profound sense of linguistic insecurity in Stephen: "The language in which we are speaking is his before it is mine. How different are the words *home, Christ, ale, master,* on his lips and on mine! I cannot speak or write these words without unrest of spirit. His language, so familiar and so foreign, will always be for me an acquired speech. I have not made or accepted its words. My voice holds them at bay. My soul frets in the shadow of his language" (205). The suggestion is that the Irish are inevitably foreigners in the dominant language of their culture. It is a familiar argument. According to Thomas O'Donnell, a prominent MP from Parnell's Irish Parliamentary Party, "Irish was the language of our people until quite recently, and although most of us speak English now, our thoughts are Irish in form. The Irish mind has been built up by the Irish language, and the Irish mind can only express itself through a medium it has specially chosen for itself."[54] The sense of English as a foreign and inadequate medium haunts both O'Donnell and Joyce's hero. But while for the former this inadequacy is an argument in favor of the Revival (in fact, only a few months earlier O'Donnell made an attempt to address the House of Commons in Gaelic), for Stephen Dedalus it is a frustrating thought that nonetheless fails to influence his rejection of Irish.

    Whereas Douglas Hyde, the founder of *Conradh na Gaeilge,* preached "the necessity for de-anglicizing Ireland," arguing that the loss of language "is our greatest blow, and the sorest stroke that the rapid Anglicisation of Ireland has inflicted upon us," for Stephen Dedalus, as for Joyce himself, the triumph of English is irreversible and beside the point.[55] In a diary entry toward the end of *A Portrait,* Stephen reasserts himself in relation to English: the dean's objection to his use of the language was unfounded; he had used the right word. "I looked it up and find it English and good old blunt English too. Damn the dean of studies and his funnel! What did he come here for to teach us his own language or to learn it from us. Damn him one way or the other!" (274) The division between "his" language and "us" persists, but so does the sense that "his" language can be mastered.

The importance of this gesture cannot be overestimated. In bracketing the question of national language and the threat of linguistic assimilation, Stephen Dedalus dismisses the single most important concern of modern ethnolinguistic nationalism. National language, as Hyde's and O'Donnell's arguments show, is the conditio sine qua non of the preservation of cultural identity. As Hyde insisted in 1909, "They in the Gaelic movement have put their finger upon the secret spring which opened the jewel drawer of Irish thought and mind . . . the secret spring of the Irish language. Wherever they have revived the language they have revived all the rest with it, including the Irish industries." Language is the crucial element of the fantasy of reestablishing the uninterrupted transmission of national spirit, by "getting into touch with the nationality of the people as it was."[56] Stephen Dedalus offers a comprehensive rejection of this fantasy.[57]

## Changing the Subject

When Stephen rejects the Irish language, he implicitly rejects not only the claim that it is possible (or desirable) to restore the lost cultural continuity, but also the most significant tool of national self-expression. According to Hyde, "The Gaelic people can never produce its best before the world as long as it remains tied to the apron-strings of another race and another island."[58] By espousing English, Stephen rejects this assumption and dissolves the bond O'Donnell established between "the Irish mind" and the "medium it has specially chosen for itself." In fact, Stephen is prepared fully to reject the discourse of authenticity that assumes, on the one hand, the existence of an immutable national essence, and, on the other, that the intrusion of foreign elements will lead to a progressive shift away from the national spirit. Stephen on Davin:

> The young peasant worshipped the sorrowful legend of Ireland. The gossip of his fellow-students which strove to render the flat life of the college significant at any cost loved to think of him as a young Fenian. His nurse had taught him Irish and shaped his rude imagination by the broken lights of Irish myth. He stood towards the myth upon which no individual mind had ever drawn out a line of beauty and to its unwieldy tales that divided against themselves as they moved down the cycles in the same attitude as towards the Roman Catholic religion, the attitude of a dull-witted loyal serf. Whatsoever of thought or of feeling came to him from England or by way of English culture his mind stood armed against in obedience to a password; and of the world that lay beyond England he knew only the foreign legion of France in which he spoke of serving. (195–96)

Davin embodies all of the crucial characteristics of Douglas Hyde's xenophobic program as Joyce perceived it: the uncritical embrace of national mythology, followed by an equally uncritical rejection of all things English, and utter ignorance of other cultural traditions. No doubt, Davin would have espoused Hyde's appeal to stand "against this constant running to England for our books, literature, music, games, fashions, and ideas."[59]

Not only does Stephen reject Davin's attraction to the "Irish myth"—one of the final entries in Stephen's diary contains a brutal parodic assault on Revivalist ethnographic escapades (274)—but he offers a clear cosmopolitan alternative to Devin's programmatic parochialism, as he contemplates a long strain of European authors, including Gerhart Hauptmann, Henrik Ibsen, Guido Cavalcanti, and Ben Jonson. Moreover, the sequence of authors Stephen invokes in *A Portrait* closely follows the logic of Joyce's attack on the Irish Literary Theatre in "The Day of the Rabblement." In this 1901 text Joyce dismisses the theater as "the property of the rabblement of the most belated race in Europe" precisely at the moment when the theater has (at least in Joyce's estimation) dropped even the pretense of interest in anything beyond the folklore and the epic past. During that year the company produced two plays based on folktales, *Diarmuid and Grania* (by George Moore and Yeats) and *Casadh an tSúgáin* (Hyde), the latter being performed in Irish.[60] Rejecting the theater's orientation, Joyce writes: "The censorship is powerless in Dublin, and the directors could have produced *Ghosts* or *The Dominion of Darkness* if they chose. Nothing can be done until the forces that dictate public judgement are calmly confronted. But, of course, the directors are shy of presenting Ibsen, Tolstoy or Hauptmann, where even [Yeats's] *Countess Cathleen* is pronounced vicious and damnable. Even for a technical reason this project was necessary. A nation which never advanced so far as a miracle-play affords no literary model to the artist, and he must look abroad."[61] And Stephen, like Joyce, will look abroad. Having rejected the essentialist assumptions behind contemporary nationalism, and having consequently rejected the notion of language as an expression of nationality, he can proceed to dismantle the claim that an artistic vocation can be only secondary to a sense of national belonging. Once again, the contrast with Davin is instructive. Davin sees himself as "an Irish nationalist, first and foremost" (219), and he offers himself as an example to Stephen: "A man's country comes first. Ireland first, Stevie. You can be a poet or a mystic later" (220). Yet, however we choose to understand this "later"—should Stephen simply forgo literature for the sake of participating in the nationalist movement, or should he subject his literary preoccupations to a national goal, thus creating an eminently Irish art?— Joyce's protagonist clearly has no intention of following Davin's advice. Instead, he chooses to renegotiate the relationship between nationality and artistic self-expression. Every time his Irishness in challenged ("Are you Irish at all?"; "Why don't you learn Irish?"), Stephen responds by simultaneously reasserting his Irish identity and expressing disdain for the political and cultural aspirations of contemporary nationalists. While at the beginning of their conversation he offers to show Davin his family tree, at the end he produces the definition of Ireland as "the old sow that eats her farrow" (220). Since Stephen's understanding of Irishness is suspended between belonging and disgust, his pronouncement that he is a product of Ireland has an ambiguous ring to it: "This race and this country and this life produced me, he said. I shall express myself as I am" (220). This creed seems to echo the doctrine of national art as expressive of a national identity. As the president of the Architectural Association of Ireland observed in 1901, "All great art must in its origin, its growth, its making, be instinct with the spirit of the country which had produced it, and, therefore, in the true meaning of the word, national."[62] Yet there is a subtle shift in emphasis in Stephen's argument: not "I shall express this race and this country," but rather "I will express myself as I have been made by my cultural situation," a situation that in, Stephen's own view, is dysfunctional, oppressive, and self-destructive.

This deliberate blurring of the lines between self-expression and the expression of collective identity is a well-known rhetorical strategy often employed in the face of various demands for national purity. In one of the best-known rebuttals of cultural nationalism, Jorge Luis Borges offers a more expansive version of the same argument: "We cannot confine ourselves to what is Argentine in order to be Argentine because either it is our inevitable destiny to be Argentine, in which case we will be Argentine whatever we do, or being Argentine is a mere affectation, a mask."[63] By way of turning national identity from an object of reverence into an assumed fact, both Joyce and Borges are offering critiques of nationalism rather than theories of national art.[64]

Above all, Stephen Dedalus responds to the nationalist fantasies of his peers by changing the subject. In the face of Davin's "Ireland first, Stevie," he invokes Aristotle's *Poetics:* "Aristotle," he pronounces, "has not defined pity and terror. I have" (221). By reinterpreting the concept of catharsis—Aristotle has famously defined the effect of tragedy as the "purgation (catharsis) of pity and fear"—Stephen offers an implicit rebuke to the nationalist imagination: to the particularist concern with national identity, with what counts as distinctly Irish, he opposes what he sees as the universal problem of the nature of aesthetic experience.[65] In fact, this reference to the *Poetics* is only the initial step in Stephen's complex and idiosyncratic commitment to aesthetic formalism. Although he borrows the problem of catharsis from Aristotle (and his vocabulary from Aquinas, whom he repeatedly references as his intellectual guide), Joyce's hero goes on to formulate an aesthetic theory rooted primarily in Kant and concerned with the question of the universal validity of aesthetic judgments.[66] In other words, he uses the Aristotelian concern with pity and fear as responses to tragedy in order to articulate a more general question about the distinct emotional and intellectual response that defines aesthetic experience. As he sees them, both pity and fear are proper aesthetic emotions because they tend to "arrest the mind": "You see I use the word ARREST. I mean that the tragic emotion is static. Or rather the dramatic emotion is. The feelings excited by improper art are kinetic, desire or loathing. Desire urges us to possess, to go to something; loathing urges us to abandon, to go from something. The arts which excite them, pornographical or didactic, are therefore improper arts. The esthetic emotion (I used the general term) is therefore static. The mind is arrested and raised above desire and loathing" (222). The purportedly Aristotelian concern with the emotional response that defines the tragic experience seamlessly transforms into a Kantian distinction between disinterested pleasure ("static" emotions in Stephen's terminology) and the vulgar desire to possess an object ("kinetic" emotions). As Kant argues, "If the question is whether something is beautiful, one does not want to know whether there is anything that is or that could be at stake, for us or for someone else, in the existence of the thing, but rather how we judge it in mere contemplation (intuition or reflection)."[67] Like Kant, Stephen believes that proper aesthetic experience must be divorced from both sensual pleasure and moral satisfaction. In demanding that the mind rise "above desire and loathing" (222) he is rearticulating the Kantian imperative of disinterested contemplation.

It is hardly surprising, then, that Stephen takes up the equally Kantian problem of the universality of aesthetic experience: "The Greek, the Turk, the Chinese, the Copt, the Hottentot, said Stephen, all admire a different type of female beauty. That seems to be a maze out of which we cannot escape" (226). He does, however, offer a solution: "Though the same object may not seem beautiful to all people, all people who admire a beautiful object find in it certain relations which satisfy and coincide with the stages themselves of all esthetic apprehension. These relations of the sensible, visible to you through one form and to me through another, must be therefore the necessary qualities of beauty" (227). The solution itself is one that is a shared property of eighteenth-century aesthetics—Stephen sees beauty not as an objective property but as a relational predicate, assuming that there is a homology between a set of broadly defined formal characteristics and the intellectual processes through which objects are perceived.[68] Yet it is the choice of the problem, rather than the solution, that is particularly interesting. Not only does Stephen respond to nationalist tirades by offering an aesthetic theory, but one of his theory's chief concerns is to solve the problem of the universal validity of the category of beauty beyond the constraints of various national cultures. Aesthetic disinterestedness, with its investment in the principle of universality, thus emerges as a form of resistance to the demands of nationalism, and, indeed, as a vital tool of Joycean politics. For Stephen Dedalus, aestheticism amounts to a dissenting political stance.[69]

## Beyond the Nation

Now, it is perhaps still possible to argue for a nationalist version of Stephen Dedalus—he does, after all, end up promising the creation of a national conscience—although it is exceedingly difficult to discover the content of his alleged nationalist project.[70] Even Yeats, whose nationalism was far less ambiguous than Joyce's, had misgivings about some elements of the Gaelic League's program. Responding to Hyde's call for a return to Irish language, Yeats rejected this demand as impractical and likely impossible: "Let us by all means prevent the decay of that tongue where we can, and preserve it always among us as a learned language to be a fountain of nationality in our midst, but do not let us base upon it our hopes of nationhood."[71] Significantly, however, Yeats criticized the Gaelic League from the position of a fellow traveler who shared the same aspiration to de-Anglicize Ireland. Despite some doubts with regard to the language question, he did not dispute the underlying essentialist understanding of nationhood, nor did he doubt the necessity of relying on inherited Irish cultural forms in the project of nation building: "The little foreign criticism of Irish literature which I have seen speaks of it as simple and primitive. They are right. There is a distinct school of Irish literature, which we must foster and protect, and its foundation is sunk in the legend lore of the people and in the National history."⁷² A recuperable history lies at the heart of both Yeats's and Hyde's projects.

Stephen, like Joyce, rejects not only the Revivalist plunge into the national myth and Gaelic language, but denies the existence of any form of redeemable past. Most nationalists resolve their dissatisfaction with the present, or with the recent development of national history, by identifying the moment in which the nation had lost its way and by committing themselves to the reconstruction of a retrospective utopia. Hyde offers a classic example of this mode of reasoning. Lamenting the fall of Ireland, formerly "one of the most classically learned and cultured nations in Europe," he comments: "I shall endeavour to show that this failure of the Irish people in recent times has been largely brought about by the race diverging during this century from the right path, and ceasing to be Irish without becoming English. I shall attempt to show that with the bulk of the people this change took place quite recently, much more recently than most people imagine, and is, in fact, still going on."⁷³ Yet when Stephen announces that his ancestors have given away their independence and their language (220), he finds no prelapsarian Ireland to return to. As Joyce puts it in "Ireland, Island of Saints and Sages," his most extensive pronouncement on the questions of Irish history, "Ancient Ireland is dead just as ancient Egypt is dead. Its death chant has been sung, and on its gravestone has been placed the seal."⁷⁴ In the same lecture, Joyce offers his most devastating critique of nationalism:

> What race, or what language (if we except the few whom a playful will seems to have preserved in ice, like the people of Iceland) can boast of being pure today? And no race has less right to utter such a boast than the race now living in Ireland. Nationality (if it really is not a convenient fiction like so many others to which the scalpels of present-day scientists have given the coup de grâce) must find its reason for being rooted in something that surpasses and transcends and informs changing things like blood and the human word. (165–66)⁷⁵

There is, however, very little in which nationalism can be rooted once Joyce is done with it: without inherited language and folk culture, without the fiction of common ancestry, with no redeemable past or a historical mission, very little remains, except, perhaps, hybridity itself. With his willingness to "look abroad" when native cultural forms seem insufficient, Joyce is approaching what the Hungarian dissident György Konrád calls "the self-expanding national strategy," which "takes what it considers non-national and delights in condemning it. The self-expanding national strategy takes anything from the outside world that can be fruitfully related to what was previously considered national and delights in integrating the two."[76] Konrád's argument reads either as a very liberal version of nationalism or as a covert defense of cosmopolitanism, in which resistance to xenophobia and cultural parochialism is declared a "national strategy." Joyce seems to walk the same fine line.

Finally, nationalism requires a commitment to service, which is precisely why it is so difficult to take Stephen Dedalus's promise of nation building at face value. When Joyce ends his "Ireland, Island of Saints and Sages" by calling for the rise of Ireland—"It is well past time for Ireland to have done once and for all with failure. If she is truly capable of reviving, let her awake, or let her cover up her head and lie down decently in her grave forever" (174)—he does so with the usual air of impatience. For Joyce, as for his hero, Ireland needs to explain herself to him: the Irish have allowed themselves to be conquered, and both the Norman invasion of Ireland in the twelfth century and the forming of the Union with Great Britain in 1800 were self-inflicted, as the Irish invited their own conquerors. "These two Facts," he concludes, "must be thoroughly explained before the country in which they occurred has the most rudimentary right to persuade one of her sons to change his position from that of an unprejudiced observer to that of a convinced nationalist" (162–63).[77] Both Joyce's and Stephen's *non serviam* violate the most important principle of modern nationalism. In Davin's not very sophisticated formulation, "a man's country comes first. Ireland first, Stevie" (220). Stephen, however, refuses to serve and participate, exempting himself from all demands of collective identity and from all communal obligations. In 1882, as the tide of nationalist sentiment was engrossing Europe, Ernst Renan wrote: "The nation, like the individual, is the outcome of long and strenuous past of sacrifice and devotion. Of all cults, the cult of ancestors is the most legitimate, since our ancestors have made us what we are. A heroic past of great men, of glory (I mean genuine glory): this is the social capital on which a national idea is established. To have common glories in the past and common will in the present; to have done great things together, and to will that we do them again—these are the conditions essential to being a people."[78] Stephen, however, cannot participate, not even in the history of collective suffering. Whereas Renan argues that "in matters of national identity, mourning has more validity than triumph, since it imposes duties which demand a common effort," to Joyce's hero national suffering presents itself as a national failure that calls for explanation, not empathy, much less service or self-sacrifice.[79]

When Stephen announces that he will create a national conscience, after declaring that he will not serve, such an announcement can only be taken as yet another form of the hero's self-assertion in the face of Ireland he rejects. It is only after he realizes he is incapable of negotiating a tolerable relationship with historic Ireland that the aspiring artist will reinvent himself as a demiurgic creator of national conscience. With his critique of nationalism so extensive, his distanciation from all tenets of national identity so far-reaching, Stephen's vacuous promise of "forging" an Irish identity is primarily an expression of disdain toward the extant Ireland. As he is preparing to go into self-imposed exile, it is a final gesture of severance and rejection. In order to be made tolerable, Ireland must be reinvented.[80]

Like Ernest Pontifex three decades earlier, Stephen responds to the pressures of collective movements through powerful acts of distancing. "Mr. Pontifex belongs to no set—not even to a club," complains Ernest's publisher in *The Way of All Flesh* (463). "I will not serve," Stephen tells Cranly, "that in which I no longer believe, whether it call itself my home, my fatherland, or my church" (268). "I cannot enter the social order," Joyce famously wrote to Nora, "except as a vagabond."[81] Yet this quest for detachment, this rejection of dominant modes of thought and collective sentiments, this deliberate self-exclusion, testifies not to the power of individualism, but rather to the unbearable pressure of new collective loyalties, a pressure that can be met only through vigorous insistence on intellectual alienation.

Writing about Victorian intellectuals, Stefan Collini has argued that the moralist "does not speak from somewhere located, mysteriously, 'outside' society, nor should we assume that criticism requires the critic to be socially marginal, politically adversarial, or morally estranged."[82] Unlike the members of Victorian intellectual elite Collini describes, European intellectuals of Joyce's generation repeatedly indulged in the fantasy of the radical autonomy of intellectual vocation. Figures like Karl Mannheim, who developed the vision of the classless, unattached intellectual, and Julien Benda, who bemoaned the crisis of intellectual independence in the wake of the "great betrayal," shared the same impulse to advocate intellectual detachment from collective commitments.[83]

We have come full circle, then. In novels like *Daniel Deronda* and *Germinal* the hero is able to submit to a cause. In *A Portrait*, national identity is a source of frustration and constraint. In many ways, Joyce's novel offers a logical conclusion to the bildungsroman's brush with social movements and ideological agendas around the turn of the century. In the period in which ideological projects have complicated the task of self-fashioning with force hitherto unknown, the bildungsroman retreats into a vision of radical autonomy from various forms of collective identity. Yet it would be too hasty to argue that this development indicates a crisis of the genre, and not only because crisis is the *norm* of bildungsroman history: Stephen Dedalus's struggle with the constraints of collectivity and his indulgence in egotistical impulses generates a particularly intense dialectic between selfhood and society. And while pride may be a cardinal sin, it is occasionally necessary for bildungsroman heroes.

# 5

# MADAME DE GUERMANTES AND OTHER ANIMALS

## Proust and the Forms of Pleasure

The exile of Stephen Dedalus at the end of Joyce's *A Portrait of the Artist as a Young Man* marks the high point of the existential crisis that the encounter with new ideological forces generated for so many of the fictional fin-de-siècle young men. But there are, of course, other paths, and not everyone takes mass movements head on. Flaubert is a case in point. Chronicling the 1848 Revolution and the fall of the Orleans monarchy, his *L'Éducation sentimentale* (*Sentimental Education,* 1869) contains all the ingredients necessary to produce a violent political drama: heated debates about the merits of democracy; incendiary speeches; enthusiastic young socialists who read Rousseau, Saint-Simon, and Fourier in hopes that the glorious events of 1789 might be replicated; even a depiction of the revolutionary mob storming the royal palace. And yet Flaubert's hero, Frédéric Moreau, takes little notice. While clashes between the revolutionaries and the army are erupting on the streets of Paris, Frédéric pays a visit to his lover, the courtesan Rosanette, so that they can observe the crowd together: "Ils passèrent l'après-midi à regarder, de leur fenêtre, le peuple dans la rue. Puis il l'emmena dîner aux Trois-Frères-Provençaux. Le repas fut long, délicat. Ils s'en revinrent à pied, faute de voiture" (They spent the afternoon watching the mob in the street from their window. Then he took her to dinner at Trois-Frères-Provençaux. The meal was lengthy and exquisite. They returned on foot, since there were no carriages; 306, 305).[1] As they make their way through the mass of men—in the meantime the government has fallen—he has very little to say: "'Ah! on casse quelques bourgeois,' dit Frédéric tranquillement" ("Ah! They're killing off a few bourgeois," said Frédéric calmly; 307, 306). Even if he experiences occasional (quite occasional!) gusts of revolutionary enthusiasm, Frédéric remains a disinterested observer of history. While Paris is still suffering from eruptions of violence in the aftermath of the revolution, he decides to go away, driven not by fear but by boredom, as a man who wants to briefly exchange the hassle of the metropolis for a weekend in the country:

> Quelquefois, ils entendaient tout au loin des roulements de tambour. C'était la générale que l'on battait dans les villages, pour aller défendre Paris—'Ah! tiens! l'émeute!' disait Frédéric avec une pitié dédaigneuse, toute cette agitation lui apparaissant misérable à côté de leur amour et de la nature éternelle. (249)

> (Sometimes they heard the roll of drums far away in the distance. It was the call to arms being beaten in the villages for the defence of Paris. 'Why, of course! It's the insurrection!' Frédéric would say with a disdainful pity, for all that excitement struck him as trivial in comparison of their love and eternal Nature.) (254)

With Rosanette he finds repose at Fontainebleau, where they pay a visit to the old royal palace, known as one of the ancient châteaux of the French monarchy, and the site of Napoleon's abdication in April 1814. This is a conspicuous choice of venue on Flaubert's part. Whereas the great Napoleonic example determines the aspirations of Stendhal's and Balzac's heroes, Frédéric Moreau is a tourist in the emperor's palace, as if both Napoleonic success and Napoleonic failure are no longer possibilities. Insufficiently ambitious to be defeated in the struggle for success and insufficiently committed to political causes to take any decisive action, Frédéric sinks into a state of blessed mediocrity, marred only by his infatuation with Mme Arnoux and by occasional outbursts of poorly directed enthusiasm: today he may try to paint; tomorrow he will start writing a history of the Renaissance; the day after that he might run for office. At the end—and contrary to what we have seen with so many other young protagonists—he will simply withdraw from each of these passing endeavors, settling for an unremarkable future.

With Frédéric Moreau, Flaubert dismantles the figure of the parvenu that plays such a pivotal role in the fictions of Stendhal and Balzac. Instead of a man adamant to succeed or die trying, we get a lackluster hero prepared to walk away not only from the 1848 Revolution, but also from any kind of serious ambition. This slip into mediocracy and indifference, however, would open a significant new door for the bildungsroman. Clearly, Flaubert could no longer take seriously the shameless quest for success that the French bildungsroman tradition explored so meticulously, but he also refused to take part in the turn to ideology that was about to sweep the late nineteenth-century bildungsroman. Social upheaval constitutes an indispensable framework of his novel, but it also fails to create an existential drama. The revolutionary violence of 1848 is simultaneously mobilized and looked away from, simultaneously present and absent from the novel—or, rather, present but inconsequential, reduced to a spectacle. Whereas the encounter with the resolute demands of national, class, or religious identity prompted novelists like James, Butler, and Joyce to turn the bildungsroman into a personal drama in which the hero struggles with collective demands and messianic ambitions, only to end up dead or self-exiled, Flaubert seems to have found an alternative answer to this problem: when there is a revolution around the corner, one can always take a romantic weekend in the country.

By withdrawing his hero both from history and from the race to the top of the social hierarchy, Flaubert poses a question of some consequence for the development of the genre: What remains of the bildungsroman once the hero abandons an active confrontation with the world? As we have seen in chapter 2, Dickens transformed the bildungsroman into a rescue narrative. Flaubert transformed it into a parody of the Balzacian drama. Proust, as I show in this chapter, will go further: leaving behind both the Balzacian analytics of success and failure and the painstaking ideological drama central to so many fin-de-siècle texts, he transforms the bildungsroman hero from an active participant in the struggle for wealth and fame into a reflective observer of his own life. In the process, the bildungsroman itself becomes a site of an aesthetic rather than a socioeconomic enquiry. Although it still inhabits the shell of a Balzacian novel, with its distinctive backdrop of aristocratic salons and their intricate rules, rites of passage, and capricious mistresses, *À la recherche du temps perdu* adamantly refuses to produce instrumental knowledge about dominant social structures and their economic basis. Instead of treating the Balzacian salon as a site of class struggle, Proust's novel treats it as an aesthetic object: the structural relations that the narrator discovers by observing the world of the Guermanteses produce a sense of gratification—a positive emotional response—consistent with aesthetic experience. In fact, as a whole, the *Recherche* is committed to exploring the possibility of engaging the external world as an object that elicits aesthetic pleasure. In this chapter I trace the various strategies this process of exploration entails, including the suppression of socioeconomic reality and the use of botanical and zoological vocabulary in an attempt to exoticize and defamiliarize the social universe and, in particular, the world of inverts. Finally, I chronicle the crisis of this project prompted by the introduction of Albertine Simonet: as the novel displaces the inquiry into the Guermanteses and male inversion with an inquiry into Albertine's lesbianism, aestheticization is displaced by paranoia.

## The Importance of Not Being Balzac

In Balzac, economy and politics are powerful, ruthless forces whose workings are analyzed in great detail. In Proust, they are theater props, pieces of stage scenery that are present but hollow. The most significant of these props is the Dreyfus affair itself. Even though the affair constitutes the natural political center of the novel obsessed with the conflict between Dreyfusards and anti-Dreyfusards, the specifics of the scandal, the full political and ideological stakes, and the underlying mechanisms of state power remain oblique.[2] Following Flaubert's treatment of the 1848 Revolution, Proust clearly refuses to mobilize the ethical and political potential of the Dreyfus case, choosing instead to relentlessly trivialize historical processes, draining them of all rationality beyond the logic of meaningless circular movement.[3]

During Marcel's early childhood, the fashionable world was profoundly conservative and adamantly antirepublican; before he first entered the salons, Jews were already admitted, until with the Dreyfus affair the tide turned, and the most fashionable salon became the one of the ultra-Catholic Austrian prince. Anti-Semitism, an overwhelming political force of late nineteenth-century France, is reduced to a contingency: "Qu'au lieu de l'affaire Dreyfus il fût survenu une guerre avec l'Allemagne, le tour du kaléidoscope se fût produit dans un autre sens" (If instead of the Dreyfus case there had come a war with Germany, the pattern of the kaleidoscope would have taken a turn in the other direction; 1:517, 2:122).[4] The irony is, of course, that a war with Germany did come, and the kaleidoscope did turn in another direction, leaving the Baron de Charlus, a key figure in the world of the *Recherche,* suspect and marginalized because of his German heritage.

For Charlus himself, the real trouble with the Dreyfus affair is that it allowed people with dubious social credentials to win a place in society solely based on their anti-Dreyfusard stance (2:586, 3:393). And while his reasoning is quickly repudiated by the narrator as a matter of the inherent "frivolité" of the Guermanteses, the *Recherche* as a whole hides an even darker secret: nothing escapes the logic of frivolity. Marcel's conversations with his friend Robert Saint-Loup in the early days of the war confirm the novel's extraordinary ability to turn everything into a spectacle, to aestheticize every event and drain it of all inherent significance. For Saint-Loup the war was an exceptional affair in distinctly aesthetic terms. As Marcel reports, during a conversation about a recent zeppelin raid, "Il me demanda si j'avais bien vu, mais comme il m'eût parlé autrefois de quelque spectacle d'une grande beauté esthétique" (He went on to ask me if I had had a good view, very much as in the old days he might have questioned me about some spectacle of great aesthetic beauty; 4:337, 6:98). This time, Marcel finds nothing frivolous in Saint-Loup's comments, as their conversation moves from zeppelins to airplanes, and to the question of whether they are more beautiful taking off or landing.

The problem is not that the members of the upper echelons of the Parisian high society interpret world-historical events in accordance with the trivializing logic of fashionable salons. The problem is that, as far as the novel is concerned, they are right. Nothing in the *Recherche*—including a world war and a major ideological conflict—escapes this logic.

> Le dreyfusisme était maintenant intégré dans une série de choses respectables et habituelles. Quant à se demander ce qu'il valait en soi, personne n'y songeait, pas plus pour l'admettre maintenant qu'autrefois pour le condamner. Il n'était plus *shocking*. C'était tout ce qu'il fallait. À peine se rappelait-on qu'il l'avait été, comme on ne sait plus au bout de quelque temps si le père d'une jeune fille fut un voleur ou non. Au besoin, on peut dire: "Non, c'est du beau-frère, ou d'un homonyme que vous parlez, mais contre celui-là il n'y a jamais eu rien à dire." De même il y avait certainement eu dreyfusisme et dreyfusisme, et celui qui allait chez la duchesse de Montmorency et faisait passer la loi de trois ans ne pouvait être mauvais. En tout cas, à tout péché miséricorde. Cet oubli qui était octroyé au dreyfusisme l'était a fortiori aux dreyfusards. Il n'y avait plus qu'eux, du reste, dans la politique, puisque tous à un moment l'avaient été s'ils voulaient être du Gouvernement, même ceux qui représentaient le contraire de ce que le dreyfusisme, dans sa choquante nouveauté, avait incarné (au temps où Saint-Loup était sur une mauvaise pente): l'antipatriotisme, l'irréligion, l'anarchie, etc. (4:305–6)

> (Dreyfusism was now integrated in a scheme of respectable and familiar things. As for asking oneself whether it was intrinsically good or bad, the idea no more entered anybody's head, now when it was accepted, than in the past when it was condemned. It was no longer *shocking* and that was all that mattered. People hardly remembered that it had once been thought so, just as, when a certain time has elapsed, they no longer know whether a girl's father was a thief or not. One can always say, if the subject crops up: "No, it's the brother-in-law, or somebody of the same name, that you were thinking of. There has never been a breath of scandal around her father." In the same way, there had undeniably been Dreyfusism and Dreyfusism and a man who was received by the Duchesse de Montmorency's and was helping to pass the three years law could not be bad. And then, as the saying goes, no sin but should find mercy. If Dreyfusism was afforded an amnesty,

so, *a fortiori*, were Dreyfusards, In fact, there no longer were Dreyfusards in politics, since at one moment every politician had been one if he wanted to belong to the government, even those who represented the contrary of what at the time of its shocking novelty—the time when Saint-Loup had been getting into bad ways—Dreyfusism had incarnated: anti-patriotism, irreligion, anarchy, etc.) (6:53–54)

To a degree, this change is a matter of political opportunism: now that Dreyfusism has become not just acceptable but a necessary condition of political success, everyone is suddenly a Dreyfusard. But beyond ideological mimicry lies the inescapable reality of forgetting: individual political allegiances, and even the entire structure of the political field, belong to the large collection of facts that no one but the narrator remembers. Once again, Proust has managed to transform a sociopolitical problem into an existential predicament: like everything else, crucial political events are falling to the destructive effects of time. In the same way that people have forgotten who was who in the salons of the 1890s, they have also forgotten that Dreyfusism was ever an issue. In the *Recherche,* history is condemned either to aestheticization or to oblivion.

Proust's refusal to perform a historical analysis of the Dreyfus case and the Great War is matched only by his refusal to engage economic reality. If history is present but trivialized, economics seems to be fully obliterated from the world of the *Recherche.* As Antoine Compagnon observes, "Proust is among the most vehement of writers in his denials of history. The very chronology of his novel is incoherent, and history is barely present in it, and then only indirectly, in bits and pieces. . . . For this reason any 'documentary' or sociological reading of the *Recherche* along the lines of Balzac's *Comédie humaine* is spurious."[5] Compagnon identifies a vital but often overlooked distinction: despite an undeniable obsession with social distinction and class status, the *Recherche* refuses to explore the economic conditions that make the privileged world of the Faubourg Saint-Germain possible.

Like Lucien de Rubempré and Eugène de Rastignac before him, Proust's narrator seeks to penetrate the elite salons and approach the grand ladies of Parisian aristocracy. Unlike *Illusions perdues* and *Le Père Goriot,* however, the *Recherche* has nothing to tell us about the cost of such conquests. In Proust, the kind of information that an earlier generation of realists gave away willingly, and in great quantities, must be extracted with utmost hermeneutic effort and the use of enhanced interrogation techniques.[6] In the fictional worlds of Balzac and Flaubert there is no reason to speculate about the sources of wealth. The reader is told, to the last franc, how much money a hero makes, and where the money is coming from. In *Illusions perdues* David Séchard needs to pay thirty thousand francs for his father's business. Lucien de Rubempré takes a thousand francs with him from Angouleme to Paris, only to realize that the money will last no more than a week, because, as he tells his sister in a letter, the simplest dinner in a fashionable restaurant costs fifty francs, while a reputable tailor never charges under a hundred. Goriot used to earn some sixty thousand livres a year, only to end up paying forty-five francs for room and board at Mme Vauquer's, while the property of Rastignac's family brings three thousand francs a year. In *L'Éducation sentimentale,* Arnoux buys Pellerin's paintings for a bargain price, only to resell them for two thousand francs. Later, Frédéric buys two thousand shares of Nord and, due to the rise of their value, manages to earn some thirty thousand francs, only to lose another sixty thousand when the shares plummet.

In Proust, while certain broad structural relations can be easily reconstructed, mechanisms of monetary exchange are oblique, and money itself is nowhere to be found in the novel. How much does it cost to throw a party in Paris? Or to take a trip to Venice? What is the extent and what are the sources of Marcel's family wealth? While not everything is unknown—for instance, the high society begins to take notice of young Gilberte Swann once she has inherited eighty million francs from Swann's uncle (3:144; 2:197)—for the most part the sources and the movements of money are difficult to trace. The statistics is implacable: *Illusions perdues* explicitly mentions *francs* just under 500 times in about 250,000 words (approximately 18 occurrences per 10,000 words) and in *Le Père Goriot* the same reference appears around 140 times in just under 100,000 words (14 per 10,000 words). In both Stendhal's *Le Rouge et le Noir* and Flaubert's *L'Éducation sentimentale* the rate of occurrence is around 7 per

10,000 words. In the *Recherche,* however, francs are mentioned just over 110 times in its 1,300,000 words. The rate of occurrence is slightly lower than 1 per 10,000 words, or approximately 20 times lower than the rate of occurrence in *Illusions Perdues.*[7] Proust's novel shows no interest in financial operations.

Having trivialized the workings of ideology, and having obscured the economic basis of social relations, Proust can proceed with the aestheticization of the aristocracy. The comparison with Balzac is, again, striking. For Lucien de Rubempré in *Illusions perdues,* the opera is the site of his first and unsuccessful Parisian initiation. Emerging on the social scene of the capital, both Lucien and Louise de Bargeton are objects of intense scrutiny, "comme deux bêtes curieuses" (as if they had been animals of some strange species; 196, 178). Dressed atrociously (and with manners to match) Lucien, of course, doesn't stand a chance of being accepted in this society. However, even as he begins to notice the first signs of rejection, ignored by the socialites to whom he was introduced a moment ago, he is at once fascinated with this world and determined to conquer it:

> Lucien vint se replacer au coin de sa loge et demeura, pendant le reste de la représentation, absorbé tour à tour par le pompeux spectacle du ballet du cinquième acte, si célèbre par son *Enfer,* par l'aspect de la salle dans laquelle son regard alla de loge en loge, et par ses propres réflexions qui furent profondes en présence de la société parisienne.—Voilà donc mon royaume! se dit-il, voilà le monde que je dois dompter. (197)

> (Lucien ensconced himself in the corner of the box, and stayed there for the rest of the performance, absorbed now by the ornate spectacle of the fifth act of the ballet, the famous *Inferno* scene, now with the green opera house itself, his eyes travelling from box to box, now by his own reflections; the sight of Paris society has stirred him to the depths.
> "This is my kingdom," he thought to himself. "This is the world I must conquer.") (185)

Confronted with the dual spectacle of the ballet and the boxes of socialites, Lucien is clearly attracted to the latter, and he is not alone in such preferences. In the *Recherche,* Marcel shares the same fascination: "Les gens du monde étaient dans leurs loges (derrière le balcon en terrasse), comme dans de petits salons suspendus dont une cloison eût été enlevée" (Society people sat in their boxes (behind the tiered circle) as in so many little suspended drawing-rooms, the fourth walls of which had been removed; 2:339, 3:43). He enters the opera hoping to witness "la vie inimaginable" (the unimaginable life; 2:337, 3:41) of Mme de Guermantes, and to step into the "royaume mythologique des nymphes des eaux" (the mythological kingdom of the water-nymphs; 2:338, 3:41) and glimpse "les blanches déités" (the white deities; 2:339, 3:44) occupying the boxes. Like Lucien, who is more interested in the Marquise d'Espard than in the events on the stage, Proust's narrator focuses on the Princess de Guermantes:

> Cependant, parce que l'acte de *Phèdre* que jouait la Berma allait commencer, la princesse vint sur le devant de la baignoire; alors, comme si elle-même était une apparition de théâtre, dans la zone différente de lumière qu'elle traversa, je vis changer non seulement la couleur mais la matière de ses parures. Et dans la baignoire asséchée, émergée, qui n'appartenait plus au monde des eaux, la princesse cessant d'être une néréide apparut enturbannée de blanc et de bleu comme quelque merveilleuse tragédienne costumée en Zaïre ou peut-être en Orosmane. (2:343)

> (But now, because the act of *Phèdre* in which Berma was playing was due to start, the Princess came to the front of the box; whereupon, as if she herself were a theatrical apparition, in the different zone of light which she traversed, I saw not only the colour but the material of her adornments change. And in the box, now drained dry, emergent, no longer a part of the watery realm, the Princess, ceasing to be a nereid, appeared turbanned in white and blue like some marvelous tragic actress dressed for the part of Zaïre, or perhaps of Orosmane.) (3:49)

But if both Lucien and Marcel are attracted to the society women, they look upon them with very different eyes and very different desires. As we have seen in chapter 1, the common (although by no means unproblematized) assumption of *La Comédie humaine* is that the path to social success leads through the salon of one of the great ladies of Parisian aristocracy. In the *Recherche,* this central Balzacian claim, reiterated in various ways in *Le Père Goriot* and *Illusions perdues,* is articulated by Charlus as a platitude that should be dismissed: "Ma belle-soeur est une femme charmante qui s'imagine être encore au temps des romans de Balzac où les femmes influaient sur la politique" (My sister-in-law is an agreeable woman who imagines that we are still living in the days of Balzac's novels, when women had an influence on politics; 2:589, 3:397). Charlus's comment marks the decisive point at which the *Recherche* disowns the Balzacian universe it has colonized. In Balzac, Lucien's first naïve showing at the opera is quickly followed by attempts to unearth the economic and political forces that shape the world of Parisian aristocracy. The *Recherche* adopts a radically different attitude: whereas *La Comédie humaine* struggles to chart the socioeconomic reality of Restoration France, Proust persistently approaches the world of aristocracy as an object of aesthetic interest. "Ma curiosité historique," Marcel admits as he is listening to the genealogies of the great families of French nobility, "était faible en comparaison du plaisir esthétique" (My historical curiosity was faint in comparison with my aesthetic pleasure; 2:831, 3:743). Whereas Lucien quickly adopts the language of conquest, threatening to subjugate the kingdom he has just discovered, Marcel seems to relish the role of the captivated observer. Aristocracy is something to be closely watched and meticulously studied, an object of longing and fascination, relentlessly pursued by the narrator's aestheticizing gaze.[8] Rather than trying to conquer *le beau monde,* in Proust the thoroughly passivized bildungsroman hero takes on the task of exploring the forms of knowledge and pleasure that can be generated by observing the social universe as a quasi-aesthetic object.

## Exoticism and the Spectacle of Aristocracy

Proust's reference to the aesthetic should be taken in the strong sense of the word—not as a mere celebration of beauty, but as a form of cognitive engagement with the world defined by the distinct forms of pleasure it affords.⁹ In the *Recherche,* the narrator is vitally preoccupied with the possibility of engaging the social world as an object whose observable characteristics constitute a source of distinct aesthetic gratification.¹⁰ This type of gratification is derived from two contradictory sources. On the one hand, he strives to reap the aesthetic and cognitive benefits implicit in the encounter with the unfamiliar, exotic, seemingly incomprehensible world of aristocracy. On the other, he derives pleasure from the mental effort invested in understanding the logic of this unfamiliar universe.

The first impulse—to revel in the unassimilable otherness of the unfamiliar—was shared by some unlikely bedfellows at the time when Proust was writing: Max Weber in "Science as a Vocation" (1917), Victor Shklovsky in "Art as Device" (1917), and Victor Segalen in his unfinished *Essay on Exoticism* (1904–18) all express a nostalgia for otherness. While Weber bemoans the "disenchantment of the world" following the triumph of scientific rationalism,¹¹ Shklovsky hails the power of art to impose the sense of unfamiliarity on the seemingly familiar, thus breaking the perilous spell of automatized perception: "Automatization," he wrote, "eats away at things, at clothes, at furniture, at our wives, and at our fear of war."¹² Finally, like Shklovsky's theory of estrangement, Segalen's work on exoticism is an attempt to describe the capacity to recognize the otherness of what appears nearer and more familiar. Segalen describes the "sensation of Exoticism, which is nothing other than the notion of difference, the perception of Diversity, the knowledge that something is other than one's self; and Exoticism's power is nothing other than the ability to conceive otherwise." And it is precisely because of this ability that exoticism "will revitalize and beautify everything."¹³

Fragmentary and underdeveloped, Segalen's exoticist aesthetics nonetheless captures a vital ambition of the *Recherche,* a text deeply invested in the project of exoticizing everything it touches. When Proust's narrator describes the inhabitants of the world of the *Recherche* as mysterious, strange, and enchanted mythological creatures, he acts as if he is following Segalen's rally to celebrate "all that until now was called foreign, strange, unexpected, surprising, mysterious, amorous, superhuman, heroic, and even divine, everything that is Other" (67). Such rhetoric is successively used to describe, first, Swann, whose name for Marcel quickly becomes "presque mythologique" (almost mythological; 1:142, 1:202); second, Gilberte, whom he describes as an "animal fabuleux" (fabulous animal; 1:554, 2:189); and, finally, Albertine and her friends, who are described as "trois immortelles accoudées au nuage" (like three immortals leaning against the clouds; 3:675, 5:220). And even before the Guermanteses became the rulers of a mythical kingdom, Marcel has already visited the mysterious domain "où Swann et sa femme menaient leur vie surnaturelle" (in which Swann and his wife led their supernatural existence; 1:499, 2:111). In the vocabulary of the *Recherche*, "mythological" stands for unfamiliar and fascinating objects that induce a particular kind of aesthetic pleasure, partly intellectual and partly sensual.

Of course, the problem is that the world of the *Recherche* is suffering from the very disease variously described by Weber, Shklovsky, and Segalen, the malaise of disenchantment: only distant and unfamiliar objects are truly exotic. This principle is articulated very early in the novel in relation to Marcel's aunt Léonie, known for her obsessive spying on all that goes on at Combray:

> À Combray, une personne "qu'on ne connaissait point" était un être aussi peu croyable qu'un dieu de la mythologie, et de fait on ne se souvenait pas que, chaque fois que s'était produite, dans la rue de Saint-Esprit ou sur la place, une de ces apparitions stupéfiantes, des recherches bien conduites n'eussent pas fini par réduire le personnage fabuleux aux proportions d'une "personne qu'on connaissait," soit personnellement, soit abstraitement, dans son état civil, en tant qu'ayant tel degré de parenté avec des gens de Combray. (1:56–57)

> (At Combray a person whom one "didn't know from Adam" was as incredible a being as any mythological deity, and indeed no one could remember, on the various occasions when one of these startling apparitions had occurred in the Rue du Saint-Esprit or in the Square, exhaustive inquiries ever having failed to reduce the fabulous monster to the proportions of a person whom one "did know," either personally or in the abstract, in his or her civil status as being more or less closely related to some family in Combray.) (1:77–78)

This corrosive process of diminishment, the transformation of semi-mythical figures into mere humans, spreads through the novel like an infection. At the end of *À l'ombre des jeunes filles en fleurs,* Albertine and her friends, the objects of Marcel's frantic observation, have lost all of their magical aura, precisely because he has managed to approach them: "Les géographes, les archéologues nous conduisent bien dans l'île de Calypso, exhument bien le palais de Minos. Seulement Calypso n'est plus qu'une femme, Minos qu'un roi sans rien de divin" (Geographers or archaeologists may conduct us over Calypso's island, may excavate the Palace of Minos. Only Calypso becomes then a mere woman, Minos a mere king with no semblance of divinity; 1:949, 2:723). This too is the fate of Mme de Guermantes. Having discovered in her salon a reality much more common than he had hoped, Marcel compares himself to a traveler who ventured to explore the remote areas of Central America and North Africa, hoping to encounter unknown, exotic forms of life, only to find out that their inhabitants are reading Voltaire's tragedies (2:814–15, 3:720).

This pervasive process through which mythical beings are diminished should not, however, be confused with mere disillusionment: the loss of the mythical aura is not the function of the objects observed but an inescapable feature of our cognitive encounter with the world.[14] As Shklovsky wrote, "After being perceived several times, objects acquire the status of 'recognition.' An object appears before us. We know it's there but we don't see it, and, for that reason, we can say nothing about it."[15] The mythical aura surrounding the Guermanteses disappears not simply because Marcel gradually manages to recognize the pettiness and triviality that defines the life of the aristocracy, but because no object can escape this fate. It also disappears because of an inherent paradox of Proustian aesthetics. The novel draws pleasure from two contradictory sources: from relentlessly othering the objects of Marcel's observation, and also from knowing them. As Monroe Beardsley puts it, "One of the central components in art experience must be the experience of discovery, of insight into connections and organizations—the elation that comes from the apparent opening up of intelligibility" (292). To connect the histories of the noble families and their names, to know who is who in the Parisian high society, who is an insider and who is not, to understand the logic and the intricate laws of salon etiquette—all these forms of knowledge produce aesthetic pleasure, which arises from what Beardsley describes as "the excitement of meeting a cognitive challenge, of flexing one's powers to make *intelligible*" (292).[16] The difficulty, however, is that the very process of inquiry that makes the Guermanteses intelligible also depletes their capacity to serve as unfamiliar objects of aesthetic fascination. Marcel hence puts a particularly difficult burden on the world of the Guermanteses, which he wants to make simultaneously enchanted and intelligible.

One solution that the *Recherche* offers for this problem is to look for new sources of fascination. No sooner has Marcel declared his disappointment with the Duchess, when Monsieur de Charlus brings to his attention the existence of an even more mysterious being, the Princess de Guermantes: "La princesse de Guermantes est supérieure à la duchesse de Guermantes?—Oh! cela n'a pas de rapport" (Is the Princesse de Guermantes superior to the Duchesse de Guermantes?—Oh! There's no comparison; 2:853, 3:775). In the *Recherche,* behind every secret and every fascination lurks another one.

The novel, however, offers a more substantial response to the challenge of disenchantment by mobilizing disciplinary formations that could plausibly unite the two types of pleasure. Proust turns to zoology and botany as disciplines that seem to be able to simultaneously maintain the sense of wonder in the face of their subject and offer the pleasure derived from understanding the rules that govern the worlds they describe. Both disciplines take pride in their commitment to meticulous observation. As Darwin writes in one of his autobiographical pieces, "I think that I am superior to the common run of men in noticing things which easily escape attention and in observing them carefully."[17] When seen through the zoological lens, the inhabitants of Faubourg St. Germain can maintain their status as exotic creatures while simultaneously being subjected to a meticulous scientific inquiry. Taking up the role of the zoologist, Marcel first places the Marquis de Palanacy into an aquarium (2:343, 3:48), and then repeats the same gesture with the socialites in Balbec, where the hotel dining room devenait comme un immense et merveilleux aquarium devant la paroi de verre duquel la population ouvrière de Balbec, les pêcheurs et aussi les familles de petits bourgeois, invisibles dans l'ombre, s'écrasaient au vitrage pour apercevoir, lentement balancée dans des remous d'or, la vie luxueuse de ces gens, aussi extraordinaire pour les pauvres que celle de poissons et de mollusques étranges (une grande question sociale, de savoir si la paroi de verre protègera toujours le festin des bêtes merveilleuses et si les gens obscurs qui regardent avidement dans la nuit ne viendront pas les cueillir dans leur aquarium et les manger). (2:41–42)

(became as it were an immense and wonderful aquarium against whose glass wall the working population of Balbec, the fishermen and also the tradesmen's families, clustering invisibly in the outer darkness, pressed their faces to watch the luxurious life of its occupants gently floating upon the golden eddies within, a thing as extraordinary to the poor as the life of strange fishes or molluscs (an important social question, this: whether the glass wall will always protect the banquets of these weird and wonderful creatures, or whether the obscure folk who watch them hungrily out of the night will not break in some day to gather them from their aquarium and devour them).) (2:353–54)

And having transformed the Balbec socialites into fish—the "social question" is articulated en passant and forgotten—he goes on to observe Robert de Saint-Loup with "la curiosité et l'admiration moitié mondaine, moitié zoologique" (curiosity and wonder, half social and half zoological; 4:281–82, 6:19), imagining his friend as a caged bird trapped in the Jardin des Plantes. Finally, in more adventurous moments, Proust will turn his narrator from an observer of caged animals into a bona fide wildlife observer, stalking his beasts in their natural habitat, or into an explorer of distant lands, "à la recherche d'habitants quelconques, qui seraient peut-être des anthropophages" (in search of possible inhabitants who might turn out to be cannibals; 3:10, 4:11). As I show in the next section, Marcel's use of scientific discourse as a tool to exoticize and defamiliarize the world he observes will culminate in his complex study of inversion.

## Beyond Inversion

The dialectic of exploration and defamiliarization culminates in Proust's description of the world of Sodom, whose inhabitants simultaneously serve as examples of exotic wildlife and as a persistent source of intellectual fascination. As the Baron de Charlus describes it about halfway through the novel, this "freemasonry of men" constitutes a "partie réprouvée de la collectivité humaine, mais partie importante, soupçonnée là où elle n'est pas étalée, insolente, impunie là où elle n'est pas devinée; comptant des adhérents partout, dans le peuple, dans l'armée, dans le temple, au bagne, sur le trône" (reprobate section of the human collectivity, but an important one, suspected where it does not exist, flaunting itself, insolent and immune, where its existence is never guessed; numbering its adherents everywhere, among the people, in the army, in the church, in prison, on the throne; 3:16, 4:23–24). This parallel universe developed around the figure of the Baron is the most enduring source of cognitive pleasure in Proust: not only does it invite careful observation and the mastery of secret codes, but, because it can never be fully explored, the freemasonry of men offers Marcel an endless repository of secrets to be discovered. What is at stake is nothing short of a cognitive revolution.

At the beginning of *Sodome et Gomorrhe,* in one of the *Recherche*'s most significant voyeuristic scenes, a queer pantomime literally displaces the Guermanteses as an object of fascination. Waiting for the Duke and the Duchess de Guermantes to appear, the narrator stakes out their courtyard, until he inadvertently stumbles on a courtship ritual between Charlus and Jupien. The process of observation is extremely meticulous, as the narrator, mimicking military tactics, changes his position repeatedly in order to see better and in order not to be seen, moving from the top of the house to the staircase, traversing the courtyard, until he finds himself eavesdropping against the wall of a shop that the couple entered: "D'après ce que j'entendis les premiers temps dans celle de Jupien et qui ne furent que des sons inarticulés, je suppose que peu de paroles furent prononcées" (From what I heard at first in Jupien's quarters, which was only a series of inarticulate sounds, I imagine that few words had been exchanged; 3:11, 4:12). The experience proves sufficient to revolutionize Marcel's understanding of the world: "Dès le début de cette scène, une révolution, pour mes yeux dessillés, s'était opérée en M. de Charlus, aussi complète, aussi immédiate que s'il avait été touché par une baguette magique. Jusque-là, parce que je n'avais pas compris, je n'avais pas vu" (From the beginning of this scene my eyes were opened by a revolutionary change in M. de Charlus, as complete and as immediate as if he had been touched by a magic wand. Until then, because I had not understood, I had not seen; 3:15, my translation, cf. 4:17). Almost melodramatic in tone, moved to the privileged position of the beginning of *Sodome et Gomorrhe,* this revelation is announced as "si importante en elle-même que j'ai jusqu'ici, jusqu'au moment de pouvoir lui donner la place et l'étendue voulues, différé de la rapporter" (in itself so important that I have until now, until the moment when I could give it the prominence and treat it with the fullness that it demanded, postponed giving any account of it; 3:3, 4;1). For the narrator, the encounter between Charlus and Jupien is a uniquely powerful source of cognitive pleasure, a paradigmatic example of what Beardsley describes as the experience of *active discovery:* "A keyed-up state amounting to exhilaration in seeing connections between precepts and between meanings, a sense (which may be illusory) of intelligibility" (288–89).

However, while Proust's attempt to turn a queer underworld into one of the key sources of cognitive pleasure in the novel is compatible with the widespread popular assumption that men who desire men constituted "a large class beneath the surface of society," the *Recherche*'s other aestheticizing tendency—namely, to portray inverts as exotic and fascinating, yet entirely natural creatures—flies in the face of the dominant view of inversion as a clearly pathological state.[18] The figure of the invert thus constitutes a peculiar epistemic challenge for Proust: while to a large extent the portrayal of the invert in the *Recherche* remains in the clutches of the emerging science of sexuality and its pathologizing view of the subject, the novel also works to naturalize and legitimize same-sex desire, simultaneously appropriating and reworking the widespread medical assumptions about inversion.

Not only in insistent descriptions of inverts as men-women, but also in the links he casually establishes between inversion, neurosis, neurasthenia, and artistic temperament, the narrator of the *Recherche* constantly reveals his debts to the medical ideas developed throughout the later part of the nineteenth century.[19] In the context of late nineteenth-century medical discourse, the concept of inversion fused the question of sexual desire, secondary sex characteristics, and gender identity. The majority of influential accounts construed the invert not as a man desiring men, but as a figure whose erotic desires and visible effeminacy betray the woman within: deep down, and often on the surface, men who wanted men were really women.[20] Such constructions of the invert followed the general tendency of psychiatric literature to link undesirable sexual practices (including homosexuality, masturbation, and fetishism), neurological disorders, temperament, and physical characteristics, all of which were often read as signs of hereditary degeneration. A particularly strong link was routinely established between a variety of unconventional sexual practices and neurasthenia, understood as a general sense of physical and mental exhaustion.[21] As George Beard writes, "I am persuaded that a nervous constitution and excessive nervous susceptibility going on to debility, tend to induce the habit of 'mental masturbation,' as well as both natural and unnatural excess in sexual indulgence. The strong, the phlegmatic, the healthy, the well-balanced temperaments—those who live outdoors and work with the muscle more than with the mind—are not tormented with sexual desire to the same degree or in the same way as the hysterical, the sensitive, the nervous—those who live indoors and use mind much and muscle very little."[22] The connection between homosexuality, neurasthenia, excessive sensitivity, and an overactive life of the mind repeatedly emerges among the inverts of the *Recherche*. The Baron de Charlus in particular serves as an embodiment of these interrelated characteristics: "Le style rapide, anxieux, charmant avec lequel M. de Charlus jouait le morceau schumannesque de la Sonate de Fauré, qui aurait pu discerner que ce style avait son correspondant—on n'ose dire sa cause—dans des parties toutes physiques, dans les défectuosités de M. de Charlus?" (Who would ever have detected that the rapid, nervous, charming style with which M. de Charlus played the Schumannesque passage of Fauré's sonata had its equivalent—one dare not say its cause—in elements entirely physical, in the Baron's nervous weaknesses?; 3:344, 4:479–80). The link between neurasthenia, artistic proclivities, and same-sex desire is further confirmed in Charlus's lover Charles Morel, a violinist, an invert, and a neurasthenic (3:699, 5:210), and in Andrée, one of Albertine's suspected lesbian lovers:

> Mais pour que j'aimasse vraiment Andrée, elle était trop intellectuelle, trop nerveuse, trop maladive, trop semblable à moi.... J'avais cru le premier jour voir sur la plage une maîtresse de coureur, enivrée de l'amour des sports, et Andrée me disait que si elle s'était mise à en faire, c'était sur l'ordre de son médecin pour soigner sa neurasthénie et ses troubles de nutrition, mais que ses meilleures heures étaient celles où elle traduisait un roman de George Eliot. (2:295)

> (But Andrée was too intellectual, too neurotic, too sickly, too like myself for me really to love her.... I had thought, that first day, that what I saw on the beach was the mistress of some racing cyclist, passionately interested in sport, and now Andrée told me that if she had taken it up, it was on orders from her doctor, to cure her neurasthenia, her digestive troubles, but that her happiest hours were those which she spent translating one of George Eliot's novels.) (2:714)

And yet, although the topoi of fin-de-siècle medical discourse maintain such a strong presence in the *Recherche,* scattered throughout the novel and concentrated in strategic locations like the beginning of *Sodome et Gomorrhe,* medicalization fails to impose itself as the exclusive explanatory model of same-sex desire. The vision of the invert as a talented neurotic that Proust emphasized in his correspondence fails to fulfill the insatiable aesthetic desires of the *Recherche*.[23] In order to turn it into the central enigma of the novel, Proust will have to reconceptualize it by invoking additional interpretative models that will allow him to build a composite and often contradictory portrait of inversion as a nervous defect, an alternative but nonpathological form of sexuality, a broad conspiracy that underlies the more transparent social networks, and an object of aesthetic appreciation.

Ironically, it is precisely through the most iconic image of fin-de-siècle medical discourse—that of the invert as a man-woman—that the project of medicalization is undermined in the *Recherche*. As we have seen, for Proust, as for many of the medical writers I have discussed, the invert is really a woman in a man's body, or, more precisely, a creature which "se rapproche trop de la femme pour pouvoir avoir des rapports utiles avec elle" (is too closely akin to woman to be capable of having any effective relations with her; 3:30–31, 3:629). Experts like Saint-Paul don't mince words when it comes to the distinctly pathological nature of this duality: "What happens in this case is what happens in all animal or vegetable species. This invert, born deformed, taking up a female form (if he is a man), or a masculine on (if he is a women), is, quite simply, a monstrosity."[24] But perhaps it is not quite that simple. Already in the mid-1860s Karl Heinrich Ulrichs has managed to conceptualize the apparently dual nature of the invert—his preferred term is *Urning*—in decisively nonpathological terms. Like so many subsequent writers, he treats the existence of homosexual desire as a result of a congenital coupling of male anatomy and female psychology. However, unlike the medical establishment, he describes this coupling not as a monstrosity, but as a complex yet natural psychosexual identity: "The Urning is not a man, but rather a kind of feminine being when it concerns not only his entire organism, but also his sexual feelings of love, his entire natural temperament, and his talents. The dominant characteristics are of femininity both in his behavior and in his body movements. These are the obvious manifestations of the feminine element that resides in him."[25] The presence of this "feminine element" is not a sign of a particular pathology—rather, of a wholly different ontological status of Urnings who constitute not a mere error of nature but "a third sex" (36). Consequently, the question of the normalcy of sexual drive is circumvented: "When I love the person I am naturally attracted to, I am not acting contrary to nature. When I, as an Urning, fall in love with a mature and handsome young man, I am not behaving contrary to nature" (36). The Urning is, quite simply, an entirely different kind of being.[26]

It is during the iconic encounter between Charlus and Jupien at the beginning of *Sodome et Gomorrhe* that the image of the invert as a neurotic gives way to a vision that approaches Ulrichs's. As he observes the scene, Marcel comments that Charlus "appartenait à la race de ces êtres, moins contradictoires qu'ils n'en ont l'air, dont l'idéal est viril, justement parce que leur tempérament est féminin, et qui sont dans la vie pareils, en apparence seulement, aux autres homes" (belonged to that race of beings, less paradoxical than they appear, whose ideal is manly precisely because their temperament is feminine, and who in ordinary life resemble other men in appearance only; 3:16, 4:19–20). Marcel's rhetoric, and in particular his use of the word *race* to describe inverts, suggests a movement away from the pathological classification of neurotic disorders and toward a taxonomy of biological varieties. Given that *race* in French corresponds both to *race* and to *breed* in English, there is a particularly strong connotation of common descent and common biological characteristics: like Ulrichs's urnings, Proust's inverts are a legitimate biological variation. Moreover, rather than a monstrosity, the invert is a strange, new, exotic form of life that circumvents familiar binaries.

The movement away from contemporary medical discourse is further emphasized by the fact that Marcel once again mobilizes zoology and botany. First, he transforms into a zoologist observing a mating ritual among birds (3:8, 4:8). Then, as he spies on Charlus and Jupien, he is fascinated by

> l'existence de la sous-variété d'invertis destinée à assurer les plaisirs de l'amour à l'inverti devenant vieux: les hommes qui sont attirés non par tous les hommes, mais—par un phénomène de correspondance et d'harmonie comparable à ceux qui règlent la fécondation des fleurs hétérostylées trimorphes, comme le *Lythrum salicoria* [sic]—seulement par les hommes beaucoup plus âgés qu'eux. De cette sous-variété, Jupien venait de m'offrir un exemple, moins saisissant pourtant que d'autres que tout herborisateur humain, tout botaniste moral, pourra observer, malgré leur rareté, et qui leur présentera un frêle jeune homme qui attendait les avances d'un robuste et bedonnant quinquagénaire, restant aussi indifférent aux avances des autres jeunes gens que restent stériles les fleurs hermaphrodites à court

style de la *Primula veris* tant qu'elles ne sont fécondées que par d'autres *Primula veris* à court style aussi, tandis qu'elles accueillent avec joie le pollen des *Primula veris* à long style. (3:30)

(the existence of the subvariety of inverts destined to guarantee the pleasures of love to the invert who is growing old: men who are attracted not by all other men, but—by a phenomenon of correspondence and harmony similar to those that govern the fertilisation of heterostyle trimorphous flowers like the *lythrum salicaria*—only by men considerably older than themselves. Of this subvariety Jupien had just furnished me with an example, one less striking however than certain others which every human herbalist, every moral botanist, will be able to observe in spite of their rarity, and which will show them a frail young man awaiting the advances of a robust and paunchy quinquagenarian, and remaining as indifferent to those of other young men as the hermaphrodite flowers of the short-styled *primula veris* remain sterile so long as they are fertilised only by other *primulae veris* of short style also, whereas they welcome with joy the pollen of the *primula veris* with the long style.) (4:39)

The main advantage of botany was that it offered a vastly different understanding of sexuality from the emerging medical study of inversion that espoused an essentially heteronormative view of sexuality: proper sex distinctions, accompanied by a sexual drive directed at the opposite sex constituted the standard of normalcy against which pathological deviations were measured. Yet while medical science was in the business of classifying pathological states, botany was in the business of providing a taxonomy of biological types. Whereas for a human to have both male and female genitals, or to have male genitals and, as it was commonly assumed about inverts, a feminine psyche, was seen as a sign of severe malformation, flowers that have both male and female genitals are by definition *perfect*. To restate the basic facts of plant reproductive morphology, not only is hermaphroditism the most widespread form of plant sexuality, but beyond the simple distinction between hermaphrodite and unisexual flowers, one can further distinguish between plants with all hermaphrodite flowers, plants with male and female flowers, with male and hermaphrodite, female and hermaphrodite, only male, only female, and finally male, female, and hermaphrodite flowers on the same plants. Thus emerges a plethora of reproductive strategies, some more complex or more cunning than others, but all natural, and delightfully so. From such a perspective, Jupien, with his attraction to older inverts, becomes not an instance of a particular pathology, but, rather, is classified in accordance with his taxonomical rank, as he belongs to a particular "subvariety" of inverts.

It matters very little that homosexual behavior in humans serves no reproductive purpose. As Barry McCrea points out, "The use of the botanical metaphor to describe a gay assignation naturalizes biologically sterile conjunctions as a legitimate template of creation."[27] Besides, the medical discourse of the late nineteenth century had already blurred the line between anatomical and psychological, and Ulrichs has offered an essentialist justification of male homosexuality. Even if the function of male homosexuality is not reproductive, it is nonetheless perfectly natural, and if it is natural, then it can serve as an object of the botanist's gaze. For the botanist, even more than the zoologist, is the quintessential benevolent observer of nature's marvels: "Botany,—the science of vegetable kingdom, is one of the most attractive, most useful, and most extensive departments of human knowledge. It is, above every other, the science of beauty. There are few plants which are not beautiful, considered as separate individuals, and in all parts of their individual organization; and there is a beauty in the grouping of plants, whether as grouped by nature, or by skillful art, to which there is nothing equal in that of any of the other productions of nature."[28] As numerous popular introductions to botany demonstrate, the discipline's self-justification tends to confound the project of scientific nomenclature and the spiritual benefits of disinterested observation: "No study is better calculated than that of plants to sharpen the powers of observation in the minds of youth, and to lead to methodical habits and accurate discrimination. There is, moreover, nothing repulsive in plants, but their beauty at once attracts attention; and as they may be found everywhere and at all seasons of the year, their study will afford an endless source of interest, and add increasing pleasure to our daily walks."[29] Marcel couldn't agree more: "Dès que j'eus considéré cette rencontre de ce point de vue, tout m'y sembla empreint de beauté" (As soon as I considered the encounter from this [botanical] point of view, everything about it seemed to me instinct with beauty; 3:29, 4:38). The narrator's view powerfully expresses the duality in the perception of botany as a discipline that owes as much to Rousseau's *Reveries of a Solitary Walker* (1776–78) as it does to Linnaeus's *Systema Naturae* (1735), and that is always on the verge of slipping into aesthetic contemplation.[30]

Proust's use of botany and zoology differs fundamentally from realist and naturalist attempts to appropriate scientific discourses.[31] When Balzac invokes zoology in his preface to *La Comédie humaine,* he does so under the assumption that bringing the resources of an exemplary natural science to bear upon the analysis of human society will bolster the quasi-scientific credentials of his own project: "Social species have always existed, and will always exist, just as there are zoological species. If Buffon could produce a magnificent work by attempting to represent in a book the whole realm of zoology, was there not room for a work of the same kind on society?"[32] As with so many other aspects of the Balzacian project, Proust simultaneously appropriates and thoroughly transforms Balzac's scientific ambitions. The method of "moral botany" with which he approaches the courtship of Charlus and Jupien displaces not only the inherent moralism of the medical discourse—after all, flowers cannot serve as objects of moral judgment—but also the instrumentality of Balzacian knowledge that has traditionally served to aid the hero's rise through the ranks of high society. The sciences of the *Recherche* are simultaneously tools of classification and defamiliarization: they enable the social universe to function as a dual source of aesthetic pleasure, an object whose structure can be glimpsed and whose various constituent elements can be classified, but that nonetheless can never be fully assimilated into the realm of the familiar.

## From Pure Judgment to Pure Speculation

Yet even the *Recherche* cannot turn everything into a source of joyous wonder. If male homosexuality has offered Proust an ideal mechanism for the production of otherness, the reality of lesbianism inverts this principle, because it finally offers a form of knowledge that resists aestheticization. While male homosexuality is exempt from ethical judgments and is referred to as a "vice" only with qualifications, when speaking about lesbianism Marcel confesses to "le profond dégoût que m'inspiraient les femmes atteintes du même vice" (the profound disgust I felt for women tainted with that vice; 2:832, 4:314)—"les plus vicieuses" (the most depraved; 2:803, 4:273) women, as he puts it elsewhere.[33] The asymmetry is simultaneously emotional and ethical. Marcel's initial encounters with Albertine, like his early encounters with Swann and the Guermanteses, are marked by the sense of wonder: Albertine and her friends first emerge as enchanted beings. As the narrator comments toward the end of *À l'ombre des jeunes filles en fleurs,* "Devant elles, je n'étais pas encore blasé par l'habitude, j'avais la faculté de les voir, autant dire d'éprouver un étonnement profond chaque fois que je me retrouvais en leur presence" (My perception of them was not yet dulled by familiarity, I still had the faculty of seeing them, that is to say of feeling a profound astonishment every time that I found myself in their presence; 2:269, 2:677). Very soon, however, it becomes apparent that Albertine belongs to an epistemic regime of her own, separate from the rest of the novel: instead of mere disenchantment, what follows is a slip into paranoid speculation.

The word *hypothesis* ("hypothèse") appears on sixty-five occasions in the *Recherche*. Nearly forty of those instances refer to Albertine and "la petite bande" of girls, and thirty instances are concentrated in *La Prisonnière* and *Albertine disparue*. In contrast, during Marcel's study of inversion in *Sodome et Gomorrhe,* hypothesizing plays no role whatsoever. The only other context in which the word *hypothesis* systematically appears is Swann's affair with Odette. This linguistic cue points to a unique exploratory mechanism reserved for Albertine. From her first appearance in *À l'ombre des jeunes filles en fleurs,* the same circular movement persists: Marcel observes, constructs hypotheses, examines their validity, seeks to produce a conclusive interpretation, and, once he fails, repeats the process. As he first observes the group of young girls whose names he still doesn't know, he struggles to determine their social standing and their proclivities and repeatedly refuses to settle for a simple interpretation.

First, he notes that one of them wears a modest hooded cape, but instead of concluding that the girl is poor, he insists that things are not what they seem and constructs an elaborate explanation of her appearance: her exceptionally modest attire suggests that the girl belongs to a family so high in the social hierarchy that its members are fully indifferent to the impression they may be making. However, Marcel quickly backtracks:

> Abandonnant l'hypothèse que la pèlerine de sa camarade m'avait fait échafauder, je conclus plutôt que toutes ces filles appartenaient à la population qui fréquente les vélodromes, et devaient être les très jeunes maîtresses de coureurs cyclistes. En tous cas, dans aucune de mes suppositions, ne figurait celle qu'elles eussent pu être vertueuses. (2:150)

> (Abandoning the hypothesis which her friend's hooded cape had prompted me to formulate, I concluded instead that all these girls belonged to the population which frequents the velodromes, and must be the very juvenile mistresses of racing cyclists. In any event, none of my suppositions embraced the possibility of their being virtuous.) (2:509)

In the early stages this hypothesizing largely resembles Marcel's attempts to ascertain the social identity of various other characters that fascinate him. However, as his relationship with Albertine develops, Marcel's hypothesizing escalates until it reaches what Leo Bersani accurately describes as "a compulsive intellectual investigation."[34] This pattern extends so far that it is perhaps justified to appeal to the common clinical understanding of compulsion as a repetitive behavior exercised in order to relieve anxiety, but that paradoxically feeds obsessive thoughts instead of relieving them: mechanisms of self-assurance are also mechanisms that reinvigorate doubt, for one wouldn't be checking if one were sure all is well.

Albertine's lesbianism constitutes the fixation that turns Marcel's hypothesizing into a self-sustaining machinery. Because lesbianism has the status of an obsessive thought in the novel, the suspicion can never be averted, despite assurances. For the same reason, however, Albertine's lesbianism cannot be conclusively proven despite all the evidence: obsessional thinking cannot tolerate certainty. This becomes particularly apparent as Marcel continues to produce contrary hypotheses about Albertine after her death (see, e.g., 4:121, 5:728). Even as he dispatches Aimé to meet with possible witnesses and participants in Albertine's lesbian adventures, even when these investigations yield not only indicative clues but unambiguous confessions, Marcel finds his way back to ambiguity. When Andrée, the cause of so many of his doubts, denies ever having an affair with Albertine, he can't bring himself to believe her. However, later on, when Andrée confesses everything, he is equally suspicious: "Mais qu'Andrée ne crût plus à la réalité d'Albertine pouvait avoir pour effet qu'elle ne redoutât plus (aussi bien que de trahir une vérité qu'elle avait promis de ne pas révéler) d'inventer un mensonge qui calomniait rétrospectivement sa prétendue complice" (But the fact that Andrée no longer believed in the reality of Albertine might mean that she no longer feared (any more than to betray a secret which she had promised not to reveal) to concoct a lie which retrospectively slandered her alleged accomplice; 4:182, 5:815).

These obsessional impulses suggest that in the *Recherche* the social world and the world of personal desires elicit fundamentally different responses from the narrator. They may occupy the same fictional universe, but in some ways they belong to different novels. A latecomer into the world of the *Recherche,* Albertine begins to take shape as a character only in 1914, the last significant addition to the novel.[35] Before her appearance, *Du côté de chez Swann* was already published in 1913, and two further volumes, *Le Côté de Guermantes* and *Le Temps retrouvé,* were planned for the following year.[36] In a word, Albertine's narrative had its own genesis, separate from the rest of the novel, and separate from the theme of inversion that was there from about 1909.

What this suggests is a unique bifurcation in the structure of the bildungsroman. Traditionally, the hero's erotic desires and the dynamics of socialization have been intertwined. In Balzac, Lucien de Rubempré's social conquest is inseparable from his infatuation with Louise de Bargeton, and the same could be said of Stendhal's Julien Sorel and his relationship with Mme de Rênal and Mathilde de la Mole. Albertine is, quite literally, a different story, integrated into the already developed project of the *Recherche* by a series of careful revisions. But while she is assimilated into the novel's fictional world, Albertine nonetheless brings with her an epistemology of her own, largely alien to the rest of the book. Instead of that relentless fascination with both otherness and knowledge that permeated Marcel's observation of the Guermanteses and of the world of inverts, she brings with her the horror of both.

The two faces of inversion are therefore the two faces of the hero's relationship to the world, a relationship split between aestheticization and paranoia. The discovery of male inversion as both a botanical miracle and a vast underworld constitutes the high point of the novel's aestheticizing and exoticizing efforts. Having suppressed the economic reality, and having reduced the Dreyfus affair to an index of the destructive workings of time, the novel chooses to treat the social world as an aesthetic object, a target of Marcel's curiosity. The difficulty is that when the same approach is extended onto Marcel's erotic desires, disinterested observation—perhaps predictably—transforms into something akin to obsessional neurosis. If the novel began by following Swann's way and the Guermantes way, it ended up describing Charlus's way and Albertine's way, embodying wonder and horror as two contesting visions of the self's relationship to the world.

Is reconciliation possible? Yes, but we should first note what a strange novelistic creature Proust has engineered. As I have repeatedly argued, he has displaced so many of the familiar elements of the Balzacian bildungsroman, and yet it appears that his inactive and sickly hero has managed to master the social universe in the traditional Balzacian sense: for all we know, he has successfully traversed the path from a timid observer of Swann and the Guermanteses to the quintessential high society insider. The irony is, of course, that he has managed to do so in a novel in which success no longer matters.

The *Recherche,* however, does maintain a uniquely strong teleological thrust, matched by very few of the novels I discuss in this book. This, of course, is possible only because the *Recherche* has a preconceived ending, with the epiphanic moment on the Guermanteses' stairs written long before all the plotlines were envisioned. Consequently, the divided worlds of the *Recherche* can be brought together only as the material and motivation for the act of writing. As Marcel admits, "En me faisant perdre mon temps, en me faisant du chagrin, Albertine m'avait peut-être été plus utile, même au point de vue littéraire, qu'un secrétaire qui eût rangé mes paperoles" (Albertine had perhaps been more useful to me, even from a literary point of view, than a secretary who would have arranged my "paperies"; 3:909, 4:319). What Marcel's aesthetic theory suggests is that the act of writing will reunite what the book in our hands has separated: the heavily aestheticized vision of the social universe and the paranoid universe of personal relations. This, of course, may appear as a forced solution that suggests that the contrary aspects of the *Recherche*'s universe can come together only in a kind of an aesthetic afterlife:

> Et certes, il n'y aurait pas que ma grand'mère, pas qu'Albertine, mais bien d'autres encore, dont j'avais pu assimiler une parole, un regard, mais qu'en tant que créatures individuelles je ne me rappelais plus; un livre est un grand cimetière où sur la plupart des tombes on ne peut plus lire les noms effacés. (3:903)

> (And certainly there were others besides my grandmother and Albertine, there were many from whom I had been able to assimilate a single phrase or look although as individual human beings I had no recollection of them; a book is a huge cemetery in which on the majority of the tombs the names are effaced and can no longer be read.) (4:310)

And yet, given the history this book has been tracing, that is perhaps where reconciliation and coherence belong—as fictions imposed by the act of writing. By imposing aesthetic form on social reality and personal history, Proust works to contain, however imperfectly, the pressures of modernity. For containment is precisely what the bildungsroman plot so rarely achieved in the nineteenth century: to see everything, to know everything, to impose structure, to exert mastery.

# EPILOGUE

## Historicizing the Bildungsroman

Published some seven years apart, Virginia Woolf's *The Voyage Out* (1915) and *Jacob's Room* (1922) both deny the bildungsroman protagonist a proper entry into adulthood. Rachel Vinrace, the heroine of *The Voyage Out*, seems particularly ill prepared for this transition. As her aunt, Helen Ambrose, muses in disbelief, "At the age of twenty-four she scarcely knew that men desired women and was terrified by a kiss."[1] Within weeks, Rachel will be engaged to an aspiring young writer, and within a few more, she will be dead, suddenly crushed by some unknown tropical ailment. In *Jacob's Room*, Jacob Flanders meets a similarly untimely death. Unlike Rachel, he knows something of the world: he goes to Cambridge, he ponders politics, he reads widely, he has an affair with an older woman. Soon, however, he simply disappears. Jacob's death in the Great War, like the death of Paul Emanuel in *Villette*, is assumed but not represented. At the end of the novel, all that is left to be done is to clean up the last scattered traces of Jacob's existence: "Nothing arranged. All his letters strewn about for anyone to read. What did he expect? Did he think he would come back?"[2] With both of Woolf's protagonists, the bildungsroman seems less a site of struggle between inward desires and outer realities and more a site of outright, even preemptive capitulation. In the nineteenth-century bildungsroman, it usually takes years of relentless fight for the hero's fate to be finally determined. Here, however, the hero quietly disappears, while the heroine suddenly falls ill and dies in a delirium, having barely encountered the trials of adulthood. It is as if their fate was a foregone conclusion.

What are we to make of these deaths? One familiar path, repeatedly taken by bildungsroman historians, would be to read them as a sign of the bildungsroman's radical transformation if not outright exhaustion in the face of the crisis of the nation-state, of expanding imperialism, of the Great War. As Moretti argues in a passage in which he dismisses Joyce's *A Portrait of the Artist as a Young Man,* "In the end nothing was left of the form of the *Bildungsroman,* a phase of Western socialization had come to an end, a phase that the *Bildungsroman* had both represented and contributed to" (244). In the twentieth century, Moretti's argument goes, the bildungsroman continued to stumble aimlessly for some time, propelled by little more than stubbornness or inertia. The form had exhausted its historical purpose; it just took a while for that realization to be fully absorbed. Less extravagant in his claims than Moretti, Jed Esty does not dismiss the modernist bildungsroman as a failure, but nonetheless sees it as kind of antithesis to what the bildungsroman normally is: "In the traditional bildungsroman, youth drives narrative momentum until adulthood arrives to fold youth's dynamism into a conceit of uneventful middle age. In the set of youth-fixated novels I have identified, though, youth retains its grip on the center of the text, disorganizing and distending the plot" (*Unseasonable Youth,* 18). While Moretti sees the bildungsroman in terms of a quasi-biological teleology in which an organism dies having fulfilled its purpose, Esty constructs a strong opposition between modernist texts—"antidevelopmental fictions," as he calls them (2)—and that elusive being, the traditional bildungsroman.

In many ways, this book has been an attempt to think about the history of the bildungsroman by eschewing some of the difficulties that follow from such theorizations. The first such difficulty is, of course, that by the mid-nineteenth century the bildungsroman had largely abandoned whatever commitment to teleology it may have had and was struggling to negotiate even a relatively favorable outcome for its heroes. To use an old cliché of narrative theory, Balzac *tells* us that Rastignac has succeeded, but doesn't really *show* us. In *David Copperfield,* Dickens manages to produce something like a narrative of successful socialization but only at the cost of persistently evading a series of urgent concerns of mid-nineteenth-century capitalism. As we have seen, however, such triumphs come amid a flurry of more unsettling outcomes, including the early deaths of Julien Sorel, Lucien de Rubempré, Roderick Hudson, Maggie Tulliver, and

Hyacinth Robinson, as well as the bitter disappointments of Lucy Snowe, Pip, Richard Feverel, and Gwendolen Harleth.

Perhaps more significantly, the nineteenth-century bildungsroman's struggle to imagine successful socialization becomes apparent at the level of narrative structure. Even before it finally ends in disaster, the story of Lucien de Rubempré follows a circular rather than linear path, with Lucien literally running in circles between Paris and the provinces. In Dickens, the bildungsroman hero repeatedly emerges as something of a puppet whose fate remains firmly in the hands of others. In Brontë's *Villette,* Lucy Snowe oscillates between audacity and withdrawal until the novel finally grants her the promise of a meaningful future with Paul Emanuel, only to have it promptly revoked. As we have seen throughout this book, the nineteenth-century bildungsroman forcefully demonstrates the excruciating difficulty of social apprenticeship as a theme and as a form.

It is in part because the nineteenth-century bildungsroman refuses to be easily assimilated to the notion of purposeful development that the opposition between the traditional and nontraditional forms of the genre is put under pressure: the subversion of the developmental process runs far too deep in the bildungsroman tradition for the modernist bildungsroman to be considered the genre's enfant terrible. The truth is, however, that there are significant difficulties on both sides of this polarity. While the fictions of French realism and of the mid-Victorian period are not quite the picture of stability they are sometimes imagined to be, the modernist bildungsroman itself maintains an uneasy relationship with the genre's past, presenting itself as an autochthonous product of the emerging century in some ways, yet remaining firmly rooted in the legacies of realism in others.

On the one hand, much of what happens in the bildungsromans written during the 1910s and 1920s can be easily attributed to the sociopolitical realities of early twentieth-century Europe. If novels such as Woolf's *Jacob's Room* or Mann's *The Magic Mountain* refuse to even entertain the possibility that young men might have a future, it is perhaps because, in the face of the great European carnage of 1914, they did not have one. As Mann's narrator tells the protagonist, Hans Castorp, at the end of the novel: "Farewell, Hans—whether you live or stay where you are! Your chances are not good. The wicked dance in which you are caught up will last many a little sinful year yet, and we would not wager much that you will come out whole."[3] Indeed, even those novels whose heroes don't end up in the trenches of the Great War (with, of course, little hope of return), seem to belong to a very different world, one characterized both by a whole new stage of technological development and, as Esty rightly points out, by a new stage in the development of imperialism (e.g., *Unseasonable Youth*, 16–17). Stephen Dedalus certainly thinks about his status as an imperial subject; Rachel Vinrace looks toward "the shooting motorcars, more like spiders in the moon than terrestrial objects" (5) and ponders female suffrage (134); and Proust opens his novel to the scenes of aerial bombing during the Great War.

On the other hand, despite all the signs that these authors belong to an altogether different modernity, technologically as well as socially, they cannot really leave behind either the narrative patterns or the ideological preoccupations of the nineteenth century. As we have seen in the final two chapters of this book, the aestheticist turn in the work of Joyce and Proust requires to be read in light of the growing power of collective loyalties that had already begun to exert considerable influence on the form of the bildungsroman in the 1870s. Proust's aestheticization of the social universe in particular constitutes an attempt to simultaneously contain the ideological tensions that surrounded the Dreyfus affair and to refashion the parvenu plot that has dominated the French bildungsroman since Stendhal.

A similar sense of continuity emerges in Woolf's *The Voyage Out*. Although Woolf can explore aspects of female subjectivity that were out of bounds for her predecessors, the ghost of the nineteenth-century courtship plot refuses to go away. In important ways Rachel Vinrace is a product of the same realities that shaped the lives of Dorothea Brooke or Gwendolen Harleth some decades earlier. Her education is limited—music, some foreign languages, some English books—and her future bound up in marriage: "She had been educated as the majority of well-to-do girls in the last part of the nineteenth-century had been educated. Kindly doctors and gentle old professors had taught her the rudiments of about ten different branches of knowledge. . . . But there was no subject in the world which she knew accurately. Her mind was in the state of an intelligent man's in the beginning of the reign of Queen Elizabeth" (26). Not only is she repeatedly patronized by men—"D'you mean to tell me you've reached the age of twenty-four without reading Gibbon?" (141)—but her concerns about marriage echo those of Eliot's Gwendolen Harleth. Whereas Gwendolen reflects on marriage as "rather a dreary state in which a woman could not do what she liked, had more children than were desirable, was consequently dull, and became irrevocably immersed in humdrum" (*Daniel Deronda,* 31), Rachel is forced to rebuke her fiancé's fantasies of family life: "I won't have eleven children," she insists (278). When Rachel dies, she is exhausted not merely by a mysterious South American illness, but by a model of femininity inherited from Victorian England.

The death of Rachel Vinrace, like Stephen Dedalus's struggle with nationalism in Joyce's *Portrait* and like the political and aesthetic concerns of the *Recherche,* fall—to borrow the phrase from Antoine Compagnon—between two centuries, therefore pushing back against the tendency to think about the modernist and realist bildungsroman in binary terms. The question is not, of course, whether the genre changes: as I have argued in chapter 4, the change was dramatic enough between 1850s and 1870s, let alone between Dickens and Joyce. The question is, rather, how do we describe and theorize this change? In part, I have approached such a question by taking a critical stance toward dominant approaches to the history of the bildungsroman. As I have argued time and again, we may be better off if we were to discard some of the common props we routinely use in order to explain the bildungsroman's historical transformations. Chief among those props are the so-called traditional bildungsroman (with its largely unproblematized teleological thrust) and its inverted image, the antibildungsroman (in which the unproblematized teleology of the former breaks down and disintegrates). Such constructions may seem useful because they distill an inherently complex history into a straightforward binary opposition, but by doing so they also impose a predetermined teleology on the bildungsroman's development. Within this teleology, the bildungsroman always moves away from a relatively unproblematic early form to a contested late one.

In this book, I have sought to dissociate the history of the bildungsroman from such a preordained teleology. Rather than a form that led a more or less healthy existence through the better part of the nineteenth century, only to implode around the turn of the twentieth, the bildungsroman, in my reading, emerges as a form in a continuous state of crisis, alternately invoking and disowning the promise of purposeful development. The shifts that the bildungsroman underwent during the nearly hundred years of literary history covered in this book involved far-reaching transformations of its structure, but not any kind of terminal breakdown, primarily because there is no master model that could break down. Instead, the bildungsroman is best understood as a genre that seeks to engage the changing demands of modern socialization. Being the parasitical form that it is, the bildungsroman latched onto a new set of issues every few decades, moving, for instance, from the obsessive concern with the logic of upward mobility in the early and the middle part of the nineteenth century, and toward an engagement with mass politics in the final decades of that century. In doing so, it did not move from stability to crisis, but from one contested state to another. Perhaps the best way to describe its development during the long nineteenth century is as a series of revisions and rewritings that were necessary precisely because the task of becoming someone, which it sought to address, is a perpetual moving target, a target at which the bildungsroman threw everything it possibly could—willful self-making, cunning, withdrawal, self-denial, compromise, aestheticization, self-invention—only to come out of it all if not empty-handed, then certainly with very mixed results. And yet it is precisely through the defeats of its heroes, through the dubious compromises, countless evasions of important issues, and manifest inadequacies of its answers that the bildungsroman offers a privileged insight into the social pressures that make modernity. It is a form that speaks most vocally when it offers partial answers and suspect solutions.

And what of the bildungsroman after Proust? This book has focused on the long nineteenth century precisely because so much of our understanding of the bildungsroman's history depends on how we conceptualize its development during this specific period: as we have seen, claims about its breakdown or radical transformation are almost always predicated on imagining the nineteenth-century European bildungsroman as a site of relatively stable socialization. While I offer no definite pronouncements on its destiny beyond European high modernism, I suspect that the further revisions of the form follow no predictable pattern. As I have suggested in my remarks on the female bildungsroman in chapter 3, historical processes tend to affect the genre in a nonlinear manner: while the twentieth-century novel has found, understandably, many new ways of denying the promise of growth and social integration, it is not at all obvious that it has grown significantly more cynical in its treatment of these promises than the founding fictions of French realism already were. Two counterintuitive examples should suffice. Despite all of its metafictional playfulness, and in spite of being written in Nazi Germany by a man who had escaped the Russian Revolution and was about to seek safety in the United States, Vladimir Nabokov's *Gift* (1938) remains remarkably—perhaps uniquely—confident in the ideal of harmonious development.[4] Conversely, despite all the complications of a colonial upbringing in Jamaica Kincaid's *Annie John* (1985), it is by no means obvious that the eponymous heroine's voyage from Antigua to England at the end of her novel is any more uncertain than Lucy Snowe's journey across the English Channel and into the hostile world of Labassecour. Indeed, the angst Annie experiences—the overwhelming desire to dissociate herself from what is meant to be home—falls neatly within a pattern established in *Great Expectations*, in *Le Rouge et le Noir*, in *Jane Eyre*, in *A Portrait of the Artist as a Young Man*. Of course, by insisting on such continuities I do not wish to argue that the vicissitudes of twentieth-century history, including the remarkable outbursts of totalitarian violence and the palpable reality of anticolonial struggle, did not affect the form of the bildungsroman. I do, however, remain confident that in our efforts to understand the bildungsroman's transformations throughout the twentieth century and into our own, we will do well to forget all about that "proper," "classical," or "traditional" nineteenth-century bildungsroman that never was.

# NOTES

## Introduction

1. David Copperfield does achieve what appears to be a personal and professional fulfillment, although, as I will show, only at the cost of suppressing various social and psychological factors that could derail his path. Rastignac does achieve unqualified social success, although it should be noted that his success is described only in scattered references throughout a variety of Balzac's subsequent novels. The most extensive treatment of Rastignac beyond *Goriot* (in which his conquest of Paris has only just begun) is in *La Maison Nucingen* (1837), but, as I argue elsewhere, even in that short book Rastignac doesn't appear as a character; instead, various elements of his life story are supplied through the conversations among a group of journalists who debate the dynamics of high society. He is literally reduced to a piece of gossip. See my "Realism, the Bildungsroman and the Art of Self-Invention: Stendhal and Balzac."

2. In my title and throughout this book I use the term *self-fashioning* in order to refer to the variety of attempts to shape personal identity coupled, alternately, with the desire for social mobility or for self-realization. In my usage the term serves as a value-neutral way of referring to the processes through which personal identity is constructed and that may range from attempts to fully realize a presumed inner potential to the construction of an alternative identity motivated by pragmatic considerations. I borrow this usage from Stephen Greenblatt, although I have little interest in retaining the Foucauldian assumptions that shape elements of his analysis in *Renaissance Self-Fashioning*. As Greenblatt observes, although there are always selves to be fashioned, there are also historical moments characterized by "an increased self-consciousness about the fashioning of human identity as a manipulable, artful process" (*Renaissance Self-Fashioning,* 2). This book, as we shall see, deals with one such period. To the best of my knowledge the term *self-fashioning* was first used in the context of the bildungsroman by Todd Kontje, but his interest lies in self-fashioning as an activity performed by the authors of the bildungsroman rather than as a process described in the novels (*Private Lives,* 8). I also prefer *self-fashioning* because it enables me to avoid certain connotations of the German term *Bildung,* which inevitably

points to Enlightenment ideals of harmonious growth, maturation, perfection, and depth of inner life.

3. See, for instance, Moretti, *Way of the World,* 216, and Esty, *Unseasonable Youth,* 6. Further references to *The Way of the World* and *Unseasonable Youth* will be given parenthetically in the text.

4. Castle, *Reading the Modernist Bildungsroman,* 30. Further references will be given parenthetically in the text. In the eloquent formulation of Todd Kontje, "Any *Bildungsroman* worth reading, including *Wilhelm Meister,* is always an *Antibildungsroman*" (*Private Lives,* 16).

5. Morgenstern, "On the Nature of the Bildungsroman," 656.

6. Humboldt, *Limits of State Action,* 16, emphasis original. Although the book didn't appear until after Humboldt's death, this chapter was published in a journal shortly after it was written in 1792.

7. Dilthey, *Poetry and Experience,* 336. Perhaps even more influential is Georg Lukács's assertion that in the case of Wilhelm Meister "a reconciliation between interiority and reality, although problematic, is nevertheless possible" (*Theory of the Novel,* 132).

8. Dilthey, *Poetry and Experience,* 336.

9. The affirmative logic of Goethe's novel has always been subject to some degree of critical skepticism. Thomas P. Saine, for instance, wonders "how much real optimism with regard to harmonious human development is actually warranted by what goes on in Goethe's novel, and whether it is not put there for the most part by its interpreters" ("Was *Wilhelm Meister's Lehrjahre* Really Supposed to Be a Bildungsroman?," 121). Undoubtedly, Wilhelm Meister is made to renounce quite a lot both personally and professionally, and the level of autonomy he exercises seems fundamentally limited once we realize that he has been directed by the Society of the Tower all along. However, it is important not to overstate this case. After all, one doesn't have to subscribe to an uncritically affirmative reading of the novel in order to recognize the difference between Wilhelm's imperfect but unmistakable reconciliation with the world and the utter destruction of the hero's prospects that will become commonplace in the nineteenth century.

10. As Marc Redfield points out, complaints about the difficulties associated with the term *bildungsroman* and its convoluted history constitute an inevitable ritual in bildungsroman studies (see Redfield, review of *Formative Fictions* by Tobias Boes, 718). My own position on conceptual and terminological issues surrounding the study of the bildungsroman closely mirrors that of Todd Kontje (see *Private Lives in the Public Sphere,* 16–17): as a term *bildungsroman* is too firmly established to allow for serious terminological questioning; as a generic concept it denotes a broad range of narrative texts that, beginning with the late eighteenth century, explore the dynamics of individualization and socialization, regardless of whether those texts bear

a meaningful relationship to the Humboldtian ideal of Bildung. Of course, this extension of the term's scope beyond the novels that maintain a meaningful connection to the intellectual legacy of the German Enlightenment is sometimes rejected as imprecise or anachronistic (see, e.g., Hardin, "Introduction," x). In my view, however, such demands for purity are not very helpful. As Fredric Jameson observes, what generic classifications require in order to be productive is not purity, but precisely their "experimental" character: "Such classifications in fact prove rewarding only as long as they are felt to be relatively arbitrary critical acts, and lose their vitality when, as with the category of the bildungsroman, they come to be thought of as 'natural' forms" (*Political Unconscious,* 132). As Karl Morgenstern correctly anticipated when he introduced the term, the preoccupations of the bildungsroman naturally change: "I just now called *Wilhelm Meister's Apprenticeship* a model of its kind, from our time and for our time. But Chronos marches quickly, leaving ruins behind him and gazing toward ever-new edifices that rise up before him. How much has changed in Germany and in the rest of Europe during the twenty-five years that have passed since the publication of the *Apprenticeship;* how much has already changed its shape and how much strives toward new forms that in some cases have been foreseen but in others come completely unexpected!" ("On the Nature of the Bildungsroman," 658). For a more contemporary version of this flexible understanding of genres as fundamentally "open systems," see Cohen, "History and Genre," 210.

11. Sammons, "Bildungsroman for Nonspecialists," 41.

12. As Thomas Pavel has shown, to speak of literary genres is always to be "subject to two temptations: one is to freeze generic features, reducing them to immutable formulas, another is to deny genres any conceptual stability" ("Genres as Norms and Good Habits," 201).

13. Sammons, "Bildungsroman for Nonspecialists," 41. On the surface, Sammons is not primarily concerned with the outcome of the educational process (he is happy to include in the bildungsroman canon Thomas Mann's novels, which offer anything but harmonious socialization of the hero), but rather with the existence of a meaningful connection to Bildung. The two are, however, difficult to disentangle: the only non-German novel Sammons is fully prepared to treat as a bildungsroman is Dickens's *David Copperfield,* whose eponymous hero very much follows the path of successful social integration. By contrast, *Great Expectations, Illusions perdues,* and *Jude the Obscure* do not make the cut.

14. As I show elsewhere, restrictive approaches to the history of the bildungsroman—that is, the ones that seek to tie the genre closely to Goethe or the intellectual context of the German Enlightenment—face insurmountable difficulties: Goethe's influence has limited reach among the major figures of French or English realism, and the reception of Bildung in Victorian culture is much more a matter of intellectual rather than literary history. Neither a search for Wilhelm Meister's "kinsmen" (to recall the

title of Susanne Howe's important book), nor the appropriation of Bildung by such figures as Mill and Arnold will do much to explain European realism's fascination with developmental fictions. For an argument why we should abandon such genealogical approaches to the bildungsroman while remaining committed to the term itself, see Stević, "The Genre of Disobedience."

15. Franco Moretti also describes a crisis of the bildungsroman around the turn of the twentieth century (*Way of the World*, 229–45). More provocatively, and much closer to the argument I will be making in this book, Gregory Castle has argued that the modernist bildungsroman constitutes something akin to a productive failure: "It is precisely the breakdown of traditional forms of identity and of normative, harmonious socialization that gives the Bildungsroman a new sense of purpose" (*Reading the Modernist Bildungsroman*, 5).

16. Castle, 8–9. See also Boes, "Beyond the *Bildungsroman*," 116. For the claim that the bildungsroman educates the reader, see, for instance, Mahoney, "Apprenticeship of the Reader," as well as Redfield, *Phantom Formations*, 54.

17. As Tobias Boes summarizes this view, "The Bildungsroman responds to these challenges [of modernity] by creating narratives of socialization, in which ambitious young protagonists work their way to the inside of the power structures that govern their time, attempt to hew for themselves a position of privilege, and characteristically fail, realizing only too late the fundamentally misguided nature of their social ambitions" ("Beyond the *Bildungsroman*," 116).

18. In doing so, I am in some ways following a path open by the theorists of the female bildungsroman. As Susan Fraiman observes at the beginning of *Unbecoming Women*, "A book on the novel of development might seem a book invested, by definition, in notions of linear progress and coherent identity. Certainly the form and most discussions of the form have tended to invoke a purposeful youth advancing toward some clarity and stability of being." Her own project is to look beyond such notions: "The *unbecoming* of my title is intended to push back against conventional assumptions about becoming and stories about becoming, and this pressure is obtained in large part by focusing on *women*" (ix, emphasis original). While Fraiman seeks to upend this sense of teleological progress by focusing on the social limitations faced by female protagonists (as opposed to the relative freedom of their male counterparts), my own project in this book can be described as an extension of this skepticism to the nineteenth-century bildungsroman as a whole. I address the methodological issues surrounding the study of the female bildungsroman in more detail in chapter 3.

19. Morgenstern, "On the Nature of the Bildungsroman," 658; Moretti, *Way of the World*, 5.

20. Bakhtin, "Bildungsroman," 23–24, emphasis original.

21. Giddens and Pierso, *Conversations with Anthony Giddens*, 94.

22. Giddens, *Modernity and Self-Identity*, 20.

23. Bakhtin, "Bildungsroman," 30.

24. Giddens, *Modernity and Self-Identity*, 20.

25. Boes, *Formative Fictions*, 5.

26. "Different strata of society," Therese tells Wilhelm halfway through the novel, "have different lifestyles that they cannot share or exchange with each other" (Goethe, *Wilhelm Meister's Apprenticeship*, 283). Tobias Boes, who argues for a more dynamic understanding of the novel's social universe, nonetheless concludes that "by revealing his characters to be relatives rather than fellow travelers down the currents of history, however, Goethe unexpectedly reaffirms the conventions not only of eighteenth-century narrative, in which such implausible revelations commonly occur even in the most 'realist' texts, but also of eighteenth-century politics" (*Formative Fictions*, 67). Boes also largely remains faithful to the opposition between Goethe and Stendhal that Moretti introduced (see *Formative Fictions*, 82, 94).

27. While I don't wish to revive the problematic claims about Germany's "special path," it seems uncontroversial to argue that in Germany certain traditional hierarchies proved quite resilient, that the state played an outsized role in the process of modernization, and that the movement toward an industrial society was generally slower than in England or France. See, for instance, Blackbourn, *Long Nineteenth Century*, 1–45, and Seigel, *Modernity and Bourgeois Life*, 244–64.

28. Berman, *All That Is Solid Melts into Air*, 18.

29. As Jerrold Seigel points out, "Many features of the world we inhabit in the twenty-first century are ones he [Marx] and other nineteenth-century observers rightly associated with bourgeois doings and aspirations: the urbanization and globalization of life, the ascendancy of market relations, the opening of new paths and opportunities for individuals, the expansion of education, the extension of political rights; all of them, now as then, combined with a litany of associated discontents, chief among them persisting social inequality" (*Modernity and Bourgeois Life*, 10).

30. As it should be clear from my discussion so far, the relationship between *Wilhelm Meister* and the subsequent tradition has been a complicated issue for bildungsroman scholarship for reasons theoretical as well as historical. Because it has long been established as the inaugural example of the genre, bildungsroman criticism has continuously circled back to *Wilhelm Meister*, only to find itself disappointed by the fact that it cannot provide a productive link between Goethe's novel and some subsequent body of work it has been analyzing. While it is, of course, possible to speak of the bildungsroman in relation to Goethe, we should also be able to perform what Lorna Ellis aptly calls a "divorce from an originary text" (*Appearing to Diminish*, 22).

31. Goethe, *Wilhelm Meister's Apprenticeship*, 3.

32. As Moretti argues, *Wilhelm Meister* ends up being Wilhelm's and not Werner's bildungsroman—an implicit rebuke to Werner's worldview (24–25).

33. Hobsbawm, *Age of Empire*, 6.

34. Bauman, *Liquid Modernity,* 32, emphasis original.

35. Wagner, *Sociology of Modernity,* xiii.

## 1. Lucien de Rubempré and the Politics of Usurpation in Post-Napoleonic France

1. The diagnosis of inadequacy and naïveté (manifest, in particular, in all the insistence on Lucien's "illusions") permeates the discourse of the narrator and seems to be repeatedly confirmed in conversations and casual remarks. As he admits to Vautrin, who served as his mentor throughout *Splendeurs,* "Vous avez voulu faire un personnage plus grand que je ne pouvais l'être" (You tried to make [me] a greater figure than I had it in me to be; 504, 398). Lucien only repeats after Daniel d'Arthez, one of his literary friends, who describes him as being "un homme de poésie et non un poète, il rêve et ne pense pas, il s'agite et ne crée pas" (very poetic, but he is not a poet; he dreams but he does not think, he acts but does not create; 504, 521). D'Arthez, in turn, echoes the narrator, who claims that Lucien is "un poète, sans réflexion profonde, allant de lumière en lumière come un papillon, sans plan fixe" (a poet incapable of deep-laid plans, flying like a moth from one candle-flame to another; 460, 473).

2. Balzac, *Correspondance,* vol. 3, 111, my translation.

3. On the composition of elites, see, in particular, Price, *Social History of Nineteenth-Century France,* 104. Tobias Boes, whose reading of Stendhal also touches on the question of political legitimacy, sums up this moment in French history as follows: "Older men who had come into power and fortune during the ancien régime confronted a rising tide of younger people whose formative experiences had coincided with the Napoleonic Wars. This clash entailed much more than a collision of values and opinions about such subjects as political emancipation and property distribution. Also at stake was a fundamental disagreement about historical narrative, about the ways in which the past should be connected to the present" (*Formative Fictions,* 82).

4. References to *Le Rouge et le Noir* point to the following editions: Stendhal, *Le Rouge et le Noir* (Paris: Gallimard, 2000) and Stendhal, *The Red and the Black: A Chronicle of the Nineteenth Century,* trans. Catherine Slater (New York: Oxford University Press, 1971); all references are given parenthetically. The first number indicates the page number in the French original, while the second indicates the one in the English translation.

5. Greenblatt, *Renaissance Self-Fashioning,* 3.

6. Greenblatt, 31.

7. Unless otherwise noted, the references to Balzac's novels are given according to the following editions: Honoré de Balzac, *Le Père Goriot* (Paris: Gallimard, 1999), and for the English translation, *Père Goriot,* trans. A. J. Krailsheimer (Oxford: Oxford University Press, 1999); *Illusions perdues* (Paris: Gallimard, 2004), and

*Lost Illusions,* trans. Kathleen Raine (New York: Modern Library, 1997); *Splendeurs et misères des courtisanes* (Paris: Gallimard, 2008), and for the English translation, *A Harlot High and Low,* trans. Rayner Happenstall (London: Penguin, 1970); all references are given parenthetically. The first number indicates the page number in the French original, while the second indicates the one in the corresponding English translation.

8. Brooks, "Balzac," 122.

9. De Barthélemy, *Noblesse en France avant et depuis 1789,* 140, my translation.

10. As the Vicomte de Bonald—one of the most important conservative voices of nineteenth-century France, and a key ideologue of the ultras—observed in his 1815 *Considérations sur la noblesse:* "Lorsqu'enfin l'hérédité du trône a été la loi constante et fondamentale, et que la couronne a été fixée dans une famille de mâle en mâle, et par ordre de primogéniture, le ministère publique de la société est devenu héréditaire et patrimonial, et il y a eu des familles nobles, comme il y a eu une famille royale" (When the heredity of the throne finally became a constant and fundamental law, and when the crown was passed in one family from male to male, end by the order of primogeniture, the public rule of society has become hereditary and patrimonial, and there were noble families, just as there was a royal family; 57, my translation). De Bonald's account stresses the interdependency of royal sovereignty and the institution of nobility. The latter mimics the logic of the former, as they are both predicated on the principle of heredity and primogeniture.

11. Higgs, *Nobles in Nineteenth-Century France,* 7.

12. *Constitutions de la France depuis 1789,* ed. Jacques Godechot, 224, my translation.

13. An anonymous pamphlet quoted in Pettiteau, *Élites et mobilités,* 142, my translation.

14. De Staël, *Considerations on the Principal Events of the French Revolution,* 573. The fundamental disagreement between Lucien and the Marquise can be explained in terms of the distinction between J. L. Austin's understanding of performative utterances and subsequent poststructuralist interpretations of performativity. In Austin's speech act theory, a valid performative utterance must be verbalized by someone with proper authority to do so. This is the view taken by the Marquise: only the king has the power to ennoble, and simply saying "I am a baron" will not do, in the same way in which saying "I pronounce you man and wife" will not make any difference unless uttered as a part of a legally sanctioned marriage ceremony. Lucien, however, senses—not altogether incorrectly—that this demand for the existence of a proper authority can be circumvented: to be a nobleman is to claim that you are a nobleman.

15. Lukács, *Studies in European Realism,* 49.

16. Prendergast, *Balzac,* 30.

17. Lukács, *Studies in European Realism,* 63–64.

18. Lukács, 54.

19. Lukács, 53.

20. For the notion of the "exchange of injuries," see Gouldner, "The Norm of Reciprocity," 172. In *Stone Age Economics,* Marshall Sahlins describes negative reciprocity as "an attempt to get something for nothing with impunity" (195). In the words of behavioral economist Colin Camerer, "Responders reciprocate unfair behavior by harming the person who treated them unfairly, at a substantial cost to themselves (provided the unfair Proposer is harmed more than they are)" (*Behavioral Game Theory,* 10). For a further discussion of the self-destructive side of negative reciprocity, see Fehr and Gächter, "Reciprocity and Economics," 846.

21. Simmel, *On Individuality and Social Forms,* 45.

22. See, for instance, the entries under "chantage" in *Trésor de la langue française.*

23. The action of the novel begins in 1824 (37, 17), while Lucien's suicide takes place in 1830.

24. Prendergast, *Order of Mimesis,* 99. For Prendergast's account of the role of contingency in *Splendeurs,* see also his *Balzac,* 80.

25. As Richard Terdiman writes in one of the most powerful articulations of this view, in *Splendeurs* "the social system over which the initiatory process has sought control thus controls the process even in the form of its seeking; the power over which control was sought turns out to be *power over those who seek power*" (*Discourse/Counter-Discourse,* 106). See also Lucey, *Misfit of the Family,* 179.

26. Miller, "Balzac's Illusions Lost and Found," 178.

27. Chauveau, *Code pénal progressif,* 457.

28. "Chambre des pairs," *Journal des débats,* March 13, 1835, 2, my translation. The provision in question is the Article 71, which remained unchanged when the Charter of 1814 was revised in 1830. However, since a number of other articles were suppressed, article 71 became article 62.

29. "Chambre des deputes," *Journal des débats,* January 16, 1834, 3, my translation. In fact, a similar suggestion was offered during the original debate about the suppression of the part of Article 259 that relates to titles: "La Charte constitutionnelle confère au roi le droit d'accorder des titres. Il est évident que ce droit serait illusoire s'il n'y avait pas une loi contré celui qui usurpe des titres que le roi a seul le droit de conférer" (The Constitutional Charter confers upon the king the right to grant titles. It is evident that that right would be illusory if there was no law against those who usurp the titles which only the king has the right to confer; quoted in Chauveau, *Code pénal progressif,* 258, my translation).

30. Collingham, *July Monarchy,* 109.

31. Furet, *Revolutionary France,* 327.

32. Barthelemy, "Patronymic Names and *Noms de Terre,*" 191.

33. Sandy Petrey has offered an interpretation of the simultaneous rise of realism and the July Monarchy that is based on an understanding of the Revolution of 1830

essentially opposite to what I have been arguing: "Julien Sorel and Louis Philippe both create presence from absence, solidity from evanescence, concrete substance from a yawning void, reality from representation" (*In the Court of the Pear King*, 120). It seems that for Petrey the July Revolution constitutes the great moment of illegitimacy within nineteenth-century French history, in which "representation constitutes reality" (132). However, I find it highly improbable that after forty years of rapidly changing regimes (regimes based on different, and often mutually opposed, concepts of legitimacy), and after what François Furet has rather eloquently called the "theatrical succession of sovereigns" (*Revolutionary France*, 280), the July Revolution should be seen as such a profound culture shock.

## 2. The Great Evasion

1. Although I emphasize the passivity of the Dickensian hero, I am not quite willing to follow Franco Moretti in considering this passivity a sign of aesthetic failure. Dismissing the Victorian bildungsroman as a "conspiracy of the innocents," Moretti argues that "in England, between the insipid normality of the hero, and a stable and thoroughly classified world, no spark will ever flash" (200). In my view, however, the introduction of the seemingly unremarkable hero and the evasion of certain kinds of conflicts in Dickens ought to be seen in a more strategic light: as I argued in the introduction, the bildungsroman as a form is equally committed to the pacification and suppression of social tensions and to their amplification. The way in which it oscillates between these two is often unpredictable. As we shall see in chapter 5, with Flaubert and especially with Proust, the French bildungsroman will also turn to strategies of suppression and containment. For a critical take on Moretti's dismissal of the English novelistic tradition, see also Duncan, *Modern Romance*, 5–6.

2. Paxton Hood, *Self-Formation*, 2.

3. Miller, "Some Aspects of the Name in Culture-History," 586.

4. Dickens, *Oliver Twist*, 7. Further references will be given parenthetically in the text.

5. In his book on family relations in the realist and modernist novel, Barry McCrea also points to the fact that Oliver Twist gets his family name from Bumble rather than from his parents. McCrea considers this act of naming in the context of a broader argument about the crisis of family genealogy in the modern novel (*In the Company of Strangers*, 26–27). My analysis is complementary to McCrea's, but I am more interested in locating Dickens's obsession with orphanhood within the context of Victorian social discourse.

6. Dickens, *David Copperfield*, 184. Further references will be given parenthetically in the text.

7. Dickens, *Great Expectations*, 136. Further references will be given parenthetically in the text.

8. This continuity did not escape some of the first readers of *Great Expectations*. As a reviewer wrote in the *Times,* "The hero of the present tale, Pip, is a sort of Oliver. He is low-born, fatherless and motherless, and he rises out of the cheerless degradation of his childhood into quite another sphere. The thieves got a hold of Oliver, tried to make him a pickpocket, and were succeeded in their friendly intentions by Mr. Brownlow.... The convict in the new story takes the place of Mr. Brownlow in the old, and supplies Master Pip with every luxury. In either tale, through some unaccountable caprice of fortune, the puny son of poverty suddenly finds himself the child of affluence" (October 17, 1861, 6, reprinted in *Charles Dickens: The Critical Heritage*, 445). For a version of this view, see also Kettle, *Introduction to the English Novel*, 123.

9. With this development the bildungsroman arguably circles back to Goethe, whose protagonist was also guided by the benevolent hand of the Society of the Tower. There are, however, two differences worth pointing out. First, it seems that in Goethe this plot twist expresses a certain confidence in the paternalism of the upper classes, whereas in Dickens, as we shall see in a moment, the focus on charitable intervention largely serves to subvert the ideology of liberal individualism. Second, in Goethe the revelation that Wilhelm has been guided by others comes late in the novel, while in Dickens this is the premise that is articulated at the beginning. As a consequence, in Goethe we witness aspects of the hero's development (e.g., Wilhelm's aesthetic education) that will be occluded in Dickens.

10. Paxton Hood, *Self-Formation,* 13–14. For various elaborations of this creed, see George Lillie Craik, *Pursuit of Knowledge under Difficulties* (1830); Capel Lofft, *Self-formation* (1st ed., London, 1837); Isaac Taylor, *Self-cultivation Recommended,* (1817); and William E. Channing, *Self-culture* (1838[?]). Although Channing was American, his lecture went through at least four English editions before the mid-1840s. Tellingly, among these terms—*self-cultivation, self-education, self-training, self-culture,* and *self-formation*—only *self-formation* can be traced back to the 1700s, while the others originated in the nineteenth century.

11. Smiles, *Self-help,* 1. This line of argument can be traced back to Joseph Townsend's highly influential *Dissertation on the Poor Laws*. "It is universally found," Townsend argues, "that where bread can be obtained without care or labour, it leads through idleness and vice to poverty" (14).

12. For a fuller account of the intellectual and institutional context of Victorian attitudes toward charity, see Owen, *English Philanthropy;* Fraser, *Evolution of the British Welfare State;* and Roberts, *Social Conscience of the Early Victorians*.

13. Highmore, *Pietas Londinensis,* 189–190.

14. *Poverty in the Victorian Age,* ed. A. W. Coats, vol. 3, 114.

15. Reid, *What Should Be Done for the People,* 14.

16. Held, *The Ethics of Care,* 86. See also Gilligan, *In a Different Voice*. A detailed elaboration of the ethics of care can be found in the works of Nel Noddings. See,

in particular, *Caring; Educating Moral People; Maternal Factor;* and Slote, *Ethics of Care and Empathy.* For a rationalist argument against the care ethics, see Nussbaum, *Sex and Social Justice,* 74–75.

17. Noddings, *Maternal Factor,* 103.

18. As F. David Roberts has noted, "Dickens, the many-sided reflector of life, could hardly not reflect paternalism, but he did so in a different manner and with strong doubts. His Cheerybles [in *Nicholas Nickleby*] and Pickwicks are not strictly paternalist. Their benevolence is diffuse and individual, not linked to the spheres of the lord's estate and the vicar's parish. It is humanitarian, not authoritarian part of London's democratic life" (*Social Conscience of the Early Victorians,* 42).

19. Noddings, *Caring,* 14; see also *Maternal Factor,* 45–47.

20. Miller, *Charles Dickens,* 243.

21. Marcus, *Dickens,* 80.

22. For a discussion of Oliver's incorruptibility, see, for instance, Gilmour, *Idea of the Gentlemen in the Victorian Novel,* 114, and Baldridge, "Instabilities of Inheritance in *Oliver Twist.*"

23. Bakhtin, "Forms of Time and Chronotope in the Novel," 247.

24. Several scholars have tried to portray *David Copperfield* as a novel seriously interested in literary professionalism. For instance, Mary Poovey writes: "While novels like *David Copperfield* and *Pendennis* tended to formulate their responses to the writer's market situation less directly than the essays in *Blackwood's* or *North British Review,* all of these discussions of literary men struggled to define the place the writer occupied in Britain's increasingly secular, capitalist society" (*Uneven Developments,* 102). Along similar lines, Jennifer Ruth suggests that "Dickens wanted readers to imagine a writing professional whose intelligence resembles capital but whose work habits reproduce the measurable rhythms of labor" (*Novel Professions,* 59). For a reading that situates *David Copperfield* within the context of mid-Victorian debates about the "Dignity of Literature," see Salmon, "Professions of Labour."

25. Welsh, *From Copyright to Copperfield,* 109. Ian Duncan makes a similar observation: "Notoriously, the 'real' or economic content of that progress—how David does his work, the conversions of fancy into industry into profit—has consistently been refused explicit representation. Authorship as material process of production, as labour and sale, is never *shown* to the reader" (*Modern Romance,* 200).

26. Buckley, *Season of Youth,* 37.

27. Hardy, *Moral Art of Dickens,* 131.

28. It is hardly surprising that a critic like Lukács was more than a little impatient with Dickens. Having described the bildungsroman's central problem as "the reconciliation of the problematic individual, guided by his lived experience of the ideal, with concrete social reality" (*Theory of the Novel,* 132). Lukács had little choice but to dismiss Dickens altogether: "He had to make his heroes come to terms, without

conflict, with the bourgeois society of his time and, for the sake of poetic effect, to surround the qualities needed for this purpose with a false, or anyway inadequate, poetic glow" (107).

29. Gilligan, *In a Different Voice,* 62.

30. In identifying caring as a specifically feminine quality, *David Copperfield* also circumscribes the social role of women: the main female figures in the novel are seen almost exclusively as caregivers. This is a difficulty Dickens shares with modern care ethicists who have been accused of setting up the "caring trap" by reducing women to caring figures. See Barnett and Rivers in *Same Difference.* For Noddings's response, see *Maternal Factor,* 25.

31. As Hillis Miller argues, "Magwitch is a nightmare permutation of Mr. Brownlow and Mr. Jarndyce [from *Bleak House*]. He is the benevolent guardian, secretly manipulating the fortunes of the hero and protecting him, turned into a condemned felon who, like a horrible old dog, gloats over his victim" (*Charles Dickens,* 255).

32. Pecora, "Inheritances, Gifts, and Expectations," 182.

33. George Orwell has offered an interpretation along these lines, arguing that Dickens's later books tend to leave behind the figure of the "superhumanly kindhearted old gentleman who 'trots' to and fro, raising his employees' wages, patting children on the head, getting debtors out of jail and in general, acting the fairy godmother." For Orwell, the absence of such figures from *Great Expectations* indicates a new social vision: "The seeming inference from the rather despondent books that Dickens wrote in the fifties is that by that time he had grasped the helplessness of well-meaning individuals in a corrupt society" (*Collected Essays,* 35–36).

## 3. Charlotte Brontë and the Governess as a Liberal Subject

1. Eliot, *Middlemarch,* 792. Further references will be given parenthetically in the text.

2. Fraiman, *Unbecoming Women,* 5–6.

3. Bonaparte, "History and the Novel of Development," 1771.

4. Moretti, *Way of the World,* ix–x.

5. While such explicit rejections of the female bildungsroman are comparatively rare, there is also a long tradition of silence around it. Jerome Buckley's 1974 *Season of Youth*—for a long time the standard account of the bildungsroman in English, and an early target of feminist critical interventions—ignores the female bildungsroman and even reads Eliot's *The Mill on the Floss* as Tom Tulliver's (rather than Maggie's) novel. Moretti offers a substantial discussion of Austen's *Pride and Prejudice* in the first chapter of *Way of the World* (though without attention to the question of gender) and briefly discusses *Jane Eyre* as a part of his general dismissal of the English bildungsroman as a kind of a fairytale (187). In his 1996 *Phantom Formations,* Marc Redfield dedicates a chapter to George Eliot, although, again, without

particular attention to the development of her heroines. More recently, Thomas Jeffers's 2005 *Apprenticeships* reads no bildungsroman written by a woman, although the book does engage the female heroines of Henry James's novels. Finally, Tobias Boes's 2012 *Formative Fictions* discusses only Eliot's *Daniel Deronda,* but again with minimal attention to gender. The female bildungsroman has generally fared better with modernist scholars. Jed Esty dedicates a substantial part of his *Unseasonable Youth* to the discussion of female writers, while Gregory Castle explicitly engages feminist theorizations of the female bildungsroman (*Reading the Modernist Bildungsroman,* 212).

6. Abel et al., *The Voyage In,* 4.

7. Abel et al., 7. Perhaps the most detailed argument along these lines was developed by Marianne Hirsch. According to Hirsch, the heroine's inability to actively engage the world has led the nineteenth-century female bildungsroman to focus disproportionally on inward psychological development. At the same time, because this more dynamic inward growth can never result in any kind of outer self-realization, the female bildungsroman violates the principle of teleological progress traditionally associated with the genre: "The plot of inner development traces a discontinuous, circular path which, rather than moving forward, culminates in a return to origins, thereby distinguishing itself from the traditional plot outlines of the Bildungsroman" ("Spiritual *Bildung,*" 26).

8. Fraiman, *Unbecoming Women,* 144.

9. Cook, "Poor Genteel Women," 513.

10. For a nuanced account of the relationship between the male and female bildungsroman, see Ellis, *Appearing to Diminish,* 15–28. Ellis insists that women don't merely "grow down," and that the opposition between male and female bildungsroman is too restrictive and ultimately misleading. While I share many of Ellis's concerns, her argument for the proximity of the male and female bildungsroman is that the latter is not quite as problematic as it sometimes seems. My argument is, rather, that the two are close to each other because they are problematic in similar ways.

11. For a reading that problematizes the common view of *Pride and Prejudice* as a text that ends with an equitable compromise (in which Darcy relinquishes his pride while Elizabeth relinquishes her prejudice), see Fraiman, *Unbecoming Women,* 59–87. As we shall see later in this chapter, in *Villette* Brontë also attempts to portray Lucy Snowe's surrender to Paul Emanuel as a kind of compromise.

12. Brontë, *Jane Eyre,* 93. Further references will be given parenthetically in the text.

13. See also chapter 2. Significantly, in *David Copperfield* the novel's single reflection on the value of active engagement with the world comes from the tyrannical figure of Edward Murdstone: "David, to the young this is a world for action, and not for moping and droning in. It is especially so for a young boy of your disposition, which requires a great deal of correcting; and to which no greater service can be done than

to force it to conform to the ways of the working world, and to bend it and break it" (130). In *David Copperfield* "action" is a byword for punishment and abandonment.

14. For interpretations of Brontë's world as one steeped in conflict, see, for instance, Auerbach, *Romantic Imprisonment*, 195, and Kucich, *Repression in Victorian Fiction*, 58.

15. Eagleton, *Myths of Power*, 30, and Armstrong, *Desire and Domestic Fiction*, 54.

16. Lanser, *Fictions of Authority*, 177.

17. Nancy Armstrong articulates this problem as follows: "In [the Brontës'] hands, domestic fiction began playing out a fierce struggle to socialize desires whose origin and vicissitudes comprised one's true identity as well as his or her possibilities for growth" (*Desire and Domestic Fiction*, 198). However, she seems to suggest that this "socialization of desire" moves their novels away from the ideal of respectability. My contention will be precisely that Charlotte Brontë worked to reconcile erotic desire to the demands of domestic ideology.

18. Gardiner, *Governess*, vol. 2, 283. Further references will be given parenthetically in the text.

19. Eliot, *Daniel Deronda*, 232. In Countess Blessington's novel, Clara's father commits suicide after an unsuccessful speculation suddenly left him bankrupt (vol. 1, 3). In Eliza Cheap's *The Nursery Governess*, the father suddenly dies, just as his speculations are about to set the family on the path to financial independence (15).

20. Pullan, *Maternal Counsels to a Daughter*, 229. Ambiguity and intermediacy were central to the discursive construction of the governess. This ambivalence of the governess's social position—a gentlewoman who has to work, and who is neither a family member nor a servant—has generally led contemporary scholars to see the governess as a disruptive figure, undoing the familiar Victorian binaries. Mary Poovey offers a classical interpretation of the governess's position along these lines: "Because the governess was like the middle-class mother in the work she performed, but like both a working-class woman and man in the wages she received, the very figure who theoretically should have defended the naturalness of separate spheres threatened to collapse the difference between them" (*Uneven Developments*, 127). M. Jeanne Peterson describes the governess's position in terms of "status incongruence" in her pioneering essay "The Victorian Governess: Status Incongruence in Family and Society," 9–11; compare Hughes, *Victorian Governess*, 86–88. For both Poovey and Hughes, this ambiguity extends both to the class status of the governess and to her sexuality, implying a link with other feminine figures that the contemporary discourse had difficulty placing, including the prostitute, the fallen woman, the spinster, and the lunatic (Poovey, *Uneven Developments*, 29–131, and Hughes, *Victorian Governess*, 118–144). As Hughes writes, "Like the prostitute, the governess was propelled into the domestic heart of the upper and upper middle class from the world of the streets, the world of financial desperation" (119). Although this is a compelling analogy that

certainly does capture some of the Victorian upper-middle-class anxieties, Brontë, as I will show, seems interested in using some altogether different possibilities inherent in the figure of the governess.

21. Martineau, "Governess," 271.
22. O'H., "Governess Mania," 61.
23. Poovey, *Uneven Developments,* 134.
24. Mill, *On Liberty and Other Essays,* 17.
25. Eagleton, *Myths of Power,* 16.
26. In his reading of *Jane Eyre* James Buzard similarly emphasizes the novel's commitment to both self-fulfillment and socialization, but he sees this commitment in opposition to the claims of classical liberalism: "Brontë's revisionary romance seeks the freedom to realize the powers of the female self within the constraints of an intersubjective order, a genuine culture, far more positive and forceful than the pale contractual models of society permitted under classical commercial liberalism" (*Disorienting Fiction,* 210). While I fully agree with Buzard about the novel's desire to enact the heroine's self-realization within an intersubjective context, I am less sure about the need to describe this process, as it is portrayed in the novel, in such stark opposition to the "contractual" logic of liberalism. In other words, while it is certainly true that the novel refuses to endorse any kind of unbridled individualism, it also appears to me that Brontë largely anticipates the central gesture of Mill's *On Liberty:* the positing of right to individual fulfillment as "one of the leading essentials of well-being," individual as well as collective (*On Liberty,* 95).
27. As Buzard points out, "Jane Eyre leads its journeying protagonist along a path that stretches not simply from homelessness to home, but from a series of *antihomes* to the idealized home these define by opposition" (*Disorienting Fiction,* 200).
28. Eagleton, *Myths of Power,* 20.
29. Sandra M. Gilbert and Susan Gubar, for instance, write that "true minds, Charlotte Brontë seems to be saying, must withdraw into a remote forest, a wilderness even, in order to circumvent the strictures of a hierarchical society" (*Madwoman in the Attic,* 369). Along similar lines, Lorna Ellis suggests that "Brontë allows her heroine to be reintegrated with 'society' by starkly limiting what that 'society' is" (*Appearing to Diminish,* 146).
30. Roy, "Unaccommodated Woman," 715. For a reading that similarly emphasizes Jane's complicity with an upper-class ideology and English nationalism, see Politi, "*Jane Eyre* Class-ified." Whereas Roy describes Jane's insistence on having genteel origins as "a little distasteful" and "snobbish" (724), Politi finds her upper-class sympathies and her distaste of poverty "hypocritical" (80). For a critique of the novel's relationship to imperialism, see Spivak, "Three Women's Texts and the Critique of Imperialism."
31. Roy, "Unaccommodated Woman," 720.

32. Mill, "Subjection of Women," 268.
33. Mill, 275.
34. Mill, 278.
35. Eagleton, *Myths of Power,* 30.
36. Fraiman, *Unbecoming Women,* 118.
37. Ironically, while the attempt to define the specifics of the female bildungsroman has been an important task of feminist literary criticism, and while *Jane Eyre* simultaneously enjoyed the status of the preeminent female bildungsroman and of the privileged text of much of feminist criticism, the category of the bildungsroman has rarely been invoked to attend to the specific interpretative problems of the novel. Gilbert and Gubar refer to *Jane Eyre* as a bildungsroman and offer a reading of the novel that is relatively easy to reconcile with the traditional definitions of the genre, but since *The Madwoman in the Attic* shows only limited interest in generic questions, they stop short of engaging the issue (339). The editors of *The Voyage In* concede that *Jane Eyre* fits such traditional definitions more readily than any other Victorian female novel, but because of the editors' investment in the distinction between the male and female bildungsroman, they pursue the matter no further ("Introduction," 15). Lorna Ellis, however, articulates the problem in full force, arguing that "*Jane Eyre* clearly fits all the traditional definitions of the *Bildungsroman,* including those based solely on texts with male protagonists" (*Appearing to Diminish,* 146).
38. Lukács, *Theory of the Novel,* 132.
39. Gilbert and Gubar, *Madwoman in the Attic,* 400.
40. John Hughes, "The Affective World of Charlotte Brontë's *Villette,*" 716. For earlier expressions of similar critical sentiment, see, for instance, Carlisle, "The Face in the Mirror," 263, and Jacobus, *Reading Women,* 41–61. Gretchen Braun has used the theoretical insights of trauma studies to explore what she describes as Lucy's "unspeakable loss." See Braun, "A Great Break in the Common Course of Confession." For an important attempt to locate protomodernist characteristics in the novel, see Auerbach, *Romantic Imprisonment,* 195–211.
41. Lucy's first role at Mme Beck's is that of a nursery governess, a position generally considered inferior to that of a "proper" governess and reserved for young women with fewer educational achievements. This is a position occupied by "well-trained and sufficiently educated young women, *between* the higher calling of the accomplished governess and the inferior services of the maid" (Cheap, *Nursery Governess,* xii). While Lucy's progression directly from a nursery governess to a schoolteacher is quite remarkable, the distinction between a governess and a classroom teacher was generally porous, and women could move back and forth between the two positions (Hughes, *Victorian Governess,* 165).
42. Garrett Stewart has offered a convincing reading of the novel's refusal to admit the death of Paul Emanuel: "We seem invited by the narrator . . . to 'pause'

on the verge of the hero's inevitable fatality while narrative averts its gaze, suppressing any explicit mention of the death, ceding instead to a populace of optimists. The reader is, however, more cornered here than capitulated to, because despite the rhetoric of avoidance, we have no real choice. There is no textually sanctioned option but to recognize the death in its full inevitability" ("Valediction for Bidding Mourning," 52).

43. Brontë, *Villette*, 62. Further references will be given parenthetically in the text.

44. Karen Lawrence has argued, along similar lines, that "one of the striking aspects of Lucy Snowe as protagonist is the degree to which she is primarily a viewer rather than viewed object, an interpreter rather than the erotic, mysterious 'other' to obsess the male gaze and fantasy" ("Cypher," 450). Lawrence sees this invisibility as empowering because it turns the tables on the male gaze. As we shall see in a moment, my reading follows a different path, arguing that Brontë wanted to push her heroine through a fundamentally different set of external pressures compared to those to which she has previously exposed Jane Eyre.

45. Buzard, *Disorienting Fiction*, 213.

46. Thormählen, *Brontës and Religion*, 50.

47. The most thorough engagement with *Villette*'s anti-Catholicism can be found in Buzard's *Disorienting Fiction*, 245–476. As he points out, "Lucy Snowe never does decisively unlearn her proclivity for regarding the Francophone Catholics among whom she lives in Villette as uncivilized savages. On the contrary, growing understanding of them tends to confirm and activate British Protestant values that were perhaps underdeveloped or dormant in her when she lived in Britain" (247). Buzard's reading touches on many of the same themes I explore in this chapter, although some of our conclusions differ, especially with regard to the novel's ending and the nature of the rapprochement between Lucy and Paul Emanuel (see pp. 110–11 in this volume; compare Buzard, *Disorienting Fiction*, 250).

48. See, for instance, Gilbert and Gubar, *Madwoman in the Attic*, 420; Jacobus, *Reading Women*, 46–47; Stokes, "Rachel's Terrible Beauty," 783; and Shuttleworth, *Charlotte Brontë and Victorian Psychology*, 237. For a more ambivalent reading of the Vashti sequence in *Villette*, see Johnson, "This Heretic Narrative." For a useful overview of Lucy's response to art, see Petermann, "'These are not a whit like nature.'"

49. Shuttleworth, *Charlotte Brontë and Victorian Psychology*, 237.

50. See, for instance, Jacobus, *Reading Women*, 47, and Johnson, "This Heretic Narrative," 627.

51. Information on Geefs's work is scant. She is mentioned in the press of the day as a fairly prolific painter who has achieved some success in Brussels and Paris. Her *Assumption of the Virgin* is exhibited in the Church of Saint Joseph in Waterloo. For basic information about her life and work, see Clement and Hutton, *Artists of the Nineteenth Century*, 288, and *Dictionnaire des femmes belges*, 123.

52. The understanding of the baroque as the art of Counter-Reformation is commonplace, although not unproblematized. For a useful overview of the issues involved, see the editors' introduction in *Hispanic Baroques,* ed. Nicholas Spadaccini and Luis Martín-Estudillo, and Burke, "Intensity and Orthodoxy."

## 4. Portrait of the Hero as an Ideologue, ca. 1885–1914

1. Drew, *Dickens the Journalist,* 14.

2. The politics of *Daniel Deronda* have become a source of considerable controversy in recent years, with a number of critics attempting to portray Daniel's political stance as an embodiment of a certain type of cosmopolitanism rather than of ethnolinguistic nationalism. While I find such attempts to be misguided, the precise characterization of Deronda's stance has little bearing on my overall argument: however we judge Daniel's ideology, there can be little doubt that the question of the hero's individual development has become inseparable from the question of ethnic belonging. I address the politics of *Daniel Deronda* in more detail in my "Convenient Cosmopolitanism."

3. Benda, *Great Betrayal,* 2. Further references to be given parenthetically in the text. While Benda's central claim about the betrayal of the intellectuals has grown increasingly contested over the years, his description of the "will to group" (2) as the key characteristic of fin-de-siècle Europe has been reiterated by later social historians. As Michael Biddis observes, "The concepts of class, nation, and race, seemed to provide the age with increasingly effective instruments both for social identification and moral orientation" (*Age of the Masses,* 111).

4. Oakeshott, *Social and Political Doctrines of Contemporary Europe,* xi.

5. On the extension of the franchise, see Biddiss, *Age of the Masses,* 38; Stone, *Europe Transformed,* 40; and Hobsbawm, *Age of Empire,* 85. Already in 1877, the *Times* was very explicit about the dangerous possibilities opened up by democratization: "There is thus certain to be distress and discontent, and whenever these exist the ground is ready for the Socialists. Manhood suffrage is alone needed for the new doctrine to assert itself" ("The German Socialists Seem to Be Increasing," *Times,* Thursday, June 7, 1877, 11). For a concise account of the interrelated forces that enabled the rise of the "age of the masses" in the late nineteenth century, see Garrard, "The Democratic Experience." As Garrard writes, "Newspapers carried voluminous reportage about all kinds of civil associations, providing vast extended platforms for those who ran them. Interests and identities could therefore be articulated and rendered available to very wide audiences, enabling people scattered across a country, or even between countries, to see their experiences and struggles as similar to those elsewhere" (160).

6. Bracher makes this point in relation to the first half of the twentieth century: "Never before," he argues, "did political systems and forms of government, or politics

itself—democratic and dictatorial alike—display such an overwhelming need to justify themselves intellectually, to establish the scope of their power in a comprehensive ideological manner and to extend it as far as possible" (*Age of Ideologies*, 2).

7. Dostoyevsky, *Crime and Punishment*, 648.

8. "It may be," reads the review of James's *The Princess Casamassima* in the *Graphic*, "that Mr. James is deeply versed in human nature and in the physiology of socialist conspiracy; but he assuredly does not succeed in making anybody believe in his characters" ("New Novels," Saturday, December 18, 1886, 646).

9. "German nationalism," wrote a Scottish newspaper, "has got into their Churches like a mighty flood, and the public mind was being rapidly infected" ("The General Assemblies," *Aberdeen Weekly Journal*, Saturday, May 27, 1882, 7). The following year the *Pall Mall Gazette* complained about the "great tide of nationalism" ("Ireland and the Viceroyalty," Thursday, June 21, 1883, 1). Compare also "The Growth of Socialism," *Ipswich Journal*, Friday, January 21, 1887, 2.

10. "The Measure for the Repression of Socialism," *Times*, Wednesday, October 16, 1878, 9.

11. "The Trial of Montceau-les-Mines Church Wreckers," *Glasgow Herald*, Monday, December 25, 1882, 4.

12. *Notebooks of Henry James*, 68. At the time, he was simultaneously working on *The Princess Casamassima* and on *The Bostonians* and felt that the sense of disorientation should be attributed to his divided attention between the two novels.

13. As Michal Ginsburg sums up the common view of the novel, "There can be little critical disagreement that thematically *The Princess Casamassima* is concerned with the relation between social engagement in the form of revolutionary activity and aesthetic experience. But what exactly is the nature of this relation? Most critics (following the lead of the characters themselves) see Hyacinth as choosing, in the course of the novel, aesthetic experience over political engagement" (*Economies of Change*, 156).

14. Scanlan, "Terrorism and the Realistic Novel," 392–93.

15. Benjamin, "Theses on the Philosophy of History," 256.

16. Budd, *Varieties of Unbelief*, 124–49.

17. "Her Oscar Schmidt," *Pall Mall Gazette*, Wednesday, December 4, 1878, n.p.

18. Burrow, *Crisis of Reason*, 46. On social Darwinism, see 92–108.

19. Kaufmann, "Socialism and Atheism," 824. Compare Upton, "Fervent Atheism," 98. On Darwinism's affinity with socialism see also "Natural Science and Free Thought," *Times*, Tuesday, Jan 29, 1878, 4, and Pearson, "Socialism and Natural Selection," 1.

20. "Science Perverted to Infidelity," *Nottinghamshire Guardian*, Friday, August 28, 1868, 6. Gradually such attitudes were being increasingly challenged. Darwin's obituary in the *Times* insisted that the initial perception according to which

Darwin's theory was "necessarily hostile to the fundamental teachings of religion" was abandoned, and rightfully so ("The Late Mr. Darwin," *Times,* Monday, Apr 24, 1882, 10).

21. Butler, *Way of All Flesh,* 435. Further references will be given parenthetically.

22. See, for instance, Bradlaugh, *Humanity's Gain from Unbelief,* and G. W. Foote, *Flowers of Freethought.*

23. On the factual accuracy of the gospels he argues: "If I instance discrepancies whilst treating the gospels, if I show them to contain inaccuracies and discrepancies, they must be incredible; for when a book I put forward as a work from God there should be nothing in it inaccurate, nothing in it incoherent, but all should be plain and straightforward." (*Credibility and Morality of the Four Gospels,* 76). In his *Genesis* (first version published in 1857), Bradlaugh offered an analogous argument regarding the Old Testament. He sought to demonstrate that the Book of Genesis is "unhistoric" and "pieced together after the lapse of many centuries, often clumsily," that "its chronological statements are, on the face of them, absurdly inaccurate, and that they are overwhelmingly contradicted by history and modern discovery," and that its moral teachings would be "destructive to human happiness" (*ix*–x).

24. Bradlaugh, *Credibility and Morality of the Four Gospels,* 78.

25. Raby, *Samuel Butler,* 134.

26. Colenso, *Pentateuch and the Book of Joshua,* 5, emphasis original. Colenso started publishing his multivolume work in 1862. Along with *Essays and Reviews* and Darwin's *Origin of Species,* Colenso's work is listed in *The Way of All Flesh* as one of the decisive intellectual influences at the time when Ernest was entering priesthood (232).

27. *Note-Books of Samuel Butler,* 328. Further references to be given parenthetically.

28. Butler, *Luck or Cunning,* 85.

29. Butler, 317.

30. Butler, *Evolution Old and New,* 360.

31. Said, *Representations of the Intellectual,* xvi.

32. Dahrendorf, "Intellectual and Society," 50. On the intellectual's oppositionary attitude, see also Shills, "Intellectuals and the Powers," 30. The view of intellectuals as exempt from the relations of power is by no means a matter of consensus. This view has been challenged at least since Antonio Gramsci introduced the notion of the "organic intellectual" as a representative of very definite class interests, and since the growing specialization of intellectual work in the second half of the twentieth century, along with the increasingly complex institutional status of intellectuals, rendered the claims to intellectual autonomy even less plausible. However, regardless of whether we accept that the unattached intellectual is a plausible social type, I rely primarily on the sociological tradition exemplified in various ways by Mannheim,

Shils, and Dahrendorf because my literary sources (Butler, and, as we shall see in a moment, Joyce) share with this tradition the investment in the project of intellectual detachment. On the development of the discipline, see Kurzman and Owens, "Sociology of the Intellectuals."

33. The publication of *A Portrait of the Artist as a Young Man* began in the *Egoist*, no. 3, February 1914.

34. Joyce, *A Portrait of the Artist as a Young Man*, 268. Further references to be given parenthetically in the text.

35. Kenner, "The *Portrait* in Perspective," 42.

36. For influential Joycean scholars like Seamus Deane, Emer Nolan, Vincent Cheng, Andrew Gibson, and Gregory Castle, the aestheticist and cosmopolitan Joyce emerges as a construction embodying the mid-century new critical ideals, if not something more sinister. As Cheng argues in a particularly forceful formulation of this view, "One effect, however, of this canonization—of the elevation of an Irish-Catholic colonial writer like Joyce into the pantheon of the Modernist greats—is hardly innocent but rather insidious: for it shifts attention away from the manifestly political content and ideological discourse of Joyce's works onto his unarguably potent role and influence in stylistic revolution.... The net effect is to neutralize the ideological potency of Joyce's texts, to defang the bite of Joyce's politics. Perhaps only in this way could an Irishman whose works bristle with bitter resentment against the imperiums of State, Church, and Academy be somehow appropriated and rendered acceptable, even revered, as a High Modernist icon of the Great English Literary Canon" (*Joyce, Race, and Empire*, 2). For a useful account of the movement from an apolitical toward a political view of Joyce, see Rabaté, *James Joyce and the Politics of Egoism*, 38–39.

37. Gibson, "'Time Drops in Decay,'" 697. In Gibson's book *The Strong Spirit*, which incorporates a revised version of this essay, the final sentence is omitted. However, the book's introduction contains a similarly determined call for a distinctly Irish contextualization of Joyce's work (2–3).

38. Gibson, *James Joyce*, 12.

39. Gibson, 17.

40. Gibson, 40.

41. As Edward Said notes, the exile "exists in a median state, neither completely at one with the new setting, nor fully disencumbered of the old, beset with half-involvements and half-detachments, nostalgic and sentimental on one level, an adept mimic or secret outcast at another" (*Representations of the Intellectual*, 49).

42. Castle, *Modernism and the Celtic Revival*, 173.

43. For instance, Emer Nolan argues that "art, for Joyce, should be autonomous, above the realm of propaganda and politics: he rejected outright the cultural nationalism of Yeats and the Irish Literary Revival. It is, however, seriously misleading to

consider Joyce's relationship to Irish politics solely in these terms" (*James Joyce and Nationalism*, 23).

44. Hobsbawm, *Age of Empire*, 142. See also Anderson, *Imagined Communities*, 7.

45. The classic version of this argument is Eric Hobsbawm's. See Hobsbawm, *Nations and Nationalism since 1870*, chapter 4. I am aware that Hobsbawm's and Anderson's theories, while immensely influential, are often vigorously challenged by scholars, such as Anthony Smith, who claim that both nations and nationalism are much less "invented" or "imagined," and much older than these dominant views would suggest. However, for the purposes of my argument, the dispute between "modernists" and "primordialists" has only limited significance, as the question I am addressing is not whether some of the crucial elements of national identity are essentially premodern. What I take from Hobsbawm is the claim, rarely disputed, that the sense of ethnic and linguistic identity became an immensely powerful political force, and a basis of a widespread populist ideology whose meteoric rise in the late nineteenth century corresponded to the emergence of mass literacy and mass male enfranchisement. For Smith's critique of "modernist" approaches to nationalism and Hobsbawm in particular, see Smith, *Nationalism and Modernism*, 125–37.

46. Smith, 106.

47. "The Irish Language," *Weekly Irish Times*, March 27, 1897, 4.

48. On this, see Zimmer, *Nationalism in Europe*, in particular chapter 3, and Gellner, *Nations and Nationalism*, 106–7.

49. "Keltic Notes," *Weekly Irish Times*, May 1, 1897, 2.

50. "Irish Language Notes," *Weekly Irish Times*, November 5, 1904, 10.

51. Gibson rightly notes this tendency when he writes that "Irish nationalists were acutely aware of the place of their political cause within this larger movement [of emerging nations against their powerful oppressors]" (*Strong Spirit*, 19). However, he doesn't seem to believe that this fact—that the Irish context also has a wider context of its own—should have any bearing on his own "microhistorical" method.

52. From a speech delivered at the Law Students' Debating Society in 1901 ("Lawyers on Gaelic," *Weekly Irish Times*, November 2, 1901, 21).

53. J. Duncan, "Imitation Englishmen," *Irish Times*, August 13, 1912, 9.

54. Thomas O'Donnell, "The Irish Language" (letter), *Weekly Irish Times*, May 11, 1901, 6.

55. Hyde, "On the Necessity for De-Anglicising Ireland," 136.

56. Douglas Hyde's speech at the opening of the Dublin University Gaelic Society in 1909, *Irish Times*, November 24, 1909, 5.

57. Christine van Boheemen-Saaf offers essentially the opposite conclusion, arguing that "in the case of an Irish writer, growing up with English as his first language, the aspiring artist is forced to allude allegorically, and in the *sermo patris* of the oppressor's language, to what can never be voiced with immediacy: the loss of a natural

relationship to language, the lack of interiority of discourse and coherent selfhood" (*Joyce, Derrida, Lacan, and the Trauma of History,* 2). Joyce's relationship to English is therefore irreparably marked by trauma: "Criticism tends to ignore the pain inscribed in his writing—the pain of linguistic dispossession, of the radical severance at the point of origin which belonged to growing up Irish around 1882" (33). However, this claim is not based on an engagement with the concrete realities of Irish history and Joyce's biography, but on an a priori, even essentialist, distinction between the language of the forefathers as the only natural and "immediate" medium whose loss constitutes a trauma, and the language of the oppressor with which the oppressed can never establish a "natural" relationship. Although Boheemen-Saff's interpretation is primarily informed by the legacy of poststructuralism, her reading actually reproduces the binary opposition between "natural" and acquired language that remains central to the discourse of ethnolinguistic nationalism and which Joyce worked to deconstruct in *A Portrait*.

58. Hyde, "On the Necessity for De-Anglicising Ireland," 161.

59. Hyde.

60. Dunleavy and Dunleavy, *Douglas Hyde,* 214.

61. *Critical Writings of James Joyce,* 70.

62. "Architectural Association of Ireland," *Irish Times,* October 9, 1901, 7.

63. Borges, "The Argentine Writer and Tradition," 427.

64. As Jean Michel Rabaté points out, Borges makes this argument by explicitly invoking the Irish example. Argentinians, like the Irish and the Jews, can hope to profit from their hybrid status as both insiders and outsiders in relation to the European literary tradition: they are in a position to borrow irreverently and productively from the entire Western culture ("Borges's Canny Laughter," 174).

65. Aristotle, *Poetics,* 1149b.

66. The Kantian sources of Stephen's theory have been acknowledged for a long time and are sometimes used to question the coherence of his theory, particularly by critics who were otherwise inclined to argue that Joyce maintained an ironic stance toward Stephen. Ever since Hugh Kenner characterized Joyce's attitude to Stephen as nothing short of "mockery," there is a persistent tradition of ironic readings of *A Portrait,* usually based on various complaints about the quality of the hero's artistic achievements and the coherence of his aesthetic theory (see Kenner, "*Portrait* in Perspective"). Although I am interested in Stephen's aesthetics primarily in the context of his rejection of nationalism, this is an appropriate moment to acknowledge that I remain unpersuaded by ironic readings of *A Portrait.* For a particularly helpful rebuttal of this critical attitude, see Yee, "Aesthetics of Stephen's Aesthetics."

67. Kant, *Critique of the Power of Judgment,* 90.

68. On the transformation of beauty into a relational predicate in eighteenth-century British aesthetics, see Jerome Stolnitz, "'Beauty': Some Stages in the History

of an Idea." For Kant's description of the judgment of taste as an instance of subjective universality, see *Critique of the Power of Judgment*, 77.

69. By emphasizing the redemptive political aspects of aesthetic disinterestedness, my analysis participates in a larger movement away from what Fredric Jameson calls "Bourdieu's blanket condemnation of the aesthetic as a mere class signal and as conspicuous consumption" (*Postmodernism*, 132). Contrary to the tradition of the "sociology of aesthetics," a field largely informed by Bourdieu's work, I follow the lead of scholars such as Amanda Anderson and Leela Gandhi, who recognize the more complex ideological implications of both aesthetic detachment and cosmopolitanism. See Anderson, *Powers of Distance,* and Gandhi, *Affective Communities.* By reasserting the significance of Joyce's aestheticism, I am not robbing *A Portrait* of its political potential but emphasizing what Anderson calls "the critical, dialogical, and even emancipatory potential of cultivated detachment" (177). For a defense of the cosmopolitan aspects of Joyce's politics as something more than "a view from nowhere, which registers only gray neutrality or abstract universality," see Valente, "James Joyce and the Cosmopolitan Sublime," 63. The most extensive recent argument emphasizing the importance of modernist cosmopolitanism and its political implications can be found in Rebecca L. Walkowitz's *Cosmopolitan Style*. Although Walkowitz is focusing on Joyce's uses of triviality rather than on Stephen's explicit aesthetic theory, my argument here complements her reading of *A Portrait* in arguing for the liberating political potential of cosmopolitanism. See *Cosmopolitan Style,* 65–70.

70. Curiously, Stephen promises the creation of national "conscience" rather than "consciousness." While the latter term unambiguously points to a sense of national identity, the former can just as easily point to a very literal understanding of collective moral concern. For instance, a 1908 editorial in the *Irish Times* speaks of the "awakening of national conscience" with respect to the dangers of tuberculosis (October 18, 1908, 4). "National conscience" quite often points to a collective sense of moral outrage or an increased awareness of some pressing concern. This suggests, I believe, that Stephen sees Ireland not just as an underdeveloped nation, but as an ethically flawed community.

71. "To the Editor of United Ireland," in Yeats, *Uncollected Prose,* vol. 1, 256.

72. Yeats, "Nationality and Literature," 273.

73. Hyde, "On the Necessity for De-Anglicising Ireland," 118.

74. *Critical Writings of James Joyce,* 173. Further references will be given parenthetically.

75. A decade earlier Douglas Hyde wrote: "We must strive to cultivate everything that is most racial, most smacking of the soil, most Gaelic, most Irish, because in spite of the little admixture of Saxon blood in the north-east corner, this island is and will ever remain Celtic at the core, far more Celtic than most people imagine, because,

as I have shown you, the names of our people are no criterion of their race" ("On the Necessity for De-Anglicising Ireland," 159).

76. Konrád, *Melancholy of Rebirth*, 167. Hyde had a very different vision of the same process: "We will become, what, I fear, we are largely at present, a nation of imitators, the Japanese of Western Europe, lost to the power of native initiative and alive only to second-hand assimilation" ("On the Necessity for De-Anglicising Ireland," 160).

77. Andrew Gibson writes that "as a whole, 'Ireland, Island of Saints and Sages' produces a richly various perspective on Irish history and culture. In its desire to do justice to Ireland when others where disinclined to, it deploys a range of implicitly contradictory positions" (*Strong Spirit*, 119). While I appreciate this insistence on Joyce's nuanced and complex attitude toward Ireland—as Gibson correctly puts it, "defence of Ireland can turn into critique of Ireland, and vice-versa" (*Strong Spirit*, 118)—I cannot escape the impression that Gibson's version of "Ireland, Island of Saints and Sages" is quite a bit more nuanced than Joyce's. John McCourt's comments on an article Joyce produced during his Trieste period do more justice to the position espoused in "Ireland, Island of Saints and Sages": "No matter how great Joyce's fascination with the Irish situation the piece shows that he neither had faith in, nor wished to serve, the Irish cause. So what is offered is an entry into the inconclusive nightmare of Irish history. Joyce the journalist/artist consciously sticks his pen into the spokes of history, into the standard temporal trajectory of most nationalist historical narratives" ("Joyce on National Deliverance," 38).

78. Renan, "What Is a Nation?" 58.

79. Renan.

80. Pericles Lewis has attempted to resolve the tension between nationalism and cosmopolitanism in *A Portrait* by arguing that Stephen really offers an alternative to more conventional versions of nationalism: "In seeking to forge in the smithy of his soul the uncreated conscience of his race, Stephen draws upon the organic nationalist conception of the intimate relationship between the individual and his ethnic group which precedes all cultural ties and fundamentally conditions the individual's experience" (*Modernism, Nationalism, and the Novel*, 41). Stephen therefore sees himself as a Christ-like martyr (50) who sacrifices his soul for Ireland (34). By subscribing to the idea of mystical unity with his race, he can paradoxically reconcile the individualist desire for self-realization with the imperative of serving his race, because they are one and the same thing: "Through his writing, then, Stephen will offer the sacrifice of his own soul to Ireland. Just as this act of martyrdom will save the Irish, however, it will also allow Stephen to achieve unfettered freedom because, in embracing his moral unity with the Irish race, he will reconcile his ethical self with his socially constructed identity" (33). My main objection to this in many ways masterful reading is that it asks us to assume that Stephen is critiquing the "merely superficial nationalism" (41) of

the Gaelic League from a position of a "deeper'" mystical nationalism that promises a much more immediate unity between the individual and his "race" (41–42). There are at least two reasons why this is difficult to accept. The first is that Stephen offers a typical liberal-cosmopolitan critique of the nationalist commitment to the purity of national myth and national language. It is hard to imagine how Stephen can utterly reject "the broken lights of Irish myth" (*A Portrait*, 195) while he simultaneously "places Irish history in the context of a mythical religious pattern that culminates in his own person" (Lewis 32). The second problem is that, in spite of the attention it affords to the debates about national identity and to Stephen's intellectual preoccupations, the novel has little to tell us about the hero's mystical nationalism, except for the vague formulation toward the end of Stephen's diary. In my view, what naturally follows from Stephen's arguments about myth, art, language, and religion is a quasi-nationalist position (expressed by Borges, Konrád, and Joyce himself) that defers nationalist objections to individualism by declaring all self-expression to be the expression of a national spirit.

81. Joyce, *Letters*, vol. 2, 48.
82. Collini, *Public Moralists*, 3.
83. Mannheim, *Ideology and Utopia*, 140. The book was first published in 1929.

## 5. Madame de Guermantes and Other Animals

1. All references to *L'Éducation sentimentale* point to the following editions: Gustave Flaubert, *L'Éducation sentimentale: historie d'un jeune home* (Paris: Garnier-Flammarion, 1969) and, for the English translation, *Sentimental Education,* trans. Robert Baldick, revised with an introduction and notes by Geoffrey Wall (New York: Penguin, 2004). The first number indicates the page number in the French original, while the second indicates the one in the English translation.

2. All this in spite of Proust's own well-documented involvement in the case. Proust was an early signatory of an appeal to free Dreyfus, he was well acquainted with prominent conservatives and anti-Dreyfusards like Léon Daudet and Charles Maurras, and at one point he even managed to have a copy of *Pleasures and Days* smuggled into colonel Picquart's cell (Carter, *Marcel Proust*, 254–56).

3. Malcolm Bowie recognized as much when he described social change in the *Recherche* as an "impersonal" and "ironic" process: "Within a generation, a prominent set of social attitudes has changed and changed again, and the responsibility for these shifts cannot be clearly assigned to individual agents or even to groups propelled by a common purpose" (*Proust among the Stars,* 139). In Bowie's interpretation, however, Proust emerged as something of an enraged moralist committed to brutally satirizing contemporary politics: "Out of the narrator's estrangement from the political sphere comes a sabre-toothed style of political critique. Having no other public role than that of a lesser courtier in a superannuated court, he develops a lucid rage against

politics at large" (133). Along similar lines, Richard Terdiman has argued that Proust offered "a radical critique of *all* social life" (*Dialectics of Isolation,* 228). In my view, however, Proust's treatment of politics has little to do with disillusionment and satire and much more with a wholesale refusal to treat ideological conflict as a governing historical force. Proust's novel is not in the business of simply unearthing the hypocrisy and the banal worldly aspirations underlying all currents of social life, but rather in the business of denying the pragmatic considerations of social life the centrality afforded to it by realists.

4. All references to the *Recherche* are given according to the Pléiade edition: Marcel Proust, *À la recherche du temps perdu,* ed. Jean-Yves Tadié, 4 vols. (Paris: Gallimard, 1987–89). Unless otherwise noted, the references to the English translation are to Marcel Proust, *In Search of Lost Time,* trans. C. K. Scott Moncrieff and Terence Kilmartin, rev. D. J. Enright, 6 vols. (New York: Modern Library, 1992–93). The first number indicates the page number in the French original, while the second indicates the one in the English translation.

5. Compagnon, *Proust between Two Centuries,* 15. Before Compagnon, René Girard has already argued that "none of the questions that interest the sociologist seem to attract Proust's attention. We conclude that this novelist is not interested in the problems of Society" (*Desire, Deceit, and the Novel,* 217).

6. Nothing underscores this absence better than the exasperation of those critics who would like to extract from the *Recherche* a clear image of socioeconomic reality. "We cannot," wrote Michael Sprinker, "brusquely ignore this massive silence, but neither ought we to dismiss it as simple lack of interest or even ignorance" (*History and Ideology in Proust,* 10). For Sprinker, the lack of specifics about the sources of wealth and the logic of class struggle in the *Recherche* is both obvious and intolerable. He concedes that the novel pays no attention to the lower classes (5), acknowledges that there are very few signs of "open economic or political warfare" among the bourgeoisie and the aristocracy (53) and is, naturally, forced to turn to speculation: "In the absence of any evidence to the contrary, it is probably fair to assume that Proust's upper class characters are mostly rentiers with holdings in land (like the Guermanteses' country estates or Swan's Tansonville) and, equally likely, considerable investment in securities" (49–50). In my view, the very fact that the critic is forced to make assumptions about such matters should alert us that something is amiss. For other attempts to read Proust as something of a Balzac of the Third Republic, see Bidou-Zachariasen, *Proust sociologue,* and Chesney, "Aristocracy and Modernism." Even Malcolm Bowie, who has otherwise argued that "it would be unwise to think of *À la recherche du temps perdu* as a documentary record of the Third Republic, or as the fictional recreation of a characteristically French political process," is ready to concede that, while uninterested in politics in the strict sense of the word, Proust "anatomises" class relations (*Proust among the Stars,* 126–27).

7. The results were generated using the ARTFL-FRANTEXT database hosted by the University of Chicago.

8. In some ways, Marcel's fascination with the aristocracy is closer to that of Goethe's Wilhelm Meister than to that of French realism. See, for instance, Goethe, *Wilhelm Meister's Apprenticeship*, 174.

9. I am drawing here on Monroe Beardsley's classic description of aesthetic experience: "A person is having an aesthetic experience during a particular stretch of time if and only if the greater part of his mental activity during that time is united and made pleasurable by being tied to the form and qualities of a sensuously presented or imaginatively intended object on which his primary attention in concentrated" (*Aesthetic Point of View*, 81; further references to be given parenthetically).

10. The fact that Marcel acts primarily as an observer rather than as an active participant in the events of his own novel has often led critics to see Proust's narrator as a voyeur and to conceptualize the connection between knowledge and pleasure in the *Recherche* in Freudian terms. Not only in the explicitly voyeuristic observation of sexual acts, but also in his exploration of the history of the Guermantes, Marcel follows the epistemophilic instinct that functions as a sublimation the sexual drive: in the final instance, all thirst for knowledge is a form of sexual desire. This is a view most explicitly articulated by Ann Gaylin, who, drawing on Peter Brooks's theorization of epistemophilia, points to "Proust's intimate association of sexual knowledge with this larger epistemological urge" (*Eavesdropping in the Novel*, 140). For various earlier descriptions of Marcel as a voyeur, see Levin, *Gates of Horn*, 387; Murray, "Mystery of Others"; Sullivan, "On Vision in Proust"; and Ladimer, "Narrator as Voyeur." While this voyeuristic paradigm is compelling in some ways, I believe that the tradition of cognitivist aesthetics offers a better opportunity to construct a theoretical model that can account for the complex relationship between knowledge and pleasure in Proust's novel: the *Recherche* is interested in both the pleasures of seeing, knowing, and understanding, and, as I show throughout this chapter, in the pleasures derived from the encounter with the unfamiliar. For similar reasons, I am reluctant to follow Leo Bersani's and Joshua Landy's approaches to the *Recherche* as an essentially philosophical exercise in epistemology. As Bersani argues, in addition to being a novel about Marcel, the *Recherche* also "purports to be about the mental processes that make knowledge impossible" (Bersani, *Marcel Proust*, 197; compare Landy, *Philosophy as Fiction*, 51). While this is true as far as it goes, Proust's novel generates an interplay between pleasure and knowledge that goes not beyond mere voyeurism but also beyond a philosophical interest in the conditions of knowing.

11. As he writes in "Science as a Vocation," the advancement of the processes of "intellectualization and rationalization" implies that "principally there are no mysterious incalculable forces that come into play, but rather that one can, in principle, master all things by calculation. This means that the world is disenchanted. One need

no longer have recourse to magical means in order to master or implore the spirits, as did the savage, for whom such mysterious powers existed" (Weber, *From Max Weber*, 139).

12. Shklovsky, *Theory of Prose*, 5.

13. Segalen, *Essay on Exoticism*, 19. Further references to be given parenthetically in the text.

14. Germaine Bree offered a classical version of the "disillusionment" argument: driven by this snobbish fascination, Marcel is attracted to various social groups until he becomes an insider and the spell breaks. Proust's aristocrats are but "automatons" devoid of all substance and fully committed only to empty social conventions, and even if they are in a way attractive, "this charm does not, however, prevent Proust from emphasizing the cruelty of the social comedy" (*Marcel Proust and Deliverance from Time*, 99).

15. Shklovsky, *Theory of Prose*, 6.

16. This cognitivist understanding of aesthetic pleasure can be traced back at least to the work of Francis Hutcheson, who was explicitly concerned with the pleasure of knowing. Writing about the beauty of theorems, Hutcheson explores various forms in which intellectual discoveries emerge as sources of pleasure regardless of any practical application such discoveries may yield: "In the Search of Nature there is the like Beauty in the Knowledge of some great Principles or universal Forces from which innumerable Effects do flow" (*Inquiry*, 34).

17. Darwin, *Evolutionary Writings*, 423. Zoological textbooks around the turn of the century naturally advocated for the emulation of this key capacity: "The student who has formed the habit of seeking the meanings of facts in natural history will carry this habit into the study of history.... The habits of observation and interpretation once formed will be carried through life and applied in every line of thought" (Colton, *Zoology*, v).

18. Carpenter, *Intermediate Sex*, 21.

19. As J. E. Rivers argues, "Most of the theories of homosexuality found in *À la recherche* were a commonplace long before Proust wrote, and many of them were adopted directly from the standard medical theories of Proust's day" (*Proust and the Art of Love*, 157). Rivers's book remains the most thoroughly researched study of homosexuality in Proust and is particularly helpful in locating the main late nineteenth-century medical sources that theorize same-sex desire. However, his interpretation of the *Recherche* suffers from some serious limitations. As Eve Sedgwick notes, Rivers's book, which is "full of interesting scholarship and awful writing, undertakes essentially to set Proust straight on gay issues—and especially on his 'negative stereotypes'—according to the latest in empirical research" (*Epistemology of the Closet*, 213–14). Antoine Compagnon offers a more nuanced account of Proust's relationship to late nineteenth-century medical literature on homosexuality, although

I think that he is going too far in trying to distance Proust from his medical sources (*Proust between Two Centuries,* 45–49).

20. As Georges Saint-Paul writes, "The first important point to immediately note is that in the weak, it's not only the spirit, the morals, and finally love (if we want to give that meaning to the word) that is feminine, but also the body. In the majority of cases this being *is* and *was* feminine in its physical complexion; it is not only the haughty, coquettish, vain character, that betrays a woman, but also the development of the hips, the pelvis, the thighs, the prominence of the breasts, the softness of eyes, the whiteness and delicacy of skin, the delicacy of wrists, allow us to affirm that he suffers from a *non-acquired, innate,* fault" (Dr. Laupts, *Perversion et perversité sexuelles,* 191–92).

21. In the words of George Beard, who is generally credited with giving this term the meaning that will dominate nineteenth-century medical literature, "If a patient complains of general malaise, debility of all the functions, poor appetite, abiding weakness in the back and spine, fugitive neuralgic pains, hysteria, insomnia, hypochondriases, disinclination for consecutive mental labor, severe and weakening attacks of sick headache, and other analogous symptoms, and at the same time gives no evidence of anoemia or of any organic disease, we have reason to that the central suspect nervous system is mainly at fault, and that we are dealing" ("Neurasthenia, or Nervous Exhaustion," 218).

22. Beard, *Sexual Neurasthenia,* 102–3. The book was translated into French in 1895 (*La neurasthénie sexuelle*). Proust's father, in his book on neurasthenia (which significantly draws on Beard as one of the traditional authorities in the field) also recognizes a powerful link between masturbation and neurasthenia. Adrien Proust and Gilbert Ballet, *L'hygiène du neurasthénique,* 154.

23. One of the most significant differences between the *Recherche* and various preparatory materials and Proust's letters is precisely that the medical discourse is contaminated by other ideas. Drafts of what eventually became the beginning of *Sodome et Gomorrhe* can be traced back as far as 1909. Parts of the early manuscript under the title *La race des tantes* are published in the *Esquisse* to the third volume of the Tadié's 1988 edition (930–33). See also Compagnon's note in the same edition, 1202. Explaining Charlus's character in an 1814 letter to Gide, Proust insisted that he "tried to portray a homosexual infatuated with virility because, without knowing it, he is a Woman" (*Selected Letters,* vol. 3, 268). A year earlier, in a letter to Louis de Robert, he insists that "this dream of masculine beauty is the result of a neurotic defect" (194). Finally, Proust goes on to describe homosexuality as "a perversion compensated for by superior gifts" (*Selected Letters,* vol. 4, 338). In the letters Proust uses the terms *homosexuality, pederasty,* and *inversion* interchangeably.

24. Dr. Laupts, *Perversion et perversité sexuelles,* 9. Tarnowsky's description of inversion as a "moral malformation" is similarly straightforward: "Just as children can

be born with anomalies of extremities, of the torso, the head or the limbs, a congenital tendency towards perverted manifestations of the reproductive instinct may reveal itself" (*L'Instinct sexuel et ses manifestations morbides*, 18).

25. Ulrichs, *Riddle of "Man-Manly" Love*, vol. 1, 36. Further references will be given parenthetically.

26. While Ulrichs's work was well known and regularly included in surveys of literature on inversion, his insistence that the condition was not pathological was ignored. Richard von Krafft-Ebing insisted that "Ulrichs failed, however, to prove that this certainly congenital and paradoxical sexual feeling was physiological and not pathological" (*Psychopathia Sexualis*, 224), while Julien Chevalier, whose book on sexual inversion contains a concise summary of Ulrichs's ideas, finds it noteworthy that Ulrichs himself failed to exhibit any signs of degeneracy: "He has shown no signs of intellectual disorders, he was very erudite, very knowledgeable about statistics, and well known in the worlds of public service and politics as an author of several scientific works" (*L'inversion sexuelle*, 143). In his comments on Proust's sources, Compagnon seems to disregard the fundamental distinction between Ulrichs's views and those of subsequent writers like Krafft-Ebing (*Proust between the Two Centuries*, 241).

27. McCrea, *In the Company of Strangers*, 205. For an alternative reading of Proust's uses of botany, see also Luckhurst, *Science and Structure*, 141–53.

28. Goodrich, *Peter Parley's Cyclopedia of Botany*, ix.

29. Bentley, *Botany*, iv. Robert Chodat captures this duality particularly well, insisting simultaneously that observing plants in their natural environment is vital because "laboratory is not the same thing as nature," but also that botanical excursions offer a variety of pleasures and, in particular, the joy of unexpected discoveries (*Excursions botaniques*, 1–2). See also *A travers champs*, vii, and Le Maout, *Botanique*, ii.

30. This duality was already noted by Kant: "Flowers are free natural beauties. Hardly anyone but a botanist knows what sort of thing a flower is supposed to be; and even the botanist, who recognizes in it the reproductive organ of the plant, pays no attention if he judges the flower by means of taste" (*Critique of the Power of Judgment*, 114).

31. A precedent for the use of botanical observation within the context of the bildungsroman can be found in Adalbert Stifter's 1857 *Indian Summer*. Stifter's protagonist begins his exploration of the world by observing nature and by studying botanical and geological classifications. However, his methodical study of nature does not serve a further purpose in advancing his understanding the social world, which remains remarkably limited (22–23).

32. *Works of Honoré de Balzac*, vol. 1, 55.

33. The distinction between Proust's treatment of male and female homosexuality is usually debated in terms of their asymmetrical relationship to medical knowledge.

As Elisabeth Ladenson argues, Gomorrah attracts little of that "sociological, taxonomic fascination, general in aim and scientific in nature," which is reserved for Sodom (*Proust's Lesbianism*, 32; compare also Luckhurst, *Science and Structure*, 162). There is no extensive theorization of lesbianism in the novel, and, as Ladenson further argues, unlike male inverts who desire men because deep down they are really women, lesbians are not simply men in female bodies. They *are* women *desiring* women, and hence the only examples of "true homosexuality" in the *Recherche* (*Proust's Lesbianism*, 30). While it is true that lesbianism is not a female analogue to inversion, its relationship to medical knowledge is more complex than Ladenson suggests. Proust's treatment of lesbianism is not entirely free of medical and cultural clichés: as we have seen, he links Andrée's sexual preferences to her neurasthenia (2:295, 2:714) and goes on to describe the exchange of signs between the two lesbian lovers (III, 245; IV, 439).

34. Bersani, *Marcel Proust*, 63. See also Levin, *Gates of Horn*, 416.

35. The character of Albertine appears already in the novel's second published volume, *À l'ombre des jeunes filles en fleurs* (1919); however, in the order of writing, she is among the latest additions. According to Tadié, the name Albertine first appears in 1913, although Proust begins to develop her narrative only in 1914 (*Marcel Proust*, 717).

36. Schmidt, "The Birth and Development of *À la recherche du temps perdu*," 66. For a more detailed treatment of this period of the *Recherche's* development, see Tadié, *Marcel Proust*, 701–21.

## Epilogue

1. Woolf, *Voyage Out*, 5. Further references will be given parenthetically in the text.

2. Woolf, *Jacob's Room*, 246. Further references will be given parenthetically in the text.

3. Mann, *Magic Mountain*, 704.

4. I make this argument in somewhat more detail in my "Bildungsroman kao Kunstlerroman," 46–47.

# BIBLIOGRAPHY

All references to nineteenth- and early twentieth-century newspapers point to electronic versions that have been accessed through the following databases: ProQuest Historical Newspapers, British Library Newspapers (Gale), the *Times* Digital Archive (Gale), and Gallica (Bibliothèque nationale de France). Full bibliographic information for individual newspaper articles is provided in the notes. Cited articles from weekly and monthly periodicals have been included in the bibliography.

Abel, Elizabeth, Marianne Hirsch, and Elizabeth Langland, eds. *The Voyage In: Fictions of Female Development.* Hanover, NH: University Press of New England, 1983.

Alter, Robert. "Proust and the Ideological Reader." *Salmagundi* 58–59 (1982–83): 347–57.

Altieri, Charles. "Organic and Humanist Models in Some English Bildungsroman." *Journal of General Education* 23 (1971): 220–39.

Anderson, Amanda. *The Powers of Distance: Cosmopolitanism and the Cultivation of Detachment.* Princeton, NJ: Princeton University Press, 2001.

Anderson, Benedict. *Imagined Communities: Reflections on the Origin and Spread of Nationalism.* London: Verso, 2003.

Anderson, Gordon K. "Old Nobles and Noblesse d'Empire 1814–1830: In Search of a Conservative Interest in Post-revolutionary France." *French History* 8, no. 2 (1994): 149–66.

Andrews, Malcolm. *Dickens and the Grown-up Child.* London: Macmillan, 1994.

Aristotle. *Poetics.* Translated by Malcolm Heath. New York: Penguin, 1997.

Armstrong, Nancy. *Desire and Domestic Fiction: A Political History of the Novel.* Oxford: Oxford University Press, 1987.

———. *How Novels Think: The Limits of Individualism from 1719–1900.* New York: Columbia University Press, 2005.

Arnold, Matthew. *Culture and Anarchy and Other Writings.* Edited by Stefan Collini. Cambridge: Cambridge University Press, 1999.

*À travers champs. Botanique pour tous, histoire des principales familles végétales, revue par J. Decaisne. Ouvrage orné de 746 vignetes.* Paris: J. Rothschild, 1884.

Auerbach, Erich. *Mimesis: The Representation of Reality in Western Literature.* Translated by Willard R. Task. Princeton, NJ: Princeton University Press, 1953.
Auerbach, Nina. *Romantic Imprisonment: Women and Other Glorified Outcasts.* New York: Columbia University Press, 1985.
Austin, J. L. *How to Do Things with Words.* Edited by J. O. Urmson and Marina Sbisà. Oxford: Clarendon, 1975.
Bakhtin, Mikhail. "The *Bildungsroman* and Its Significance in the History of Realism (Toward a Historical Typology of the Novel)." In *Speech Genres and Other Late Essays,* edited by Caryl Emerson and Michael Holquist, translated by Vern W. McGee, 10–59. Austin: University of Texas Press, 1986.
——. "Forms of Time and Chronotope in the Novel." In *The Dialogic Imagination: Four Essays,* edited by Michel Holquist, translated by Michael Holquist and Caryl Emerson, 84–258. Austin: University of Texas Press, 1981.
Baldridge, Cates. "The Instabilities of Inheritance in *Oliver Twist.*" *Studies in the Novel* 25, no. 2 (1993): 184–95.
Balzac, Honoré de. *César Birotteau.* Paris: Gallimard, 1975.
——. *Correspondance.* Vol. 3. Edited by Roger Pierrot. Paris: Garnier Frères, 1964.
——. *La Cousine Bette.* Paris: Gallimard, 1972.
——. *Un début dans la vie.* Paris: Gallimard, 2003.
——. *A Harlot High and Low.* Translated by Rayner Happenstall. London: Penguin, 1970.
——. *Illusions perdues.* Paris: Gallimard, 2004.
——. *Lost Illusions.* Translated by Kathleen Raine. New York: Modern Library, 1997.
——. *Le Père Goriot.* Paris: Gallimard, 1999.
——. *Père Goriot.* Translated by A. J. Krailsheimer. Oxford: Oxford University Press, 1999.
——. *Splendeurs et misères des courtisanes.* Paris: Gallimard, 2008.
——. *The Works of Honoré de Balzac.* Vol. I. Translated by Ellen Marriage. Philadelphia: Avil, 1901.
Barnett, Rosalind, and Caryl Rivers. *Same Difference: How Gender Myths Are Hurting Our Relationships, Our Children, and Our Jobs.* New York: Basic Books, 2004.
Barthélemy, Édouard de. *Noblesse en France avant et depuis 1789.* Paris: Librairie Nouvelle, 1858.
Barthelemy, Tiphaine. "Patronymic Names and *Noms de Terre* in the French Nobility of the Eighteenth and the Nineteenth Centuries." *History of the Family* 5, no. 2 (2000): 181–97.
Barthes, Roland. "An Idea of Research." In *The Rustle of Language,* translated by Richard Howard, 271–76. Berkeley: University of California Press, 1989.

Bauman, Zygmunt. *Liquid Modernity*. Cambridge: Polity, 2006.
Beard, George. "Neurasthenia, or Nervous Exhaustion." *Boston Medical Journal* 3, no. 13 (April 19, 1869): 217–21.
———. *La neurasthénie sexuelle: hygiène, causes, symptômes et traitement*. Translated by Paul Rodet. Paris: Société d'éditions scientifiques, 1895.
———. *Sexual Neurasthenia [Nervous Exhaustion]: Its Hygiene, Causes, Treatment, and Symptoms, with a Chapter on the Diet for the Nervous*. New York: E. B. Treat, 1884.
Beardsley, Monroe C. *The Aesthetic Point of View: Selected Essays*. Edited by Michael J. Wreen and Donald M. Callen. Ithaca, NY: Cornell University Press, 1982.
Beebe, Maurice. *Ivory Towers and Sacred Founts: The Artist as Hero in Fiction from Goethe to Joyce*. New York: New York University Press, 1964.
Beddow, Michael. *The Fiction of Humanity: Studies in the Bildungsroman from Wieland to Thomas Mann*. Cambridge: Cambridge University Press, 1982.
Benda, Julien. *The Great Betrayal*. Translated by Richard Aldington. London: George Routledge & Sons, 1928.
Benjamin, Walter. "The Image of Proust." In *Illuminations: Essays and Reflections,* edited by Hannah Arendt, translated by Harry Zohn, 201–16. New York: Shocken, 2007.
———. "Theses on the Philosophy of History." In *Illuminations: Essays and Reflections,* 253–64.
Bentham, Jeremy. *Writings on the Poor Laws*. Vol. 1. Edited by Michael Quinn. Oxford: Clarendon, 2001.
Bentley [Robert]. *Botany*. London: Society for the Promotion of Christian Knowledge, 1875.
Berman, Jessica. *Modernist Fiction, Cosmopolitanism, and the Politics of Community*. Cambridge: Cambridge University Press, 2001.
Berman, Marshall. *All That Is Solid Melts into Air: The Experience of Modernity*. New York: Penguin, 1988.
Bersani, Leo. "The Culture of Redemption: Marcel Proust and Melanie Klein." *Critical Inquiry* 12, no. 2 (1986): 399–421.
———. *Marcel Proust: The Fictions of Life and Art*. New York: Oxford University Press, 1969.
Biddis, Michael D. *The Age of the Masses: Ideas and Society in Europe since 1870*. Atlantic Highlands, NJ: Humanities, 1977.
Bidou-Zachariasen, Catherine. *Proust sociologue: De la maison aristocratique au salon bourgeois*. Paris: Descartes et Scie, 1997.
Blackbourn, David. *The Long Nineteenth Century: A History of Germany, 1780–1918*. Oxford: Oxford University Press, 1998.

Bodenheimer, Rosemarie. *The Politics of Story in Victorian Social Fiction.* Ithaca, NY: Cornell University Press, 1988.

Boes, Tobias. "Apprenticeship of the Novel: Bildungsroman and the Invention of History ca. 1770–1829." *CLS* 45, no. 3 (2008): 269–88.

———. "Beyond the *Bildungsroman:* Character Development and Communal Legitimation in the Early Fiction of Joseph Conrad." *Conradiana* 39, no. 2 (2007): 113–34.

———. *Formative Fictions: Nationalism, Cosmopolitanism, and the Bildungsroman.* Ithaca, NY: Cornell University Press, 2012.

———. "*A Portrait of the Artist as a Young Man* and the 'Individuating Rhythm' of Modernity." *ELH* 75, no. 4 (2008): 267–85.

Boheemen-Saaf, Christine Van. *Joyce, Derrida, Lacan, and the Trauma of History: Reading, Narrative, and Postcolonialism.* Cambridge: Cambridge University Press, 1999.

Bonald, Louis de. *Réflexions sur l'intérêt général de l'Europe, suivies de quelques considerations sur la noblesse.* Paris: Le Normant, 1815.

Bonaparte, Felicia. "History and the Novel of Development." *PMLA* 108, no. 5 (1993): 1171–72.

Borges, Jorge Luis. "The Argentine Writer and Tradition." In *Selected Nonfictions,* edited by Eliot Weinberger, translated by Esther Allen, Suzanne Jill Levine, and Eliot Weinberger, 420–26. New York: Viking, 1999.

Bourdieu, Pierre. "The Forms of Capital." Translated by Richard Nice. In *The Sociology of Economic Life,* edited by Mark Granovetter and Richard Swedberg, 96–111. Boulder, CO: Westview, 2001.

———. *The Rules of Art: Genesis and Structure of the Literary Field.* Translated by Susan Emanuel. Stanford, CA: Stanford University Press, 1996.

Bowers, Rick. "Stephen's Practical Artistic Development." *James Joyce Quarterly* 21, no. 3 (1984): 231–43.

Bowie, Malcolm. *Proust among the Stars.* London: HarperCollins, 1998.

Bracher, Karl Dietrich. *The Age of Ideologies: A History of Political Thought in the Twentieth Century.* Translated by Ewald Osers. New York: St. Martin's, 1984.

Bradlaugh, Charles. *Genesis: Its Authorship and Authenticity.* 3rd ed. London: Watts, 1882.

———. *Humanity's Gain from Unbelief.* London: Freethought, 1889.

Brantlinger, Patrick. *The Spirit of Reform: British Literature and Reform, 1832–1867.* Cambridge, MA: Harvard University Press, 1977.

Braudel, Fernand, and Ernest Labrousse, eds. *Historie économique et sociale de la France.* Vol. 3:2. Paris: Presses Universitaires de France, 1976.

Braun, Gretchen. "'A Great Break in the Common Course of Confession': Narrating Loss in Charlotte Brontë's *Villette*." *ELH* 78, no. 1 (2011): 189–212.

Bree, Germaine. *Marcel Proust and Deliverance from Time*. Translated by C. J. Richards and A. D. Truitt. New Brunswick, NJ: Rutgers University Press, 1969.
Bresnick, Adam. "The Paradox of Bildung: Balzac's *Illusions Perdues*." *MLN* 113, no. 4 (1998): 823–50.
Brodsky Lacour, Claudia. "Narrate or Educate: *Le Père Goriot* and the Realist Bildungsroman." In *Approaches to Teaching Balzac's* Old Goriot, edited by Michal Ginsburg, 32–44. New York: Modern Language Association of America, 2000.
Brontë, Charlotte. *Jane Eyre*. Edited by Richard Dunn. New York: W. W. Norton, 2001.
———. *Villette*. Edited by Herbert Rosengarten and Margaret Smith. Oxford: Clarendon, 1984.
Brooks, Peter. "Balzac: Epistemophilia and the Collapse of the Restoration." *Yale French Studies* 101 (2001): 119–31.
———. *The Melodramatic Imagination: Balzac, Henry James, Melodrama, and the Mode of Excess*. New Haven, CT: Yale University Press, 1976.
———. *Reading for the Plot: Design and Intention in Narrative*. New York: Alfred A. Knopf, 1984.
———. *Realist Vision*. New Haven, CT: Yale University Press, 2005.
Bruford, W. H. *The German Tradition of Self-Cultivation: "Bildung" from Humboldt to Thomas Mann*. New York: Cambridge University Press, 1975.
Bryne, Paul. *Social Movements in Britain*. London: Routledge, 1997.
Buckley, Jerome Hamilton. *Season of Youth: The Bildungsroman from Dickens to Golding*. Cambridge, MA: Harvard University Press, 1974.
Bucknall, Barbara J. *The Religion of Art in Proust*. Urbana: University of Illinois Press, 1969.
Budd, Susan. *Varieties of Unbelief: Atheists and Agnostics in English Society, 1850–1960*. London: Heinemann, 1977.
Burke, Marcus B. "Intensity and Orthodoxy in Iberian and Hispanic Art of the Tridentine Era, 1550–1700." In *A Companion to Renaissance and Baroque Art*, edited by Babette Bohn and James M. Saslow, 484–504. Chichester: Wiley-Blackwell, 2013.
Burrow, J. W. *The Crisis of Reason: European Thought, 1848–1914*. New Haven, CT: Yale University Press, 2000.
Butler, Samuel. *Evolution Old and New*. London: Hardwicke & Bogue, 1879.
———. *Luck or Cunning, as the Main Means of Organic Modification? An Attempt to Throw an Additional Light on the Late Mr. Charles Darwin's Theory of Natural Selection*. London: Trübner, 1887.
———. *The Note-Books of Samuel Butler*. Edited by Henry Festing Jones. New York: E. P. Dutton, 1917.
———. *The Way of All Flesh*. New York: E. P. Dutton, 1917.

Buzard, James. *Disorienting Fiction: The Autoethnographic Work of Nineteenth-Century British Novels.* Princeton, NJ: Princeton University Press, 2005.

Camerer, Colin F. *Behavioral Game Theory: Experiments in Strategic Interaction.* Princeton, NJ: Princeton University Press, 2003.

Cargill, Oscar. "*Princess Casamassima:* A Critical Reappraisal." *PMLA* 71, no. 1 (1956): 97–117.

Carlisle, Janice. "The Face in the Mirror: *Villette* and the Conventions of Autobiography." *ELH* 46, no. 2 (1979): 262–89.

Carpenter, Edward. *The Intermediate Sex: A Study of Some Transitional Types of Men and Women.* New York: Mitchell Kennerley, 1921.

Carter, William C. *Marcel Proust: A Life.* New Haven, CT: Yale University Press, 2000.

Castle, Gregory. *Modernism and the Celtic Revival.* Cambridge: Cambridge University Press, 2001.

———. *Reading the Modernist Bildungsroman.* Gainesville: University of Florida Press, 2006.

Channing, William E. *Self-Culture: An Address Introductory to the Franklin Lectures, Delivered at Boston, United States.* London: J. Cleave, 1838[?].

Charcot, Jean-Michel, and Valentine Magnan. "Inversions du sens génital." *Archives de neurologie* 3, no. 7 (1882): 56–60.

———. "Inversions du sens génital (suite)." *Archives de neurologie* 4, no.10 (1882): 296–322.

Chauveau, Adolphe. *Code pénal progressif: commentaire sur la loi modificative du Code penal.* Paris: L'Editeur, 1832.

Cheap, Eliza. *The Nursery Governess.* London: Seeley, Burnside & Seeley, 1845.

Cheng, Vincent J. *Joyce, Race, and Empire.* Cambridge: Cambridge University Press, 1995.

Chevalier, Julien. *L'inversion sexuelle: psycho-physiologie, sociologie, tératologie, aliénation mentale, psychologie morbide, anthropologie, médecine judiciaire.* Paris: G. Masson, 1893.

———. *Une maladie de la personnalité: Inversion sexuelle.* Paris: G. Masson, 1893.

Chodat, Robert. *Excursions botaniques en Espagne et au Portugal.* Genève: Imprimerie Eugène Froreisen, 1909.

*Christianity and Secularism: Which Is the Better Suited to Meet the Wants of Mankind? A Written Debate between the Rev. George Sexton, M.A., L.L.M., and Charles Watts, Esq.* London: Smart & Allen, 1881.

*Christianity or Secularism: Which Is True? The Verbatim Report of a Four Nights' Debate between Rev. Dr. James McCann and Mr. G.W. Foote.* London: Progressive, 1886.

Clark, Priscilla P. "Proustian Order and the Aristocracy of Time Past." *French Review* 47, no. 6 (1974): 92–104.
Clement, Clara Erskine, and Laurence Hutton. *Artists of the Nineteenth Century.* Vol. 1. Boston: Houghton, Mifflin, 1887.
Coats, A. W., ed. *Poverty in the Victorian Age.* 4 vols. Westmead: Gregg International, 1973.
Cohen, Margaret. *The Sentimental Education of the Novel.* Princeton, NJ: Princeton University Press, 2002.
Cohen, Monica F. *Professional Domesticity in the Victorian Novel: Women, Work, and Home.* Cambridge: Cambridge University Press, 1998.
Cohen, Ralph. "History and Genre." *New Literary History* 17 (1986): 203–18.
Cohn, Dorrit. "Proust's Generic Ambiguity." *Genre: Forms of Discourse and Culture* 29, no. 3 (1996): 359–81.
Colenso, John William. *The Pentateuch and the Book of Joshua, Critically Examined.* London: Longman, 1865.
Collingham, H. A. C. *The July Monarchy: A Political History of France, 1830–1848.* London: Longman, 1988.
Collini, Stefan. *Public Moralists: Political Thought and Intellectual Life in Britain, 1850–1930.* Oxford: Clarendon, 1991.
Collins, Philip, ed. *Charles Dickens: The Critical Heritage.* New York: Routledge, 1986.
———. *Dickens and Crime.* New York: St. Martin's, 1994.
———. *Dickens and Education.* London: Macmillan, 1963.
Colón, Susan E. *Professional Ideal in the Victorian Novel: The Works of Disraeli, Trollope, Gaskell, and Eliot.* Basingstoke: Palgrave Macmillan, 2007.
Colton, Buel Preston. *Zoology: Descriptive and Practical. Part I: Descriptive.* Boston: D. C. Heath, 1903.
Compagnon, Antoine. *Proust between Two Centuries.* Translated by Richard E. Goodkin. New York: Columbia University Press, 1992.
Cook, Eliza. "Poor Genteel Women." *Littell's Living Age* 32 (March 13, 1852): 513.
Craik, George Lillie. *The Pursuit of Knowledge under Difficulties; Illustrated by Anecdotes.* London: Charles Knight, 1830.
*The Credibility and Morality of the Four Gospels: The Only Authorized and Verbatim Report of the Five Nights' Discussion between Rev. T. D. Matthias, Baptist Minister and Iconoclast.* London: Farrah, Wilks & Dunbar, 1860.
Crotch, W. Walter. *Charles Dickens Social Reformer: The Social Teachings of England's Great Novelist.* London: Chapman & Hall, 1913.
Curtius, Ernst Robert. *Marcel Proust.* Translated from the German by Armand Pierhal. Paris: La Revue novelle, 1928.

Dahrendorf, Ralf. "The Intellectual and Society: The Social Function of the 'Fool' in the Twentieth Century." In *On Intellectuals: Theoretical Studies, Case Studies,* edited by Philip Rieff, 48–56. Garden City, NY: Doubleday, 1969.

Daleski, H. M. *Dickens and the Art of Analogy.* London: Faber & Faber, 1970.

Darwin, Charles. *Evolutionary Writings: Including the Autobiographies.* Edited by James A. Secord. Oxford: Oxford University Press, 2010.

DeLaura, David. "Heroic Egotism: Goethe and the Fortunes of *Bildung* in Victorian England." In *Johann Wolfgang von Goethe: One Hundred Years of Continuing Vitality,* edited by Ulrich Goebel and W. T. Zyla, 41–60. Lubbock: Texas Tech University Press, 1984.

Deleuze, Gilles. *Proust and Signs: The Complete Text.* Translated by Richard Howard. Minneapolis: University of Minnesota Press, 2000.

Derrida, Jacques. "Declarations of Independence." In *Negotiations: Interventions and Interviews, 1971–2001,* edited and translated by Elizabeth Rottenberg, 46–54. Stanford, CA: Stanford University Press, 2002.

DeVine, Christine. "Revolution and Democracy in the *London Times* and *The Princess Casamassima.*" *Henry James Review* 23, no. 1 (2002): 53–71.

Diani, Mario. "The Concept of Social Movement." *Sociological Review* 40, no. 1 (1992): 1–25.

Dickens, Charles. *American Notes.* Boston: Ticknor & Fields, 1967.

———. *David Copperfield.* Edited by Nina Burgis. Oxford: Clarendon, 1981.

———. *Great Expectations.* Edited by Margaret Cardwell. Oxford: Oxford University Press, 1998.

———. *Oliver Twist.* Edited by Kathleen Tillotson. Oxford: Oxford University Press, 1999.

———. *The Speeches of Charles Dickens.* Edited by Paul Fideler. Oxford: Clarendon, 1960.

*Dictionnaire des femmes belges: XIXe et XXe siècles.* Bruxelles: Editions Racine, 2006.

*Dictionnaire historique de la langue française.* Paris: Dictionnaires Le Robert, 1993.

Dilthey, Wilhelm. *Poetry and Experience.* Selected Works, vol. 5. Edited by Rudolf A. Makkreel and Frithjof Rodi. Princeton, NJ: Princeton University Press, 1985.

*Discussion on Atheism: Report of a Public Discussion between Rev. Brewin Grant, B.A., and Mr. C. Bradlaugh, Esq.* London: Anti-Liberation Society, 1890.

Dostoyevsky, Fyodor. *Crime and Punishment.* Translated by David McDuff. London: Penguin, 2003.

Drew, John M. L. *Dickens the Journalist.* Houndmills: Palgrave Macmillan, 2003.

Duncan, Ian. *Modern Romance and Transformations of the Novel: The Gothic, Scott, Dickens.* Cambridge: Cambridge University Press, 1992.

Dunleavy, Janet Egleson, and Gareth W. Dunleavy. *Douglas Hyde: A Maker of Modern Ireland*. Berkeley: University of California Press, 1991.

Eagleton, Terry. *The English Novel: An Introduction*. Malden, MA: Blackwell, 2005.

———. *Myths of Power: A Marxist Study of the Brontës*. Houndmills: Palgrave Macmillan, 2005.

Easley, Keith. "Self-Possession in *Great Expectations*." *Dickens Studies Annual* 39 (2008): 177–222.

Elias, Norbert. *The Civilizing Process: The History of Manners*. Translated by Edmund Jephcott. Oxford: Blackwell, 1978.

Eliot, George. *Daniel Deronda*. Edited by Graham Handley. Oxford: Oxford University Press, 1998.

———. *Middlemarch*. Oxford: Oxford University Press, 2008.

———. *The Mill on the Floss*. Edited by Carol T. Christ. New York: W. W. Norton, 1994.

Ellis, Lorna. *Appearing to Diminish: Female Development and the British* Bildungsroman, *1750–1850*. Lewisburg, PA: Bucknell University Press, 1999.

Ellis, William. "Eight Report of the Commissioners appointed by Parliament to inquire respecting Charities." *Westminster Review* 2 (July 1824): 97–121.

Esty, Jed. "The Colonial Bildungsroman: *The Story of an African Farm* and the Ghost of Goethe." *Victorian Studies* 49, no. 3 (2007): 407–30.

———. *Unseasonable Youth: Modernism, Colonialism, and the Fiction of Development*. Oxford: Oxford University Press, 2012.

Fehr, Ernst, and Simon Gächter. "Reciprocity and Economics: The Economic Implications of *Homo Reciprocans*." *European Economic Review* 42 (1998): 845–59.

Fideler, Paul. *Social Welfare in Pre-Industrial England: The Old Poor Law Tradition*. Basingstoke: Palgrave Macmillan, 2006.

Finlayson, Geoffrey. *Citizen, State, and Social Welfare in Britain, 1830–1990*. Oxford: Clarendon, 1993.

Flaubert, Gustave. *L'Éducation sentimentale: historie d'un jeune home*. Paris: Garnier-Flammarion, 1969.

———. *Sentimental Education*. Revised with an introduction and notes by Geoffrey Wall. Translated by Robert Baldick. New York: Penguin, 2004.

Foote, G. W. *Flowers of Freethought*. London: R. Forder, 1893.

Forest, Jean. *L'Aristocratie balzacienne*. Paris: Librairie J. Corti, 1972.

Forster, E. M. *The Longest Journey*. Edited by Elizabeth Heine. London: Penguin, 2006.

Forster, John. *The Life of Charles Dickens*. Vol. 1. Philadelphia: J. B Lippincott, 1872.

Foucault, Michel. *The History of Sexuality, Vol. 1: An Introduction*. Translated by Robert Hurley. New York: Vintage, 1990.

———. *The History of Sexuality, Vol. 2: The Use of Pleasure.* Translated by Robert Hurley. New York: Vintage, 1990.

———. *The History of Sexuality, Vol. 3: The Care of the Self.* Translated by Robert Hurley. New York: Vintage, 1988.

Fowler, Alastair. *Kinds of Literature: Introduction to the Theory of Genres and Modes.* Cambridge, MA: Harvard University Press, 1982.

Fraiman, Susan. *Unbecoming Women: British Women Writers and the Novel of Development.* New York: Columbia University Press, 1993.

Fraser, Derek. *The Evolution of the British Welfare State: A History of Social Policy since the Industrial Revolution.* 2nd ed. London: Macmillan, 1984.

Freud, Sigmund. "Notes upon a Case of Obsessional Neurosis." In *The Standard Edition of the Complete Psychological Works of Sigmund Freud*, 153–318. Vol. 10. London: Hogarth, 1955.

Furet, François. *Revolutionary France, 1770–1880.* Translated by Antonia Nevill. Oxford: Blackwell, 1992.

Gallagher, Catherine. *The Industrial Reformation of English Fiction: Social Discourse and Narrative Form, 1832–1867.* Chicago: University of Chicago Press, 1985.

Gandhi, Leela. *Affective Communities: Anticolonial Thought, Fin-de-Siècle Radicalism, and the Politics of Friendship.* Durham, NC: Duke University Press, 2006.

Gardiner, Margaret [the Countess of Blessington]. *The Governess.* 2 vols. London: Longman, Orme, Brown, Green & Longmans, 1839.

Garrard, John. "The Democratic Experience." In *A Companion to Nineteenth-Century Europe, 1789–1914,* edited by Stefan Berger, 149–63. Malden, MA: Blackwell, 2006.

Gaylin, Ann. *Eavesdropping in the Novel from Austen to Proust.* Cambridge: Cambridge University Press, 2002.

Gellner, Ernest. *Nations and Nationalism.* Oxford: Blackwell, 1983.

———. "La trahison de la trahison des clercs." In *The Political Responsibility of Intellectuals,* edited by Ian Maclean, Alan Montefiore, and Peter Winch, 17–28. Cambridge: Cambridge University Press, 1990.

Geertz, Clifford. *Interpretation of Cultures: Selected Essays.* New York: Basic Books, 2000.

Gibson, Andrew. *James Joyce.* London: Reaktion, 2006.

———. *The Strong Spirit: History, Politics, and Aesthetics in the Writings of James Joyce, 1898–1915.* Oxford: Oxford University Press, 2013.

———. "'Time Drops in Decay': *A Portrait of the Artist* in History (ii), Chapter 2." *James Joyce Quarterly* 44, no. 4 (2007): 697–717.

Giddens, Anthony. *The Consequences of Modernity.* Stanford, CA: Stanford University Press, 1991.

———. *Modernity and Self-Identity: Self and Society in the Late Modern Age.* Stanford, CA: Stanford University Press, 1991.
———, and Christopher Pierso. *Conversations with Anthony Giddens: Making Sense of Modernity.* Stanford, CA: Stanford University Press, 1999.
Gilbert, Sandra M., and Susan Gubar. *The Madwoman in the Attic: The Woman Writer and the Nineteenth-Century Literary Imagination.* New Haven, CT: Yale University Press, 1979.
Gilligan, Carol. *In a Different Voice: Psychological Theory and Women's Development.* Cambridge, MA: Harvard University Press, 1982.
Gilmour, Robin. *The Idea of the Gentlemen in the Victorian Novel.* London: George Allen & Unwin, 1981.
Ginsburg, Michal Peled. "Dickens and the Uncanny: Repression and Displacement in *Great Expectations.*" *Dickens Studies Annual* 13 (1984): 115–24.
———. *Economies of Change: Form and Transformation in the Nineteenth-Century Novel.* Stanford, CA: Stanford University Press, 1996.
Girard, René. *Desire, Deceit, and the Novel: Self and Other in Literary Structure.* Translated by Yvonne Freccero. Baltimore, MD: Johns Hopkins University Press, 1976.
Giraud, Raymond. *The Unheroic Hero in the Novels of Stendhal, Balzac, and Flaubert.* New Brunswick, NJ: Rutgers University Press, 1957.
Gissing, George. *The Immortal Dickens.* London: Cecil Palmer, 1925.
Godechot, Jacques, ed. *Les Constitutions de la France depuis 1789.* Paris: Garnier-Flammarion, 1970.
Goethe, Johann Wolfgang von. *Wilhelm Meister's Apprenticeship.* Vol. 9, *The Collected Works.* Edited and translated by Eric A. Blackall with Victor Lange. Princeton, NJ: Princeton University Press, 1994.
Goldmann, Lucien. *Towards a Sociology of the Novel.* Translated by Alan Sheridan. London: Tavistock, 1975.
Gomart, Hélène. *Opérations financières dans le roman réaliste: lectures de Balzac et de Zola.* Paris: Champion, 2004.
Goodrich, Samuel Griswold. *Peter Parley's Cyclopedia of Botany: Including Familiar Descriptions of Trees, Shrubs, and Plants: with Numerous Engravings.* Boston: Otis, Broaders, 1838.
Gouldner, Alvin W. "The Norm of Reciprocity: A Preliminary Statement." *American Sociological Review* 25, no. 2 (1960): 161–78.
Greenblatt, Stephen. *Renaissance Self-Fashioning: From More to Shakespeare.* Chicago: University of Chicago Press, 1980.
Greg, W. R. "Charity, Noxious and Beneficent." *Westminster Review* 59 (January 1853): 62–88.

Halperin, David M. *One Hundred Years of Homosexuality and Other Essays on Greek Love.* London: Routledge, 1989.

Hardin, James. "An Introduction." In *Reflection and Action: Essays on the Bildungsroman,* edited by James Hardin, ix–xxvii. Columbia: University of South Carolina Press, 1991.

Hardy, Barbara. *The Moral Art of Dickens.* New York: Oxford University Press, 1970.

Hardy, Thomas. *Jude the Obscure.* Oxford: Oxford University Press, 2008.

Harris, José. *Private Lives, Public Spirit: A Social History of Britain, 1870–1914.* Oxford: Oxford University Press, 1993.

Harrison, J. F. C. *Late Victorian Britain, 1875–1901.* New York: Routledge, 1991.

Harvey, David. *Paris, Capital of Modernity.* New York: Routledge, 2003.

Held, Virginia. *The Ethics of Care: Personal, Political, and Global.* Oxford: Oxford University Press, 2006.

Higgs, David. *Nobles in Nineteenth-Century France: The Practice of Inegalitarianism.* Baltimore, MD: Johns Hopkins University Press, 1987.

Highmore, A. *Pietas Londinensis: The History, Design, and Present State of the Various Public Charities in and Near London.* London: R. Phillips, 1810.

Himmelfarb, Gertrude. *The Idea of Poverty: England in the Early Industrial Age.* New York: Alfred A. Knopf, 1984.

Hirsch, Marianne. "Spiritual *Bildung:* The Beautiful Soul as Paradigm." In *The Voyage In: Fictions of Female Development,* edited by Elizabeth Abel, Marianne Hirsch, and Elizabeth Langland, 23–48. Hanover, NH: University Press of New England, 1983.

Hobsbawm, Eric. *The Age of Capital: 1848–1875.* New York: Vintage, 1996.

———. *The Age of Empire: 1875–1914.* New York: Vintage, 1989.

———. *The Age of Revolution: 1789–1848.* New York: Vintage, 1996.

———. *Nations and Nationalism since 1780: Programme, Myth, Reality.* Cambridge: Cambridge University Press, 1992.

Hocquenghem, Guy. *Homosexual Desire.* Translated by Daniella Dangoor. Durham, NC: Duke University Press, 1993.

Horkheimer, Max, and Theodor W. Adorno. *Dialectic of Enlightenment: Philosophical Fragments.* Edited by Gunzelin Schmid Noerr. Translated by Edmund Jephcott. Stanford, CA: Stanford University Press, 2002.

Hollier, Dennis, ed. *A New History of French Literature.* Cambridge, MA: Harvard University Press, 1998.

Hood, Edwin Paxton. *Self-Formation: Twelve Chapters for Young Thinkers.* 3rd ed. London: Jude & Glass, 1858.

House, Humphry. *The Dickens World.* 2nd ed. Oxford: Oxford University Press, 1979.

Howe, Susanne. *Wilhelm Meister and His English Kinsmen: Apprentices to Life.* New York: Columbia University Press, 1930.
Hughes, Edward J. "The Mapping of Homosexuality in Proust's *Recherche*." *Paragraph: A Journal of Modern Critical Theory* 18, no. 2 (1995): 148–62.
———. "Proustian Metamorphosis: The Art of Distortion in *À la recherche du temps perdu*." *Modern Language Review* 94, no. 3 (1999): 660–72.
Hughes, H. Stuart. *Consciousness and Society: The Reorientation of European Social Thought, 1890–1930.* New York: Knopf, 1958.
Hughes, John. "The Affective World of Charlotte Brontë's *Villette*." *SEL* 40, no. 4 (2000): 711–26.
Hughes, Kathryn. *The Victorian Governess.* London: Hambledon & London, 2001.
Humboldt, Wilhelm von. *The Limits of State Action.* Edited by J. W. Burrow. Cambridge: Cambridge University Press, 2009.
Hutcheson, Francis. *An Inquiry into the Original of Our Ideas of Beauty and Virtue, in Two Treatises.* London: D. Midwinter, 1738.
Hyde, Douglas. "On the Necessity for De-Anglicising Ireland." In, *The Revival of Irish Literature and Other Addresses,* by Charles Gavan Duffy, George Sigerson, and Douglas Hyde, 117–61. London: T. Fisher Unwin, 1894.
*Is the Bible Divine? A Six Nights' Discussion between Mr. Charles Bradlaugh and Mr. Robert Roberts.* London: F. Pitman, 1876.
Jacobus, Mary. *Reading Women: Essays in Feminist Criticism.* New York: Columbia University Press, 1986.
James, Henry. *The Notebooks of Henry James.* Edited by F. O. Matthiessen and Kenneth Murdock. Chicago: University of Chicago Press, 1981.
———. *The Princess Casamassima.* Edited by Derek Brewer. Harmondsworth: Penguin, 1987.
———. *The Portrait of a Lady.* Oxford: Oxford University Press, 1998.
———. *Roderick Hudson.* London: Penguin, 1986.
Jameson, Fredric. *The Political Unconscious: Narrative as a Socially Symbolic Act.* Routledge: New York, 2003.
———. *Postmodernism, or, the Cultural Logic of Late Capitalism.* Durham, NC: Duke University Press, 1991.
Jeffers, Thomas L. *Apprenticeships: The Bildungsroman from Goethe to Santayana.* New York: Palgrave Macmillan, 2005.
Johnson, Christopher H. "1830 in French Economic History." In *1830 in France,* edited by John Merriman, 141–43. New York: New Viewpoints, 1975.
Johnson, Paul. *The Birth of the Modern: World Society, 1815–1830.* London: Phoenix, 1992.
Johnson, Patricia E. "'This Heretic Narrative': The Strategy of the Split Narrative in Charlotte Brontë's *Villette*." *SEL* 30, no. 4 (1990): 617–31.

Jordan, John O. "Partings Welded Together: Self-Fashioning in *Great Expectations* and *Jane Eyre.*" *Dickens Quarterly* 13, no. 1 (1996): 19–33.

———. "The Social Sub-text of *David Copperfield.*" *Dickens Studies Annual* 14 (1985): 39–61.

Jones, Peter. "Knowledge and Illusion in *À la recherche du temps perdu.*" *Forum for Modern Language Studies* 5 (1969): 303–22.

Joyce, James. *The Critical Writings of James Joyce.* Edited by Ellsworth Mason and Richard Ellmann. New York: Viking, 1959.

———. *The Letters of James Joyce.* 2 vols. Edited by Richard Ellmann. New York: Viking, 1966.

———. *A Portrait of the Artist as a Young Man.* Edited by Seamus Deane. New York: Penguin, 2003.

———. *Stephen Hero.* Norfolk, CT: New Directions, 1963.

———. *Ulysses.* Edited by Hans Gabler. New York: Vintage, 1986.

Kant, Immanuel. *Critique of the Power of Judgment.* Translated by Paul Guyer and Eric Matthews. Cambridge: Cambridge University Press, 2000.

Karabel, Jerome. "Towards a Theory of Intellectuals and Politics." *Theory and Society* 25, no. 2 (1996): 205–23.

Kaufmann, Moritz. "Socialism and Atheism." *Contemporary Review* 47 (June 1885): 823–40.

Kelly, Dorothy. *Telling Glances: Voyeurism in the French Novel.* New Brunswick, NJ: Rutgers University Press, 1992.

Kelly, George A. "Liberalism and Aristocracy in the French Restoration." *Journal of the History of Ideas* 26, no. 4 (1965): 509–30.

Kenner, Hugh. "The Portrait in Perspective." In *Joyce's Portrait: Criticisms and Critiques,* edited by Thomas E. Connolly, 25–59. New York: Appleton-Century-Crofts, 1962.

Kettle, Arnold. *An Introduction to the English Novel.* Vol. 1. London: Hutchinson's University Library, 1951.

Kincaid, Jamaica. *Annie John.* New York: Farrar, Strauss & Giroux, 1997.

Kincaid, James R. "Performance, Roles, and the Nature of the Self in Dickens." In *Dramatic Dickens,* edited by Carol Hanbery MacKay, 11–26. New York: St. Martin's, 1989.

Konrád, György. *The Melancholy of Rebirth: Essays from Post-Communist Central Europe, 1989–1994.* Translated by Michael Henry Heim. San Diego: Harcourt Brace, 1995.

Kontje, Todd. *The German Bildungsroman: History of a National Genre.* Columbia, SC: Camden House, 1993.

———. *Private Lives in the Public Sphere: The German Bildungsroman as Metafiction.* University Park: Pennsylvania State University Press, 1992.

Krafft-Ebing, Richard. *Psychopatia Sexualis, with Special Reference to the Contrary Sexual Instinct: A Medico-Legal Study.* Translated from the 7th German edition by Charles Gilbert Chaddock. London: F. J. Rebman, 1894.
Kucich, John. *Repression in Victorian Fiction: Charlotte Brontë, George Eliot, and Charles Dickens.* Berkeley: University of California Press, 1987.
Kurzman, Charles, and Lynn Owens. "The Sociology of the Intellectuals." *Annual Review of Sociology* 28 (2002): 63–90.
Ladenson, Elizabeth. *Proust's Lesbianism.* Ithaca, NY: Cornell University Press, 1999.
Ladimer, Bethany. "The Narrator as Voyeur in *À la recherche du temps perdu*." *Critical Quarterly* 19, no. 3 (1977): 5–20.
Landy, Joshua. *Philosophy as Fiction: Self, Deception, and Knowledge in Proust.* Oxford: Oxford University Press, 2004.
———. "Proust, His Narrator, and the Importance of the Distinction." *Poetics Today* 25, no. 1 (2004): 91–135.
Lanser, Susan Sniader. *Fictions of Authority: Women Writers and Narrative Voice.* Ithaca, NY: Cornell University Press, 1992.
Laupts, Dr. [Georges Saint-Paul]. *Perversion et perversité sexuelles: tares et poisons.* Preface by Émile Zola. Paris: G. Carré, 1896.
Lawrence, D. H. *Sons and Lovers.* Oxford: Oxford University Press, 2009.
Lawrence, Karen. "The Cypher: Disclosure and Reticence in *Villette*." *Nineteenth-Century Literature* 42, no. 4 (1988): 448–66.
Laybourn, Keith. *The Evolution of British Social Policy and the Welfare State c. 1800–1993.* Keele: Keele University Press, 1995.
Leavis, F. R. *The Great Tradition: George Eliot, Henry James, and Joseph Conrad.* New York: New York University Press, 1969.
———, and Q. D. Leavis. *Dickens the Novelist.* London: Chatto & Windus, 1970.
Lees, Lynn Hollen. *The Solidarities of Strangers: The English Poor Laws and the People, 1700–1848.* Cambridge: Cambridge University Press, 1998.
Le Maout, Emmanuel. *Botanique: organographie et taxonomie: histoire naturelle des familles végétales et des principales espèces, suivant la classification de M. Adrien de Jussieu. Avec l'indication de leur emploi dans les arts, les sciences et le commerce.* Paris: L. Curmer, 1854.
Levin, Harry. *The Gates of Horn: A Study of Five French Realists.* Oxford: Oxford University Press, 1963.
———. "Proust, Gide, and the Sexes." *PMLA* 65, no. 4 (1950): 648–52.
Levine, George. *Dying to Know: Scientific Epistemology and Narrative in Victorian England.* Chicago: University of Chicago Press, 2002.
Lévi-Strauss, Claude. *The Elementary Structures of Kinship.* Translated by James Harle Bell, John Richard von Sturmer, and Rodney Needham. Boston: Beacon, 1969.

Lewis, Pericles. *Modernism, Nationalism, and the Novel.* Cambridge: Cambridge University Press, 2000.
Lofft, Capel. *Self-Formation; or, The History of an Individual Mind: Intended as a Guide for the Intellect through Difficulties to Success. By a Fellow of a College.* Boston: W. Crosby & H. P. Nichols, 1846.
Lucey, Michael. *The Misfit of the Family: Balzac and the Social Forms of Sexuality.* Durham, NC: Duke University Press, 2003.
———. *Never Say I: Sexuality and the First Person in Colette, Gide, and Proust.* Durham, NC: Duke University Press, 2006.
Luckhurst, Nicola. *Science and Structure in Proust's* À la recherche du temps perdu. Oxford: Oxford University Press, 2000.
Lukács, Georg. *The Historical Novel.* Lincoln: University of Nebraska Press, 1983.
———. *Realism in Our Time: Literature and Class Struggle.* Translated by John and Necke Mander. New York: Harper & Row, 1964.
———. *Studies in European Realism.* Translated by Edith Bone. London: Hillway, 1950.
———. *The Theory of the Novel.* Transated by Anna Bostock. Cambridge, MA: MIT Press, 1971.
Magnan, Valentin. *Des Anomalies, des aberrations et des perversions sexuelles: Communication faite à l'Académie de médecine dans la séance du 13 janvier 1885.* Paris: Progrès Médical, 1885.
Magraw, Roger. *France, 1800–1914: A Social History.* London: Longman, 2002.
Mahoney, Dennis F. "The Apprenticeship of the Reader: The Bildungsroman of the 'Age of Goethe.'" In *Reflection and Action: Essays on the Bildungsroman,* edited by James Hardin, 97–117. Columbia: University of South Carolina Press, 1991.
Malthus, Thomas Robert. *An Essay on the Principle of Population: and, a Summary View of the Principle of Population.* Edited by Antony Flew. London: Penguin, 1985.
Mann, Thomas. *The Magic Mountain.* Translated by John E. Woods. New York: Vintage, 1996.
Mannheim, Karl. *Ideology and Utopia.* New York: Routledge, 2002.
Martineau, Harriet. "The Governess." *Once a Week,* September 1, 1860, 267–72.
Martini, Fritz. "Bildungsroman—Term and Theory." In *Reflection and Action: Essays on the Bildungsroman,* edited by James Hardin, 1–25. Columbia: University of South Carolina Press, 1991.
Mayhew, Henry. *London Labour and the London Poor: A Cyclopedia of the Conditions and Earnings of Those That Will Work, Those That Cannot Work, and Those That Will Not Work.* 3 vols. London: Griffin, Bohn, 1861–62.
Marcus, Steven. *Dickens: From Pickwick to Dombey.* London: Chatto & Windus, 1965.

Markovits, Stefanie. *The Crisis of Action in Nineteenth-Century English Novel.* Columbus: Ohio State University Press, 2006.
Maupassant, Guy. *Bel Ami.* Paris: Gallimard, 1999.
Mayer, Arno J. *The Persistence of the Old Regime: Europe to the Great War.* New York: Pantheon, 1981.
McColl Chesney, Duncan. "Aristocracy and Modernism: Signs of Aristocracy in Marcel Proust's *À la recherche du temps perdu.*" *MLN* 120, no. 4 (2005): 871–95.
McCourt, John. "Joyce on National Deliverance: The View from 1907 Trieste." *Prospero: Rivista di Letterature Straniere, Comparatistica e Studi Culturali* 5 (1998): 27–48.
McCrea, Barry. *In the Company of Strangers: Family and Narrative in Dickens, Conan Doyle, Joyce, and Proust.* New York: Columbia University Press, 2011.
Meckier, Jerome. "*Great Expectations* and *Self-Help:* Dickens Frowns on Smiles." *Journal of English and Germanic Philology* 100, no. 4 (2001): 537–54.
Meredith, George. *The Ordeal of Richard Feverel: A History of Father and Son.* Edited by Edward Mendelson. London: Penguin, 1998.
Miles, Andrew. *Social Mobility in Nineteenth- and Early Twentieth-Century England.* New York: St. Martin's, 1999.
Mill, John Stuart. *On Liberty and Other Writings.* Edited by Stefan Collini. Cambridge: Cambridge University Press, 2000.
———. *Principles of Political Economy: With Some of Their Applications to Social Philosophy.* 2 vols. London: J. W. Parker, 1848.
———. "The Subjection of Women," In *Essays on Equality, Law, and Education,* edited by John M. Robson, 259–320. London: Routledge & Kegan Paul, 1984.
Miller, D. A. "Balzac's Illusions Lost and Found." *Yale French Studies* 67 (1984): 164–81.
———. *The Novel and the Police.* Berkeley: University of California Press, 1989.
Miller, J. Hillis. *Charles Dickens: The World of His Novels.* Cambridge, MA: Harvard University Press, 1965.
———. "The Other's Other: Jealousy and Art in Proust." *Qui Parle: Literature, Philosophy, Visual Arts, History* 9, no. 1 (1995): 119–40.
Miller, Nathan. "Some Aspects of the Name in Culture-History." *American Journal of Sociology* 32, no. 4 (1927): 585–600.
Minden, Michael. *The German Bildungsroman: Incest and Inheritance.* Cambridge: Cambridge University Press, 1997.
Moretti, Franco. *Modern Epic: The World System from Goethe to Garcia-Marquez.* Translated by Quintin Hoare. London: Verso, 1996.
———. *Signs Taken for Wonders: Essays in the Sociology of Literary Forms.* Translated by Susan Fischer, David Forgacs, and David Miller. London: NLB, 1983.

———. *The Way of the World: The Bildungsroman in European Culture.* Translated by Albert Sbraglia. London: Verso, 2000.

———, ed. *Novel.* 2 vols. Princeton, NJ: Princeton University Press, 2007.

Morgenstern, Karl. "On the Nature of the Bildungsroman." Translated by Tobias Boes. *PMLA* 124, no. 2 (2009): 650–59.

Morris, Pam. *Imagining Inclusive Society in Nineteenth-Century Novels: The Code of Sincerity in the Public Sphere.* Baltimore, MD: Johns Hopkins University Press, 2004.

Murray, Jack. "The Mystery of Others." *Yale French Studies* 34 (1965): 65–72.

Nabokov, Vladimir. *The Gift.* New York: Vintage, 1991.

Noddings, Nel. *Caring: A Feminine Approach to Caring and Moral Education.* Berkeley: University of California Press, 1984.

———. *Educating Moral People: A Caring Alternative to Character Education.* New York: Teachers College, 2002.

———. *The Maternal Factor: Two Paths to Morality.* Berkeley: University of California Press, 2010.

Nolan, Emer. *James Joyce and Nationalism.* New York: Routledge, 1995.

Oakeshott, Michael. *The Social and Political Doctrines of Contemporary Europe.* Cambridge: Cambridge University Press, 1939.

O'Brian, Justin. "Albertine the Ambiguous: Notes on Proust's Transposition of Sexes." *PMLA* 64, no. 5 (1949): 933–52.

O'H., E. "The Governess Mania." *London Journal,* September 27, 1851, 61.

Orwell, George. *Collected Essays.* London: Secker & Warburg, 1975.

Osteen, Mark. "The Great Expectations of Stephen Dedalus." *James Joyce Quarterly* 41, nos. 1–2 (2003–4): 169–83.

Owen, David. *English Philanthropy, 1660–1960.* Cambridge, MA: Belknap Press of Harvard University Press, 1964.

Owen, Robert. *A New View of Society: Or, Essays on the Formation of the Human Character.* 3rd ed. London: Longman, 1817.

Pavel, Thomas. "Genres as Norms and Good Habits." *New Literary History* 34 (2003): 201–10.

Pearson, Karl. "Socialism and Natural Selection." *Fortnightly Review* 56 (July 1894): 1–21.

Pecora, Vincent P. "Inheritances, Gifts, and Expectations." *Law & Literature* 20, no. 2 (2008): 177–96.

Petermann, Emily. "'These are not a whit like nature': Lucy Snowe's Art Criticism in *Villette.*" *Bronte Studies* 36, no. 3 (2011): 279–90.

Peterson, M. Jeanne. "The Victorian Governess: Status Incongruence in Family and Society." In *Suffer and Be Still: Women in the Victorian Age,* edited by Martha Vicinus, 3–19. Bloomington: Indiana University Press, 1972.

Petrey, Sandy. *In the Court of the Pear King: French Culture and the Rise of Realism.* Ithaca, NY: Cornell University Press, 2005.

———. *Realism and Revolution: Balzac, Stendhal, Zola, and the Performances of History.* Ithaca, NY: Cornell University Press, 1988.

Pettiteau, Natalie. *Élites et mobilités: la noblesse d'Empire au XIXe Siècle (1808–1914).* Paris: La Boutique de l'Historie, 1997.

"The Philanthropy of the Age and its Relation to Social Evils." *Westminster Review* 35 (April 1869): 437–57.

Polletta, Francesca, and James M. Jasper. "Collective Identity and Social Movements." *Annual Review of Sociology* 27 (2001): 283–305.

Politi, Jina. "*Jane Eyre* Class-ified." In *Jane Eyre,* edited by Heather Glen, 78–91. Basingstoke: Macmillan, 1997.

Pope, Norris. *Dickens and Charity.* New York: Columbia University Press, 1978.

Poovey, Mary. *Making a Social Body: British Cultural Formation, 1830–1864.* Chicago: University of Chicago Press, 1995.

———. *Uneven Developments: The Ideological Work of Gender in Mid-Victorian England.* London: Virago, 1989.

Porta, Donatella della, and Mario Diani. *Social Movements: An Introduction.* Malden, MA: Blackwell, 2006.

Prendergast, Christopher. *Balzac: Fiction and Melodrama.* London: Edward Arnold, 1978.

———. "Melodrama and Totality in *Splendeurs et miseres des courtisanes.*" *Novel: A Forum on Fiction* 6 (1973): 152–62.

———. *The Order of Mimesis: Balzac, Stendhal, Nerval, and Flaubert.* Cambridge: Cambridge University Press, 1986.

Price, Roger. *A Social History of Nineteenth-Century France.* London: Hutchinson, 1987.

Proust, Adrien, and Gilbert Ballet. *L'hygiène du neurasthénique.* Paris: Masson et Cie, 1897.

Proust, Marcel. *À la recherche du temps perdu.* Edition publiée sous la direction de Jean-Yves Tadié. 4 vols. Paris: Gallimard, 1987–89.

———. *In Search of Lost Time.* 6 vols. Translated by C. K. Scott Moncrieff and Terence Kilmartin. Revised by D. J. Enright. New York: Modern Library, 1992–93.

———. *Selected Letters.* Vol. 3: 1910–1917. Edited by Philip Kolb. Translated by Terence Kilmartin. London: HarperCollins, 1992.

———. *Selected Letters.* Vol. 4: 1918–1922. Edited by Philip Kolb. Translated by Joanna Kilmartin. London: HarperCollins, 2000.

Pugh, Martin. *State and Society: A Social and Political History of Britain, 1870–2007.* London: Hodder Arnold, 2008.

Pullan, Mrs. *Maternal Counsels to a Daughter.* London: Darton, 1855.

Rabaté, Jean-Michel. "Borges's Canny Laughter: 'a joyce for ever.'" In *Cy-Borges: Memories of the Posthuman in the Work of Jorge Luis Borges,* edited by Stephen Herbrechter and Ivan Callus, 164–77. Lewisburg, PA: Bucknell University Press, 2009.

———. *James Joyce and the Politics of Egoism.* Cambridge: Cambridge University Press, 2001.

Raby, Peter. *Samuel Butler: A Biography.* Iowa City: University of Iowa Press, 1991.

Redfield, Marc. *Phantom Formations: Aesthetic Ideology and the Bildungsroman.* Ithaca, NY: Cornell University Press, 1996.

———. Review of *Formative Fictions: Nationalism, Cosmopolitanism, and the Bildungsroman,* by Tobias Boes. *Monatshefte* 105, no. 4 (2013): 718–20.

Reid, Hugo. *What Should Be Done for the People: An Appeal to the Electors of the United Kingdom.* London: Simpkin, Marshall, 1848.

Renan, Ernest. "What Is a Nation?" In *Nationalism in Europe, 1815 to the Present: A Reader,* edited by Stuart Woolf, 48–60. London: Routledge, 1996.

*Report from His Majesty's Commissioners for Inquiring into the Administration and Practical Operation of the Poor Laws. Pub. by Authority.* London: B. Fellowes, 1834.

"Reports of the Society for the Suppression of Mendicity, 1838–1839." *Quarterly Review* 64 (October 1839): 341–69.

Rivers, J. E. *Proust and the Art of Love: The Aesthetics of Sexuality in Life, Times, and Art of Marcel Proust.* New York: Columbia University Press, 1980.

Roberts, David F. *The Social Conscience of the Early Victorians.* Stanford, CA: Stanford University Press, 2002.

Rosario, Vernon A., III. "Pointy Penises, Fashion Crimes, and Hysterical Mollies: The Pederast's Inversion." In *Homosexuality in Modern France,* edited by Jeffrey Merrick and Bryant T. Ragan Jr., 146–76. Oxford: Oxford University Press, 1996.

Rose, Jacqueline. *Proust among the Nations: From Dreyfus to the Middle East.* Chicago: University of Chicago Press, 2011.

Roy, Parama. "Unaccommodated Woman and the Poetics of Property in *Jane Eyre.*" *SEL* 29, no. 4 (1989): 713–27.

Royle, Edward. *Radicals, Secularists and Republicans: Popular Freethought in Britain, 1866–1915.* Manchester: Manchester University Press, 1980.

Ruth, Jennifer. *Novel Professions: Interested Disinterest and the Making of the Professional in the Victorian Novel.* Columbus: Ohio State University Press, 2006.

Sahlins, Marshall. *Stone Age Economics.* Chicago: Aldine-Atherton, 1972.

Said, Edward. *Representations of the Intellectual.* New York: Vintage, 1996.

Saine, Thomas P. "Was *Wilhelm Meisters Lehrjahre* Really Supposed to Be a Bildungsroman?" In *Reflection and Action: Essays on the Bildungsroman,* edited by James Hardin, 118–41. Columbia: University of South Carolina Press, 1991.
Salmon, Richard. "Professions of Labour: David Copperfield and the 'Dignity of Literature.'" *Nineteenth-Century Contexts* 29, no. 1 (2007): 35–52.
Samuels, Maurice. *Inventing the Israelite: Jewish Fiction in Nineteenth-Century France.* Stanford, CA: Stanford University Press, 2010.
———. *The Spectacular Past: Popular History and the Novel in Nineteenth-Century France.* Ithaca, NY: Cornell University Press, 2004.
Sammons, Jeffrey L. "Bildungsroman for Nonspecialists: An Attempt at a Clarification." In *Reflection and Action: Essays on the Bildungsroman,* edited by James Hardin, 26–45. Columbia: University of South Carolina Press, 1991.
———. "The Mystery of the Missing Bildungsroman; Or, What Happened to Wilhelm Meister's Legacy?" *Genre: Forms of Discourse and Culture* 14, no. 2 (1981): 229–46.
Sanders, Andrew. *Dickens and the Spirit of the Age.* Oxford: Clarendon, 1999.
Scanlan, Margaret. "Terrorism and the Realistic Novel: Henry James and *The Princess Casamassima.*" *Texas Studies in Literature and Language* 34, no. 3 (1992): 392–93.
Schlicke, Paul. "Bumble and the Poor Law Satire of *Oliver Twist.*" *Dickensian* 71 (1975): 149–56.
Schmidt, Marion. "The Birth and Development of *À la recherche du temps perdu.*" In *The Cambridge Companion to Proust,* edited by Richard Bales, 58–73. Cambridge: Cambridge University Press, 2001.
Scholes, Robert. "Stephen Dedalus, Poet or Esthete?" *PMLA* 79, no. 4 (1964): 485–89.
———, and Richard M. Kain, eds. *The Workshop of Daedalus: James Joyce and the Raw Materials for* A Portrait of the Artist as a Young Man. Evanston, IL: Northwestern University Press, 1965.
*Secularism: Unphilosophical, Immoral, and Anti-Social: Verbatim Report of a Three Nights' Debate between the Rev. Dr. Mccann and Charles Bradlaugh.* London: Freethought, 1882.
Sedgwick, Eve Kosofsky. *The Epistemology of the Closet.* Berkeley: University of California Press, 1990.
Segalen, Victor. *Essay on Exoticism: An Aesthetics of Diversity.* Edited and translated by Yaël Rachel Schlick. Durham, NC: Duke University Press, 2002.
Seigel, Jerrold. *Modernity and Bourgeois Life: Society, Politics, and Culture in England, France, and Germany since 1750.* Cambridge: Cambridge University Press, 2012.

Shills, Edward. "The Intellectuals and the Powers: Some Perspectives for Comparative Analysis." In *Intellectuals: Theoretical Studies, Case Studies,* edited by Philip Rieff, 24–48. Garden City, NY: Doubleday, 1969.

———. "The Theory of Mass Society." *Diogenes* 10, no. 39 (1962): 25–66.

Shklovsky, Victor. *Theory of Prose.* Translated by Benjamin Sher. Normal, IL: Dalkey Archive, 1998.

Shuttleworth, Sally. *Charlotte Brontë and Victorian Psychology.* Cambridge: Cambridge University Press, 1996.

Simmel, Georg. *On Individuality and Social Forms: Selected Writings.* Edited by Donald E. Levine. Chicago: University of Chicago Press, 1971.

———. *Simmel on Culture: Selected Writings.* Edited by David Patrick Frisby and Mike Featherstone. London: Sage, 1998.

Slaughter, Joseph R. *Human Rights, Inc.: The World Novel, Narrative Form, and International Law.* New York: Fordham University Press, 2007.

Slote, Michael. *The Ethics of Care and Empathy.* New York: Routledge, 2007.

———. *Moral Sentimentalism.* New York: Oxford University Press, 2009.

Smiles, Samuel. *Self-Help; With Illustrations of Character and Conduct.* London: John Murray, 1859.

Smith, Anthony D. *Nationalism and Modernism: A Critical Survey of Recent Theories of Nations and Nationalism.* London: Routledge, 1998.

Sorokin, Pitirim Aleksandrovich. *Social Mobility.* New York: Harper & Brothers, 1927.

Spadaccini, Nicholas and Luis Martín-Estudillo, eds. *Hispanic Baroques: Reading Cultures in Context.* Nashville, TN: Vanderbilt University Press, 2005.

Spivak, Gayatri Chakravorty. "Three Women's Texts and the Critique of Imperialism." *Critical Inquiry* 12, no. 1 (1985): 243–61.

Sprinker, Michael. *History and Ideology in Proust: À la recherche du temps perdu and the Third French Republic.* Cambridge: Cambridge University Press, 1994.

Staël, Germaine de. *Considerations on the Principal Events of the French Revolution.* Edited by Aurelian Craiut. Indianapolis: Liberty Fund, 2008.

Stefanowsky, Dimitry. "Sur la symptomatologie de l'inversion sexuelle." *Archives d'anthropologie criminelle de criminologie et de psychologie normale et pathologique* (1894): 741–44.

Stendhal. *The Red and the Black: A Chronicle of the Nineteenth Century.* Translated by Catherine Slater. Oxford: Oxford University Press, 1971.

———. *Le Rouge et le Noir.* Paris: Gallimard, 2000.

Stević, Aleksandar. "Convenient Cosmopolitanism: *Daniel Deronda,* Nationalism, and the Critics." *Victorian Literature and Culture* 45, no. 3 (2017): 593–614.

———. "Fatal Extraction: Dickensian Bildungsroman and the Logic of Dependency." *Dickens Studies Annual* 45 (2014): 63–95.

———. "The Genre of Disobedience: Is the Bildungsroman beyond Discipline?" In "Genres of Obedience," edited by Martin Wagner and Elystan Griffiths, special issue, *Seminar: A Journal of Germanic Studies* 56, no. 2: 2020 (forthcoming).
———. "*Künstlerroman* kao *Bildungsroman*: moć i nemoć teorije žanra." txt 5–6 (2004): 40–54.
———. "Realism, the Bildungsroman, and the Art of Self-Invention: Stendhal and Balzac." In *A History of Modern French Literature from the Fifteenth to the Twentieth Century,* edited by Christopher Prendergast, 414–35. Princeton, NJ: Princeton University Press, 2017.
———. "Stephen Dedalus and Nationalism without Nationalism." *Journal of Modern Literature* 41, no. 1 (2017): 40–57.
Stewart, Garrett. "A Valediction for Bidding Mourning: Death and the Narratee in Brontë's *Villette*." In *Death and Representation,* edited by Sarah Webster Goodwin and Elisabeth Bronfen, 51–79. Baltimore, MD: Johns Hopkins University Press, 1993.
Stifter, Adalbert. *Indian Summer.* Translated by Wendell Frye. Bern: Peter Lang, 2009.
Stokes, John. "'Rachel's Terrible Beauty': An Actress among the Novelists." *ELH* 51, no. 4 (1984): 771–93.
Stokes, Peter M. "Bentham, Dickens, and the Uses of the Workhouse." *SEL: Studies in English Literature, 1500–1900* 41 (2001): 711–27.
Stolnitz, Jerome. "'Beauty': Some Stages in the History of an Idea." *Journal of the History of Ideas* 22, no. 2 (1961): 185–204.
Stone, Norman. *Europe Transformed, 1878–1919.* Oxford: Blackwell, 1999.
Sullivan, Dennis G. "On Vision in Proust: The Icon and the Voyeur." *MLN* 84, no. 4 (1969): 646–61.
Swales, Martin. "The German Bildungsroman and 'The Great Tradition.'" *Comparative Criticism: A Yearbook* 1 (1979): 91–105.
———. *The German Bildungsroman from Wieland to Hesse.* Princeton, NJ: Princeton University Press, 1978.
———. "Irony and the Novel: Reflections on the German Bildungsroman." In *Reflection and Action: Essays on the Bildungsroman,* edited by James Hardin, 46–65. Columbia: University of South Carolina Press, 1991.
Tadié, Jean-Yves. *Marcel Proust.* Paris: Gallimard, 1996.
———. *Proust et le roman: Essai sur les formes et techniques du roman dans "À la recherche du temps perdu."* Paris: Gallimard, 1971.
———. "Proust, lecteur de Balzac." *L'Année Balzacienne* 14 (1993): 311–20.
Tardieu, Ambroise. *Étude médico-légale sur les attentats aux moeurs.* 3rd ed. Paris: J. B. Baillière, 1859.

Tarnowsky, Benjamin. *L'Instinct sexuel et ses manifestations morbides au double point de vue de la jurisprudence et de la psychiatrie.* Paris: Charles Carrington, 1904.
Taylor, Isaac. *Self-Cultivation Recommended: Or, Hints to a Youth Leaving School.* London: Fenner, 1817.
Taylor, Charles. *Modern Social Imaginaries.* Durham, NC: Duke University Press, 2004.
Terdiman, Richard. *The Dialectics of Isolation: Self and Society in the French Novel from the Realists to Proust.* New Haven, CT: Yale University Press, 1976.
———. *Discourse/Counter-Discourse: The Theory and Practice of Symbolic Resistance in Nineteenth-Century France.* Ithaca, NY: Cornell University Press, 1985.
———. *Present Past: Modernity and the Memory Crisis.* Ithaca, NY: Cornell University Press, 1993.
*Theism or Atheism: Which Is More Reasonable? A Public Debate between Mr. W. T. Lee and Mr. G. W. Foote.* London: R. Forder, 1896.
Thormählen, Marianne. *The Brontës and Religion.* Cambridge: Cambridge University Press, 1999.
Tilly, Charles. *Social Movements, 1768–2004.* Boulder, CO: Paradigm, 2004.
Townsend, Joseph. *A Dissertation on the Poor Laws: By a Well-Wisher to Mankind.* London: C. Dilly, 1786.
Tratner, Michael. *Modernism and Mass Politics: Joyce, Woolf, Eliot, Yeats.* Stanford, CA: Stanford University Press, 1995.
*Trésor de la langue française: dictionnaire de la langue du XIXe et du XXe siècle, 1789–1960.* Paris: Editions du Centre national de la recherche scientifique, 1971–1994.
Trilling, Lionel. "*The Princess Casamassima.*" In *The Liberal Imagination: Essays on Literature and Society,* 55–88. Garden City, NY: Doubleday, 1957.
Ulrichs, Karl Heinrich *The Riddle of "Man-Manly" Love.* Vol. 1. Translated by Michael A. Lombardi-Nash. Buffalo, NY: Prometheus, 1994.
Upton, Charles B. "Fervent Atheism." *Modern Review: A Quarterly Magazine* 1 (1880): 98–124.
Valente, Joseph. "James Joyce and the Cosmopolitan Sublime." In *Joyce and the Subject of History,* edited by Mark A. Wollaeger, Victor Luftig, and Robert Spoo, 59–80. Ann Arbor: University of Michigan Press, 1996.
Vanden Bossche, Chris, R. "Cookery, Not Rookery: Family and Class in *David Copperfield.*" *Dickens Studies Annual* 15 (1986): 87–109.
Van Ghent, Dorothy. *The English Novel: Form and Function.* New York: Harper & Row, 1961.
Wagner, Peter. *A Sociology of Modernity: Liberty and Discipline.* New York: Routledge, 1994.

Walkowitz, Rebecca L. *Cosmopolitan Style: Modernism beyond the Nation*. New York: Columbia University Press, 2006.
Weber, Max. *From Max Weber: Essays in Sociology*. Edited and translated by H. H. Gerth and C. Wright Mills. New York: Oxford University Press, 1946.
———. *The Protestant Ethics and the Spirit of Capitalism and Other Writings*. Edited by Peter Baehr. Translated by Peter Baehr and Gordon C. Wells. London: Penguin, 2002.
Welsh, Alexander. *From Copyright to Copperfield: The Identity of Dickens*. Cambridge, MA: Harvard University Press, 1987.
Williams, Raymond. *The English Novel from Dickens to Lawrence*. London: Chatto & Windus, 1970.
———. *Politics of Modernism*. London: Verso, 2007.
Wilson, Stephen. "Proust's *À la recherche du temps perdu* as a Document of Social History." *Journal of European Studies* 1 (1971): 213–43.
Woolf, Virginia. *Jacob's Room*. Edited by Kate Flint. Oxford: Oxford University Press, 1992.
———. *The Voyage Out*. London: Penguin, 1992.
———. *The Waves*. Oxford: Oxford University Press, 2008.
Yeats, W. B. *Uncollected Prose*. Vol. 1. Edited by John P. Frayne. London: Macmillan, 1970.
Yeazell, Ruth Bernard. "Why Political Novels Have Heroines: *Sybil, Mary Barton,* and *Felix Holt.*" *Novel: A Forum on Fiction* 18 (1985): 126–44.
Yee, Cordell D. K. "The Aesthetics of Stephen's Aesthetics." In *Critical Essays on Joyce's* A Portrait of the Artist as a Young Man, edited by Philip Brady and James F. Carens, 68–82. New York: G. K. Hall, 1998.
Zimmer, Oliver. *Nationalism in Europe, 1890–1940*. Houndmills: Palgrave Macmillan, 2003.
Zola, Émile. *Germinal*. Edited by Henri Mitterand. Paris: Gallimard, 1999.
———. *Germinal*. Translated by Havelock Ellis. London: Dent, 1964.

# INDEX

Abel, Elizabeth, 79
aestheticism: in James, 118, 121–23, 205n13; in Joyce, 133, 142–44, 207n36, 209n66, 209–10nn68–69; in Proust, 152–53, 155, 157, 159–63, 166, 168, 169, 173, 174, 177, 178, 182, 183, 184, 214nn9–10, 215n16
aesthetics, 68, 144, 162, 209n66, 209–10nn68–69, 214nn9–10
à Kempis, Thomas, 100
anarchism, 114, 116–18, 119, 123–24, 127
*ancien régime*, 50, 192n3
Anderson, Amanda, 210n69
Anderson, Benedict, 208n45
Aquinas, Thomas, 142
aristocracy, 10–11, 15, 24–25, 30, 33–37, 42–46, 49–50, 118, 120, 126, 152, 156–57, 159–60, 162, 193n9, 213n6, 214n8, 215n14; in Balzac, 15, 24–25, 30, 33–37, 43–46, 49–51, 117–20, 124; French, 24–25, 33–36, 49–50; in Goethe, 10–11, 214n8; in James, 117–25; in Proust, 152, 155–56, 157–60, 162, 213n6, 214n8, 215n14; titles of, 28, 34–36, 46, 49–50, 78, 194n29
Aristotle, 142, 209n65
Armstrong, Nancy, 84, 200n17
asceticism, 90–92, 100–103, 106, 111
atheism, 126. *See also* secularism
Austen, Jane, 10, 79, 81, 109, 198n5
Austin, J. L., 193n14

Bakhtin, Mikhail, 9, 51, 65, 67
Bakunin, Mikhail, 125

Balzac, Honoré de, 12, 14, 16, 17, 21, 52, 63, 67, 84, 116, 150, 151, 152, 177, 180, 213n6; *La Comédie humaine*, 23, 43, 112, 159, 173; *Illusions perdues*, 1, 5, 7, 8, 11, 13, 15, 17, 18, 19, 20, 23–26, 28, 30–48, 51, 66, 68–69, 97, 118, 119, 155–59, 176, 189n13, 192n1, 193n14; *Le Père Goriot*, 1, 17, 29–31, 155–56, 159, 180, 187n1; *Splendeurs et misères des courtisanes*, 1, 15, 17, 18, 19, 23–26, 37, 43–49, 51, 97, 192n1, 194nn23–25
baroque, 104–6, 204n52
Barthélemy, Édouard de, 34
Bauman, Zygmunt, 13
Beard, George, 167, 216nn21–22
Beardsley, Monroe, 162–63, 166, 214n9
Benda, Julien, 113–14, 116, 136, 148, 204n3
Benjamin, Walter, 121, 123
Berman, Marshall, 11
Bersani, Leo, 175, 214n11
Bible, 26, 128–29, 206n23
Biddis, Michael, 204n3
Bildung, 3–5, 7, 187n2, 189n10, 189–90nn13–15
bildungsroman: and Bildung, 3–5, 7, 187n2, 188n10, 189–90nn13–15; "classical," 6–7, 79–80, 95–96, 180, 181, 183, 185, 199n7, 202n37; contemporary, 185; failure in, 1–8, 14, 18, 23, 24, 26, 42, 43, 47–48, 62, 63, 73, 74, 127, 150, 151; female, 18, 19, 20, 77–84, 182, 185, 190n18, 198n5, 199n7, 199n10, 202n37;

bildungsroman (*continued*)
  and mass politics, 12, 15, 20, 112–25, 130–48, 149–55, 184, 204nn2–6, 205nn8–9, 205n13; modernist, 2, 6–7, 8, 10, 13, 20, 180, 181–84; realist, 2, 6–7, 10–13, 19, 67, 113, 156, 181, 183–85, 187n1, 189n14, 194n33, 213n3
biology, 116, 129, 170–72, 180. *See also* botany; zoology
Blackbourn, David, 191n27
blackmail, 38, 40–42, 46–47
Blessington, Lady, 85–88
Boes, Tobias, 10, 190n17, 191n26, 192n3, 199n5
Bonaparte, Felicia, 78
botany, 152, 163, 170–72, 177, 217nn27–31
bourgeoisie, 11–13, 15, 19, 50, 55, 67, 86, 116, 150, 164, 191nn27–29, 198n28, 213n6
Bowie, Malcolm, 212n3, 213n6
Bradlaugh, Charles, 128–29, 206n23
Britain, 5, 14, 32, 117, 127, 146, 197n24, 203n47, 209n68. *See also* England
Brontë, Charlotte, 79, 82, 88–89, 92, 220n14, 200n17, 201n20; *Jane Eyre*, 18, 20, 66, 81, 82–84, 87–96, 97–101, 105, 107, 109, 111, 185, 198n5, 201nn26–30, 202n37, 203n44; *Villette*, 1, 17, 18, 20, 84, 88, 96–111, 179, 181, 199n11, 202n40, 203nn47–48
Brontë, Emily, 88
Brooks, Peter, 30, 214n10
Buckley, Jerome Hamilton, 198n5
Budd, Susan, 125
Bulwer-Lytton, Edward, 71
Burrow, J. W., 126
Butler, Samuel: *The Evidence for the Resurrection of Jesus Christ, as Given by the Four Evangelists, Critically Examined*, 129; *Note-Books*, 130–31; *The Way of All Flesh*, 20, 113, 115, 116, 127–29, 131–32, 133, 151, 207n32

capitalism, 11, 13, 14, 16, 26, 52; as destructive economy in Balzac, 37–43; suppression of in Dickens, 16, 18, 52, 67, 83, 180

care, 15, 16, 53, 58–61, 63, 66, 70–75
care ethics, 58–61
Castle, Gregory, 2, 6–8, 135, 190n15, 198n5, 207n36
Catholicism, 102–10, 134, 135, 140, 153, 203n47, 207n36
Channing, William E., 196n10
Charity Commission, 57
Charter of 1814, 34, 50, 194nn28–29
Charter of 1830, 49–50, 194nn28–29
Chevalier, Julien, 217n26
Christianity, 91–92, 100–101, 113, 115–16, 126–32, 206n20, 211n80. *See also* asceticism; Catholicism; Protestantism; Puritanism
class, 11–12, 25, 56, 63, 78, 84–86, 89, 93, 113, 115–25, 151, 155, 196, 200n20, 201n30, 204n3, 206n32, 210n69, 213n6. *See also* aristocracy; bourgeoisie; social mobility
Colenso, John William, 130, 206n26
Collini, Stefan, 148
Compagnon, Antoine, 155, 183, 215n19, 216n23, 217n26
Conrad, Joseph, 6
*Contemporary Review*, 126
Counter-Reformation, 105, 204n52

D'Annunzio, Gabriele, 134
Darwin, Charles, 125, 126, 127, 130–31, 163, 205n20, 206n26
Darwin, Erasmus, 130
Darwinism, 116, 125–28, 130–31, 205nn18–20
Deane, Seamus, 207n36
Declaration of the Rights of the Man and of the Citizen, 34
defamiliarization, 152, 164, 165, 173
de Robert, Louis, 216n23
Dickens, Charles, 12, 14–15, 16–19, 52–56, 80, 81–83, 87, 89, 97, 112–13, 127, 151, 181, 183, 195n1, 196n9, 197n18, 197n28, 198n30, 198n33; *David Copperfield*, 1, 13, 16, 18, 19, 52, 53, 54, 55, 58–63, 65–71, 72, 74, 75, 83, 97, 118, 180, 187n1, 189n3,

# INDEX

197nn24–25, 198n30, 199n13; *Great Expectations,* 1, 11, 14, 15, 16, 17–20, 53–55, 59, 71–76, 97, 185, 189n13, 196n8, 198n31, 198n33; *Oliver Twist,* 15, 17, 18, 19, 53, 55, 57–61, 63–65, 72, 75, 85, 112, 195n5, 196n8, 197n22

Dilthey, Wilhelm, 3–5, 95
Dostoevsky, Fyodor, 115
Dreyfus Affair, 17, 152–55, 177, 182, 212n2
Duncan, Ian, 195n1, 197n25

Eagleton, Terry, 84, 88, 91, 95
education, 4, 7, 18, 21, 43, 49, 55, 56, 127, 134, 136, 191n29; aesthetic, 196n9; female, 182; suppression of in Dickens, 63–66, 69, 70, 75; tyrannical, 71
Eliot, George, 63, 79, 86, 93, 133, 168, 198n5; *Daniel Deronda,* 17, 20, 21, 63, 77, 80, 81, 86, 93–94, 113, 115, 148, 181, 182, 183, 199n5, 204n2; *Middlemarch,* 77–78, 80, 81, 82, 93, 95, 182; *The Mill on the Floss,* 1, 77, 80, 100–101, 198n5
Empire (French), 36, 49
England, 15, 20, 67, 81, 85, 90, 92, 96, 109, 130, 132, 140, 183, 185, 195n2. *See also* Britain; Victorian age
Enlightenment, 7, 116, 188n2, 189n10, 189n14
Esty, Jed, 2, 6, 7, 180, 182, 198n5
Europe, 5, 8–10, 14, 15, 25, 32, 78, 113–14, 117, 134, 136–37, 140, 145, 146, 148, 181, 189n10, 190n14, 204n3, 211n76
exoticism, 152, 159–66, 170, 177

failure: aesthetic, 180, 190n15, 195n1; of bildungsroman hero, 1–8, 14, 18, 23, 24, 26, 42, 43, 47–48, 62, 63, 73, 74, 127, 150, 151; national, 145, 147, 184
female bildungsroman, 18, 19, 20, 77–84, 182, 185, 190n18, 198n5, 199n7, 199n10, 202n37
feminist criticism, 79–80, 93, 96, 198n5, 202n37

Flaubert, Gustave, 12, 21, 68; *L'Éducation sentimentale,* 13, 17, 68, 149–52, 156, 195n1
Foote, G. W., 128
Foucault, Michel, 187n2
Fraiman, Susan, 78, 80, 95, 190n18, 199n11
France: *ancien régime,* 50, 192n3; aristocracy in, 24–25, 33–36, 49–50; Charter of 1814, 34, 50, 194nn28–29; Charter of 1830, 49–50, 194nn28–29; Declaration of the Rights of the Man and of the Citizen, 34; Dreyfus Affair, 17, 152–55, 177, 182, 212n2; French Empire, 36, 49; French Revolution, 11, 24–25, 34; July Monarchy, 50–51, 149, 194n33; Louis XVIII, 33; Louis-Philippe I, 49, 194n33; Napoleon, 14, 24–26, 28, 32–36, 112, 150; Paris, 14, 18, 20, 24, 25, 26, 30, 31, 32, 35–38, 40, 42–45, 119, 149–50, 153, 156–57, 159, 162, 181, 187n1, 203n51; political legitimacy in, 15, 19, 25, 32–36, 45, 46, 48, 50, 51, 192n3, 195n33; Restoration, 23–24, 33–36, 46, 48–51, 159
freethought, 113, 115, 126, 128–29. *See also* secularism
French Revolution, 11, 24–25, 34
Furet, Francois, 194n33

Gaelic Revival, 20, 135–39, 144–45, 210n75
Gaylin, Ann, 214n10
Geefs, Fanny, 104–5, 203n51
Germany, 3–5, 114, 117, 136, 137, 153, 185, 189n10, 191n27, 205n9
Gibson, Andrew, 134–35, 207nn36–37, 208n51, 211n77, 212n80
Giddens, Anthony, 9–10
Gide, André, 216n23
Gilligan, Carol, 71, 196n16
Glais-Bizoin, Alexandre, 49–50
Goethe, Johann Wolfgang von, *Wilhelm Meister's Apprenticeship,* 3–5, 7, 9–12, 63, 66, 68, 188n4, 188n7, 188–89nn9–10, 189n14, 191n26, 191nn30–32, 196n9, 214n8

247

# INDEX

governess, 18, 84–89, 97, 200n20, 202n41
Greenblatt, Stephen, 26–27, 187n2

Hardy, Barbara, 69
Hardy, Thomas, 1, 63
Hauptmann, Gerhart, 140, 141
Highmore, Anthony, 57–58
Hirsch, Marianne, 79, 199n7
Hobsbawm, Eric, 11, 13, 135–36, 208n45
homosexuality, 167, 169, 172–74, 215n19, 216n23, 217n33. *See also* inversion; lesbianism
Hooker, Joseph Dalton, 127
Humboldt, Wilhelm Von, 3–5, 188n6
Hyde, Douglas, 137–40, 141, 144–45, 210–11nn75–76

Ibsen, Henrik, 134, 140, 141
imperialism, 180, 182, 201n30
inversion, 152, 164, 166–72, 174, 176–77, 216nn23–24, 217n26, 218n33
Ireland, 20, 133–42, 144–47, 207nn36–37, 207n43, 208n51, 208n57, 209n64, 210n70, 210–11nn75–77, 211n80
*Irish Times*, 137, 210n70

James, Henry: *The Ambassadors*, 125; *The Bostonians*, 205n12; *The Golden Bowl*, 125; *Portrait of a Lady*, 117; *The Princess Casamassima*, 1, 16–17, 20, 113, 116, 115–25, 131, 205n8, 205nn12–13
Jameson, Fredric, 188n10, 210n69
Jesuits, 81, 108–11, 116
Johnson, Paul, 11
journalism, 13, 24, 37, 38, 40–43, 70, 211n77
July Monarchy, 50–51, 149, 194n33

Kant, Immanuel, 143, 209n66, 209n68, 217n30
Kaufmann, Moritz, 126
Kenner, Hugh, 133, 209n66
Kettle, Arnold, 196n8
Kincaid, Jamaica, 185

Kipling, Rudyard, 6
Konrád, Georg, 146, 212n80
Kontje, Todd, 187n2, 188n4, 188n10
Kropotkin, Peter, 125
*Künstlerroman*, 6, 218n4

Lamarck, Jean-Baptiste, 130
Landy, Joshua, 214n10
Langland, Elizabeth, 79
legitimacy, political, 15, 19, 25, 32–36, 45, 46, 48, 50, 51, 192n3, 195n33
lesbianism, 152, 168, 174–76, 218n33
Lévi-Strauss, Claude, 39–40
Levin, Harry, 214n10
Lewis, Pericles, 211n80
Lofft, Capel, 196n10
London, 20, 55, 57, 64, 66, 74, 75, 99, 117, 123, 134, 197n18
Louis XVIII, 33
Louis-Philippe I, 49, 194n33
Lukács, Georg, 37–39, 95, 188n7, 197n28

Mahoney, Dennis F., 190n16
Mann, Thomas: *Doktor Faustus*, 68; *Magic Mountain*, 116, 181–82
Mannheim, Karl, 148, 206n32
Marcus, Steven, 64
Marx, Karl, 125–26, 191n29
Marxism, 116
McCrea, Barry, 172, 195n5
Meredith, George, 1
Mill, John Stuart, 88, 94–95, 190n14, 210n26
Miller, D. A., 48–49
Miller, J. Hillis, 63, 198n31
Miller, Nathan, 53
modernism, 2, 6–10, 13, 19, 20, 134, 135, 180, 181, 183, 185, 190n15, 195n5, 199n5, 202n40, 207n36, 210n69
modernity, 8–14, 16, 17, 52, 67, 82, 134, 178, 182, 184, 190n17
moral sentimentalism, 17, 19, 58, 63, 75, 197n15

## INDEX

Moretti, Franco, 2, 7–8, 9, 10–11, 27, 78, 180, 190n15, 191n26, 191n32, 195n1, 198n5
Morgenstern, Karl, 3–5, 9, 189n10
Murillo, Bartolomé Esteban, 105
mythology, 135, 140, 145, 158, 160–62, 212n80

Nabokov, Vladimir, 185
Napoleon, 14, 24–26, 28, 32–36, 112, 150
nationalism, 12, 15, 20, 21, 113, 151, 183, 201n30, 204n2, 205n9, 208n45; Irish, 20, 133–42, 144–48, 207n43, 208n51, 208n57, 209n66, 210n30, 210n70, 211n77, 211n80. *See also* Gaelic Revival
Nazism, 185
negative reciprocity (Balzac), 40, 42, 45, 47, 194n20
neurasthenia, 167–68, 216nn21–22, 218n33
nobility. *See* aristocracy
Noddings, Nell, 60–61, 196n16, 198n30
Nolan, Emer, 207n36, 207n43

Oakeshott, Michael, 113
O'Donnell, Thomas, 138–39
opera, 30, 32, 43, 157–59

*Pall Mall Gazette,* 126, 205n9
painting, 27, 102–6, 109, 203n51
Parnell, Charles Stewart, 138
Paris, 14, 18, 20, 24, 25, 26, 30, 31, 32, 35–38, 40, 42–45, 119, 149–50, 153, 156–57, 159, 162, 181, 187n1, 203n51
Pavel, Thomas, 189n12
Paxton Hood, Edwin, 53, 56
Pecora, Vincent, 73
performativity, 36, 46, 51, 193n14
Petrey, Sandy, 194n33
poststructuralism, 193n14, 209n57
Prendergast, Christopher, 37, 48, 194n24
Propp, Vladimir, 55
Protestantism, 107–9, 111, 203n47
Proust, Adrien, 216n22

Proust, Marcel, 121, 184, 195n1, 212n2; *À la recherche du temps perdu,* 17, 21, 151–52, 155–78, 182, 212n3, 213nn5–6, 214n10, 215n14, 215n19, 216n23, 217nn26–27, 217n33, 218nn35–36; and Dreyfus affair, 17, 152–55, 177, 182, 212n2; homosexuality in works of, 167–76, 215n19, 216n23, 217n33; lesbianism in works of, 152, 168, 174–76, 218n33
publishing, 38, 40, 41, 43
Puritanism, 111

race, 131, 133, 135, 139, 140–42, 145, 170, 204n3, 207n36, 210n75, 211n80
Redfield, Marc, 188n10, 190n16, 198n5
Restoration (France), 23–24, 33–36, 46, 48–51, 159
revolutions: cognitive (in Proust), 165–66; French, 11, 24–25, 34; July Revolution, 194n33; proletarian (in James), 121–25; Revolution of 1848, 149–51, 152; Russian, 185
Rivers, J. E., 215n19
Rousseau, Jean-Jacques, 28, 149, 173
Roy, Parama, 93, 201n30
Rubens, Peter Paul, 103

Said, Edward, 132, 207n41
Saine, Thomas P., 188n9
Saint-Paul, Georges, 216n20
Sammons, Jeffrey, 5, 189n13
Schreiner, Olive, 6
science, 115, 116, 125–32, 160, 163, 164, 166, 171–73, 205nn19–20, 218n33
Scott, Walter, 101
secularism, 114, 127, 128, 197n24
Segalen, Victor, 160, 161
Seigel, Jerrold, 191n27, 191n29
self-cultivation, 56, 196n10
self-culture, 56, 196n10
self-denial. *See* asceticism
self-education, 56, 196n10

self-fashioning, 26–29, 43, 48, 61, 63, 64, 70, 111, 118, 133, 148, 187n2
self-formation, 56, 196n10
self-help, 53, 56–58, 61, 63, 196n11
self-invention, 24–29, 31, 35–37, 42–43, 48, 50–51, 184, 187n1
self-training, 56, 196n10
Shklovsky, Victor, 160, 161, 162
Simmel, Georg, 40
Slaughter, Joseph, 9
Smiles, Samuel, 56
Smith, Anthony, 208n45
socialism, 15, 114, 116, 125–27, 149, 204n5, 205nn8–10, 205n19
socialization, 6–8, 10, 12, 14, 15, 18, 19, 21, 24, 26, 27, 75, 79, 80, 82, 95, 96, 114, 176, 180, 181, 184, 185, 188n10, 189n13, 190n15, 190n17, 200n17, 201n26
social mobility, 11, 14–16, 18, 19, 21, 23–26, 28, 19, 31, 32, 36, 37, 48, 49, 72–75, 78–83, 87, 88, 99, 120, 184, 187n2
Spencer, Herbert, 125
Spivak, Gayatry Chakravorty, 201n30
Sprinker, Michael, 213n6
Stendhal, *Le Rouge et le Noir,* 1, 8, 10, 12, 14, 21, 26–28, 44, 48, 63, 150, 151, 156, 176, 182, 187n1, 181n26, 192nn3–4

Thormählen, Marianne, 102
*Times* (London), 117, 196n8, 204n5, 205nn19–20
Tolstoy, Leo, 67, 141

Ulrichs, Karl Heinrich, 169–70, 172, 217n26

Victorian age, 15, 67–68, 148, 181, 183, 197n24; bildungsroman in, 189n14, 195n1; conceptions of duty in, 91, 100–102; domestic ideology in, 18, 19, 77–88, 93–96, 183, 200n20; liberal individualism in, 52–53, 56–58, 196n1

Wagner, Peter, 14
Weber, Max, 160, 161, 214n11
Woolf, Virginia: *Jacob's Room,* 179, 181; *The Voyage Out,* 179, 182
World War I, 2, 13, 153, 155, 179, 180–82

Yeats, William Butler, 126, 133, 135, 141, 144–45, 207n43

Zola, Emile, 20, 113, 115, 116, 125
zoology, 152, 163–64, 170, 172–73, 215n17
Zurbarán, Francisco de, 105

www.ingramcontent.com/pod-product-compliance
Lightning Source LLC
Chambersburg PA
CBHW021351300426
44114CB00012B/1172